Amish
Cooking

Books of Similar Interest from Random House Value Publishing

AMISH: A PHOTOGRAPHIC TOUR

AS AMERICAN AS APPLE PIE

CHRISTMAS MEMORIES WITH RECIPES

COMFORT FOOD

THE FANNY FARMER BAKING BOOK

THE FRUGAL GOURMET

THE PIONEER LADY'S COUNTRY CHRISTMAS

Amish
Cooking

GRAMERCY BOOKS
New York

This 1999 edition is published by Gramercy Books™, an imprint of Random House Value Publishing, Inc. 201 East 50th Street, New York, N.Y. 10022, by arrangement with Herald Press, Scottdale, Pa.

Gramercy Books™ and design are trademarks of Random House Value Publishing, Inc.

Editor: Mark Eric Miller
Illustrations: Donald V. Sands
Food Consultant: Dorothy Ferguson
Design: First Image

Random House
New York • Toronto • London • Sydney • Auckland
http://www.randomhouse.com/

Printed and bound in the United States of America.

Library of Congress Cataloging–in–Publication Data
Amish cooking / [editor, Mark Eric Miller ; illustrations, Donald
V. Sands].
      p.   cm.
Originally published: Scottdale, Pa. : Herald Press, c1980.
Includes index.
ISBN 0-517-19458-9 (hardcover)
1. Cookery, Amish.   I. Miller, Mark Eric.
TX721.A54   1999
641.5'66—dc21   99-20228
                                                       CIP

8 7 6

TABLE OF CONTENTS

USING METRIC MEASUREMENTS

As foods and kitchen implements are increasingly sold in metric sizes, it may be a good idea to try to accustom yourself to using metric measures. It is easy to do and requires a minimum of new equipment.

Liquid measuring cups already have liter markings on the right side. For dry food measuring (where you can level off the top for accurate measuring) you will need a set of three milliliter measures: 250, 125 and 50. As well, a set of five small milliliter measures will be handy: 25, 15, 5, 2 and 1. As we are already accustomed to measuring by weight in the case of meats, butter, cheese, chocolate etc., we have only to adjust from pounds and ounces to kilograms, grams and milligrams. Otherwise, measuring is still done by volume.

If you wish to convert the recipes in this book to metric, the following tables may be helpful. It is important to note that baking recipes may not work by doing an exact conversion from Imperial to metric. Measure as closely as you can, and learn through trial and error.

Metric		Imperial
Measurements		
1 kilogram	*replaces*	2 pounds
500 grams	*replace*	1 pound
1 liter	*replaces*	1 quart
250 milliliters	*replace*	1 cup
125 milliliters	*replace*	½ cup
50 milliliters	*replace*	⅓ to ¼ cup
15 milliliters	*replace*	1 tablespoon
5 milliliters	*replace*	1 teaspoon
Baking Dishes		
2-liter square baking pan	*replaces*	8-inch square baking pan
2.5-liter square baking pan	*replaces*	9-inch square baking pan
1.3-liter round cake pan	*replaces*	8-inch round cake pan
1.5-liter round cake pan	*replaces*	9-inch round cake pan
1.5-liter loaf pan	*replaces*	8 x 4-inch loaf pan
2-liter loaf pan	*replaces*	9 x 5-inch loaf pan
3.5-liter rectangular pan	*replaces*	9 x 13-inch rectangular pan
22.5-centimeter pie plate	*replaces*	9-inch pie plate

Oven Conversion Temperatures

100°C	=	200°F	(warming)
140°C	=	275°F	(fruitcake)
150°C	=	300°F	(soufflé)
160°C	=	325°F	(roasting)
180°C	=	350°F	(cakes)
190°C	=	375°F	(quickbread)
200°C	=	400°F	(muffins)
220°C	=	425°F	(tea biscuits)
230°C	=	450°F	(fish)

TABLE OF EQUIVALENT MEASURES

1 stick (¼ pound) butter or margarine = ½ cup
1 square chocolate = 3 tablespoons cocoa
2 large eggs = 3 small eggs
1 cup macaroni = 2¼ cups cooked
1 cup buttermilk = 1 or 2 tablespoons vinegar with sweet milk to fill cup (let stand 5 minutes)
1 tablespoon quick-cooking tapioca = 1 tablespoon cornstarch or 1⅓ to 1½ tablespoons flour
1 package active dry yeast = 1 tablespoon
1 package plain gelatin = 1 tablespoon
1 pound granulated sugar = 2 cups
1 pound brown sugar = 2¼ to 2½ cups (packed)
1 pound confectioner's or icing sugar = 4 to 4½ cups (sifted)
1 pound all-purpose flour = 4 cups
1 pound butter = 2 cups
1 can soup = 1¼ cups

AMISH BEGINNINGS

The Amish are one of the few minority groups which have escaped the great "melting pot" of North America. Because they have been able to retain a group identity, they have become very visible to the general public. As a result, many books, magazine features, newspaper accounts and sociological studies of the Amish have been published. However, not all that has been written is accurate, leaving the question in many people's minds, "Who really are the Amish?"

The Amish (pronounced "AH-mish") are the direct descendants of the Swiss Brethren, who in 1525 left both the Catholic Church and the Protestant Reformed Church. The Swiss Brethren or "Anabaptists," as they were often called, did not believe in infant baptism, taking oaths, fighting wars, or dressing in stylish clothing. Another of their main tenets was complete separation of church and state, a principle taken for granted in many nations today but unheard of in sixteenth-century Europe.

Because of their religious views, many of the Amish forbears were martyred. To escape this persecution they migrated across the Swiss border into Alsace, today a part of France. There, between 1693 and 1700, the Swiss Brethren experienced a division among themselves. Bishop Jacob Ammann, from whom the Amish derive their name, felt the congregations were becoming lax and called for a stricter observance. His followers became know as "Amish" and the others as "Mennonites" after Menno Simons, a Dutch Anabaptist bishop of the sixteenth century. Today many people confuse these two groups which in fact are separate and distinct denominations even though they share a common historical connection.

When King Louis XIV expelled the Amish from France in 1712, they were forced to migrate to Germany, which at the time was composed of several independent states. Over the following 100 years, the Amish settled in various areas of Germany, where they were tolerated by local rulers. But as early as 1727 some Amish immigrated to America, where they settled in the present area of Pennsylvania. Most, however, made the journey after 1800, and by 1824 some Amish began to immigrate to Canada, settling in Ontario. Eventually so many Amish left Europe that congregations there became extinct. Of the 130,000 Amish in North America today, 97 per cent live in the United States, primarily in Pennsylvania, Ohio, and Indiana, and in 19 other states, while the remainder live in Ontario.

The Amish are a rural people who have retained many older customs, such as the horse and buggy as their means of transportation, and their distinctive cooking and eating habits. All Amish farmhouses have vegetable gardens and truck patches beside them which provide the families with a year-round supply of vegetables. The result is cellars lined with shelves of canned goods—not the kind from the supermarket but glass ones containing the produce from their own land and labor.

As homecooked meals are the center of each Amish family's day, it is an infrequent event for them to eat in restaurants. Thus it is only natural that recipes would be shared among the Amish to provide wholesome yet varied meals, and that these recipes would eventually be collected in book form.

Amish Cooking did not originate from any one Amish person or Amish region. It contains recipes from areas throughout the United States and Canada. Originally the book appeared in 1965 as *Favorite Amish Family Recipes* and contained recipes mainly from the Amish settlement in Mifflin County, Pennsylvania. Then, in 1977, it appeared with its new title, *Amish Cooking*, containing about half the recipes from the former book. Other recipes were selected from the Amish monthly magazine, *Family Life,* which has a section of recipes from a wide range of regions and generations in each issue. Some of these recipes have been handed down from grandmother to granddaughter, while others were taken from farm magazines over the years. None would be selected for gourmet cooking, but all are simple and hearty. These recipes are time-tested by a people who know about delicious yet practical cooking. You will enjoy them too.

David Luthy
Aylmer, Ontario

BREADS

HINTS FOR BREADS

- Some recipes call for cake yeast and others for dried yeast—they are interchangeable. One package of yeast is the same as one cake of yeast. If bulk yeast is used, 1 tablespoon is the equivalent of 1 package.

- Adding a little sugar to the liquid used to dissolve the yeast will make it more active.

- All milk used in bread recipes should be scalded then cooled to lukewarm before using.

- For many bread and roll recipes, the steps may be simplified if all the liquid, sugar, salt and even the shortening is put into a bowl and the yeast sprinkled or crumbled in to dissolve it. When the yeast is dissolved or becomes bubbly, add the rest of the ingredients that the various recipes call for.

- When making bread or rolls, always have the flour at room temperature before mixing. This will help keep the dough at a warm temperature and encourage it to rise.

- Always use all-purpose flour with any recipe that calls for yeast. To many people this is simply known as bread flour. It is made from hard wheat. Some common brands are Maple Leaf, Five Roses, Pillsbury, Gold Medal and Robin Hood. Use any brand you prefer.

- If your bread loaves get flat instead of nice and round, try making a stiffer dough.

- For a finer textured bread, try letting the dough rise in a place where it is a little cooler.

- Using milk instead of another liquid usually gives a softer crust which becomes a richer brown when baked.

- People who bake regularly will not need to grease their bread pans before baking if:
  -they do not wash the pans between bakings
  -they work out the loaves with greased hands
  -new or cleaned pans are seasoned by greasing them well for a few bakings and setting them aside without washing.

- Bread will then slip easily out of the pans, leaving them clean and ready for the next time.

- For best results with bread, have the water very warm, but not hot, about 115°.

- For extra flavor in your homemade bread, use cooking oil instead of lard.

- Bread is better when worked down twice or more.

- If bread is baked before it rises to double size, it will not crumble so easily.

  Replace ⅛ of the water with vinegar in your bread recipe if you do not make the dough too stiff. The dough should be sticky so that you have to use shortening on your hands to work it.

  You can add whole wheat flour to any bread recipe if you do not make the dough too stiff. Again, the dough should be sticky so that you have to use shortening on your hands to work it.

- When taking bread from the oven, grease the top to make the crust softer.

GENERAL BREAD MAKING DIRECTIONS

After mixing the ingredients as directed in the recipe, grease your hands and knead the dough vigorously for about five to ten minutes, or until the dough squeaks. You may wish to turn the dough out on a floured table top for kneading. Place the dough in a greased bowl and grease the top of it. Cover it and set it in a warm place, out of drafts, and let it rise until double in size. Knead it lightly. Again grease the bowl and the top of the dough and let it rise until double. Repeat this procedure until the dough has risen two or three times (or whatever the recipe calls for).

Divide the dough into the required portions and form them into loaves. Bang each loaf hard with the palm of your hand to get rid of air bubbles. Place the loaves, smooth side up, into greased loaf pans, brush the top of each loaf with grease and prick them deeply with a fork to release any further air bubbles. Let them rise until double in size, and bake as directed. Grease the top of each loaf again immediately after removing it from the oven. Remove the loaves from the pans and cool them on racks.

Sealing bread in plastic bags before it has completely cooled will keep the crust nice and soft.

AYLMER BREAD

For each loaf use:
1 cup very warm water
1 teaspoon melted lard or cooking oil
1 teaspoon salt (scant)
(milk may be used as part of liquid, if
    desired)

1 tablespoon sugar
1 teaspoon dry yeast
3 cups all-purpose flour

Combine the first 5 ingredients in the order given. Let the mixture stand until the yeast dissolves. Stir in ½ of the flour, beat it until smooth, then add the remaining flour. Work the dough on a greased board or in a bowl, kneading it vigorously with both hands for 5 to 10 minutes, or until the dough squeaks. Grease your hands lightly if the dough sticks to them while working. Cover the dough and set it in a warm place (out of any draft) to rise until double in size. Knead the dough lightly, then let it rise again until double in size. Knead once again. After you have let the dough rise again, punch it down and divide it into loaves. Brush grease over each loaf and prick it deeply with a fork. This will release air bubbles. Let the loaves rise until they are double in size. Bake them for 30 minutes or until done: 15 minutes at 400°, and the remaining 15 minutes at 350°.

Grease the top of the loaves when you remove them from the oven. Take them out of their pans, and cool them on racks.

For 8 loaves, use 2 rounded tablespoons of yeast.

BROWN BREAD

3 cups lukewarm water
2 tablespoons sugar
6 tablespoons cake yeast
1⅓ cups milk
1¼ cups honey (or brown sugar)

2 tablespoons salt
⅔ cup butter or corn oil
5 to 6 cups whole wheat flour
White (unbleached) flour

Pour the water into a large bowl, adding the sugar and yeast, then let it stand for 10 minutes without stirring.

Scald the milk and add to it the honey, salt and melted butter. Set it aside to cool, then add it to the yeast mixture and mix well. Stir in 5 to 6 cups of whole wheat flour. Then add enough white flour to make a soft dough. Knead it for 15 minutes or until the dough is smooth and elastic. Divide the dough into loaves, and bake them at 350° for 45 minutes. This recipe makes 6 medium-sized loaves.

HEALTH-CONSCIOUS HOUSEWIFE BREAD

2 cups stone ground whole wheat flour
2 cups rye flour
2 cups unbleached white flour
1 pint buttermilk, whey, or sweet milk
2 tablespoons brown sugar

1 tablespoon dark molasses
½ teaspoon salt
2 rounded tablespoons dry yeast
1 cup warm water
1 teaspoon brown or white sugar
¾ cup lard

Mix all 3 flours in a large bowl and have the mixture ready to use. Heat the 1 quart of liquid to more than lukewarm, but not hot, before pouring it into a large bowl. Then add the 2 tablespoons of brown sugar, the molasses and salt, stirring well until they are dissolved. Melt the yeast in the 1 cup of warm water, adding to it 1 teaspoon of brown or white sugar. (This makes it rise faster). When the yeast is dissolved and beginning to rise, add it to the liquid mixture.

With a large spoon, stir in enough of the previously mixed flours to make a stiff batter. Then add the melted lard and beat the dough until it is smooth. Let the dough rise for 12 minutes, a step which is very important if you want a soft brown bread. After this time has elapsed, add more flour to form a bread dough the same as for white bread—if this is not enough, add more unbleached or white flour to finish. This recipe makes 3 medium-sized loaves.

If flour is left over, you can always store it for use in the next batch. Bread made by this method never gets stiff or hard with age. Never bake it in a too hot oven—350° is about right, for 1 hour (although oven thermometers tend to vary).

POTATO BREAD

1 medium–sized potato	2 packages dry yeast
1 quart water	1 teaspoon sugar
2 tablespoons butter	1 cup warm water
3 teaspoons salt	11 to 12 cups sifted all-purpose flour

Cook the diced, peeled potato in the quart of water until it is tender. Drain the potato, reserving the water, and mash it until no lumps remain. Add the mashed potato to the reserved water, and stir in the butter and salt. Let this mixture cool until it is lukewarm. Dissolve the yeast and sugar in the 1 cup of warm water, and let it stand for 5 to 10 minutes. Gradually add 6 cups of the flour to the potato water, beating it until it is smooth. Mix in the dissolved yeast/sugar mixture, and beat it thoroughly. Cover and let the dough rise in a warm place for about 2 hours. Then work in enough of the remaining flour to make a soft dough.

On a floured surface, knead the dough until it is smooth and satiny. Put it into a greased bowl, greasing the top of the dough. Cover, then let it rise until it is double in size, which should take about 1½ hours. Punch down the dough and divide it into 3 portions. Form each portion into a loaf and place each loaf in a greased pan. Cover and let the loaves rise until they are double in size, for about 30 to 40 minutes. Bake them at 375° for 40 minutes, then allow the loaves to cool.

Variations: For Raisin Bread add 1 pound of dark seedless raisins, ½ teaspoon of cloves, and 2 teaspoons of cinnamon after all the flour has been worked in. Also add ½ cup more of sugar. Frost the bread with confectioner's (icing) sugar.

OATMEAL BREAD

4 cups boiling water	4 tablespoons butter or margarine
2 cups instant oatmeal	2 packages dry yeast
1 cup whole wheat flour	1 cup warm water
½ cup brown sugar	10 cups all-purpose or bread flour
2 tablespoons salt	(approximate)

Mix the oatmeal, whole wheat flour, sugar, salt and butter with the boiling water, then cool the batter until it is lukewarm. Dissolve the yeast in the warm water and add it to the batter. Add enough white flour to make an elastic dough. Place it in a bowl and let it rise before punching it down and letting it rise again until double in size. Shape the dough into 4 loaves, and let them rise again until they are about double. Bake them at 350° for 30 minutes or longer, until done.

RAISIN OATMEAL BATTER BREAD

1 package active dry yeast
2 cups warm water
1½ teaspoons salt
3 tablespoons sugar
2 tablespoons soft shortening

2 cups all-purpose flour
1 cup rolled oats
2 cups whole wheat flour
½ cup seedless raisins

In a large mixing bowl, dissolve the yeast in the warm water. Stir in the salt, sugar and shortening, plus 2 cups of the flour, and the rolled oats. Beat this mixture for 3 minutes, then stir in the rest of the flour and the raisins, mixing it until the batter is smooth and satiny. Cover it with a cloth and let it rise in a warm place until it is double in size. Stir it down while counting slowly to 15, then spoon the batter into a greased loaf pan. Cover it with a cloth and let it rise before baking it in 2 greased loaf pans at 350° for 50 minutes.

HONEY OATMEAL BREAD

2 packages dry yeast
1 cup warm water
2½ cups boiling water
2 cups instant oatmeal
1 cup honey (or part corn syrup)

¾ cup cooking oil
4 beaten eggs
2 tablespoons salt
2 cups or more whole wheat flour
White unbleached flour

Dissolve the yeast in the cup of warm water. Pour the boiling water over the oatmeal and set it aside to cool until it is lukewarm. Then, being sure that everything is just warm before adding, mix together with the oatmeal the rest of the ingredients except the yeast and flour, and beat the mixture well. Add the yeast, and work in enough white flour (preferably unbleached) to make a nice spongy dough that is not sticky. Grease the top of the dough before letting it rise, then knead it and let it rise again. Divide it into 3 loaves, and bake them at 400° for 10 minutes, then at 350° for 25 to 30 minutes.

This is a delicious, nourishing bread.

BEST WHOLE WHEAT BREAD

2 cups milk
⅓ cup, plus 2 tablespoons shortening
⅓ cup sugar
1 tablespoon salt
2 cups whole wheat flour

3 tablespoons yeast
1 cup very warm water
1 cup cold water
White unbleached flour

Scald the milk, then add the shortening, sugar and salt, stirring until it is dissolved. Add the whole wheat flour and beat it rapidly with a spoon. Dissolve the yeast in the warm water, then add it, with the cold water, to the mixture. Mix it well, then add enough white flour to mike a nice, soft dough. Knead it for 10 minutes. Let it rise until it is double in size, then punch it down and turn it over in a greased bowl. Let it rise again until double, then shape the dough into 3 loaves and spank them quite hard to remove all the air bubbles. Cover them for 15 minutes, letting the dough rise until double, then bake them at 350° for 50 to 60 minutes.

WHOLE WHEAT BREAD

1 cake yeast
¼ cup lukewarm water
2 tablespoons sugar
2 cups milk, scalded

1 tablespoon salt
3¼ cups sifted whole wheat flour
2 tablespoons cooking oil
2¼ cups all-purpose flour

Crumble the yeast into the lukewarm water and add 1 teaspoon of sugar. Stir it well, then let it stand in a warm place until foamy. Pour the milk into a mixing bowl, adding the remaining sugar, and salt. Cool this mixture until it is lukewarm, then add the yeast. Add 3 cups of the whole wheat flour, beating it thoroughly, then add the cooking oil. Stir in enough of the all-purpose flour to make a soft dough. Let it stand for 10 minutes before turning it onto a floured board. Knead the dough for 10 minutes while working in the remaining whole wheat flour, until it is soft but not sticky. Place it in a bowl and let the dough rise. Knead it again, then shape it into 2 loaves. Let them rise until double in bulk. Bake them at 400° (a hot oven) for 10 minutes, then reduce the heat to 375° and bake them for 40 minutes more.

QUICK YEAST ROLLS

2 tablespoons sugar
2 tablespoons shortening, melted and
   cooled
1½ teaspoons salt

1 cake yeast or 1 package granules
1 cup lukewarm water
3¼ cups sifted bread flour

Add the sugar, shortening, salt and crumbled yeast to the lukewarm water before adding 1 cup of the flour and beating it with a rotary beater until smooth. Then mix in the remaining flour. Place the dough on a slightly floured board and let it rest for about 5 minutes. Knead the dough until it is smooth, then place it in a greased bowl, cover it and allow it to rise for about 1 hour. Follow the directions for Chelsea Buns (see page 18) to roll the dough into buns. Bake them in a hot oven (450°) for 12 to 15 minutes. This recipe makes 18 medium-sized rolls.

CORNMEAL ROLLS

⅓ cup cornmeal
½ cup sugar
1 teaspoon salt
½ cup melted shortening
2 cups milk

2 eggs, beaten
1 package yeast
¼ cup lukewarm water
4 cups all-purpose flour

Combine the cornmeal, sugar, salt, shortening and milk in a double boiler, cooking the mixture until it is thick, stirring it often. Cool it to lukewarm, adding the eggs, and the yeast dissolved in water. Beat the mixture well. Let it rise in a greased bowl for 2 hours, then add the flour to form a soft dough. Knead it lightly, letting it rise in a greased bowl for 1 hour. Knead the dough again before rolling it out and cutting it with a biscuit cutter. Brush the dough pieces with fat, crease them, and fold them like Parkerhouse rolls. Place them on an oiled sheet to rise for 1 hour, then bake them at 375° for 15 minutes. This recipe makes a very soft dough. It yields 3 dozen rolls, which may be made in different shapes—use flour generously when handling and shaping them.

PULL BUNS ("PLUCKETS")

⅓ cup sugar
⅓ cup melted butter
½ teaspoon salt
1 cup scalded milk

1 yeast cake
¼ cup lukewarm water
3 eggs, well-beaten
3¾ cups all-purpose flour
(approximate)

Add the sugar, butter and salt to the scalded milk. When it becomes lukewarm, add the yeast (which has been dissolved in the ¼ cup lukewarm water), the eggs and just enough flour to make a stiff batter. Cover and let it rise until the mixture doubles in bulk, then knead it down and let it rise again. Roll the dough into small balls, about the size of walnuts, and dip them into melted butter. Then roll each ball in a mixture of the following:

¾ cup sugar
½ cup ground nut meats
3 teaspoons cinnamon

Pile the balls loosely in an ungreased angel food cake pan and let them rise again for 30 minutes. (Do not use a pan with a removable bottom.) Bake the buns until they are brown, about 40 minutes, beginning at 400° and decreasing the heat after 10 minutes to 350°. Turn the pan upside down and remove them immediately, serving them while still warm.

The buns will be stuck together and that's the way you serve them. Everyone plucks his bun right from the central supply. (If you want these for dinner, start the recipe in the morning.)

CHELSEA BUNS

½ cup cooled mashed potatoes
½ cup lukewarm water
1 teaspoon sugar
1 package dry yeast
⅓ cup melted shortening

2 well-beaten eggs
⅓ cup sugar
½ teaspoon salt
2½ cups all-purpose flour
  (approximate)

Combine the potatoes, water and 1 teaspoon of sugar, then sprinkle the yeast on top. Let it stand until the yeast is dissolved. Add the rest of the ingredients, stirring in enough flour to make a soft dough (less stiff than bread dough). Knead it until it is smooth, then let it rise until double in bulk before rolling the dough out to a 9 x 15-inch rectangle.

2 tablespoons soft butter
¾ cup brown sugar
¼ cup corn syrup

½ teaspoon vanilla
½ cup chopped nuts

Mix together the above ingredients except the nuts, and spread the mixture in a greased 9 x 13-inch pan. Then sprinkle the nuts over this mixture and set it aside. This is equally good if you substitute raisins for the nuts, or even if you don't use either ingredient.

¼ cup soft butter
¾ cup brown sugar

1 tablespoon cinnamon
1 cup washed raisins

(See Illustration 1-.) Spread the butter on the rolled rectangle of dough and sprinkle it with the sugar, cinnamon and raisins. (See Illustration 2-.) Roll it up like a jelly roll and cut it into 15 one-inch slices (-see Illustrations 3 and 4). (See Illustration 5-.) Place the slices cut-side down in the previously prepared pan. Cover and let them rise until they fill the pan, then bake them at 375° for about 40 minutes. Cool the buns for 3 minutes before inverting the pan to remove them.

1. Roll a portion of the dough into a 9 x 15-inch rectangle about ¼ inch thick. Spread with the soft butter and sprinkle with sugar, cinnamon and raisins.

2. Roll up as you would for a jelly roll.

3. To slice, slip a length of regular sewing thread under the roll, placing the thread to make slices about 1 inch thick.

4. Cross the two ends above the roll and pull. You will have a perfect, clean-cut slice.

5. Place the slices, cut side down, in the previously prepared 9 x 13-inch cake pan, about ½ inch apart.

SWEET BUNS

3 cups lukewarm water
1½ cups sugar
1 cake yeast

1 tablespoon lard
1 tablespoon salt
All-purpose flour

Mix together the first 5 ingredients until the yeast is dissolved. Then stir in enough flour (about 8 cups) to make a fairly stiff dough. Let it rise in a warm place for 2 hours. Punch down the dough and form it into balls the size of a small egg. Place them on a greased baking pan and let them rise until double in size. Bake them at 400° for 10 to 15 minutes, or until they are golden brown.

For sandwich buns, make the dough balls slightly larger and flatten them with your hands.

COFFEE BUNS

Dissolve 1 package of dry yeast in ¼ cup of lukewarm water. Mix the following like pie crumbs;

4 cups bread flour
1 cup shortening
¼ cup sugar

Then add and mix thoroughly along with the dissolved yeast;

2 eggs
1 cup milk, scalded and cooled
1 teaspoon salt
½ teaspoon lemon extract

Let the dough rise in the refrigerator overnight. Then divide it into 3 parts, rolling them out and spreading them with melted butter and sprinkling them with brown sugar and cinnamon. Roll the dough up like a jelly roll and slice it very thinly (it is not necessary to let it rise again) before baking it at 350° for 15 minutes or until brown.

Top it with powdered sugar icing if preferred: Dissolve 1 cup of powdered sugar in a very small amount of hot water, then dribble it over the hot buns.

BUTTERHORNS

1 cake yeast
½ cup sugar
3 eggs, beaten
1 cup lukewarm water

½ cup melted margarine
1 teaspoon salt
4½ to 5 cups sifted all-purpose flour

Blend the yeast with 1 tablespoon of the sugar, then add the beaten eggs and the rest of the sugar. Add the rest of the ingredients, the flour last, and put it into the refrigerator overnight. The next morning, roll out the dough like a pie dough, cut it into pie-wedge shapes and roll them up before dipping them into melted margarine. Let them rise for 3 hours before baking them at 325° for 15 to 20 minutes.

If you leave the dough in the refrigerator for awhile, punch it down each day.

NO-KNEAD ROLLS

4 cups milk
11 tablespoons margarine
2 or 3 packages cake yeast, OR
2 heaping tablespoons dry yeast
⅓ cup sugar
1 cup warm water

1½ cups sugar
5 eggs, beaten
2 teaspoons salt
All-purpose flour
Butter
Cinnamon

Scald the milk, then add the margarine. While this mixture cools to lukewarm, mix the yeast with the ⅓ cup of sugar in the cup of warm water. When the milk mixture has cooled to about 115° (lukewarm), add the 1½ cups of sugar, the eggs, salt and the yeast and water mixture. Add the flour, 1½ cups or more for each cup of liquid—it should make a dough soft enough to stir with a spoon. Let it rise, then stir it down and let it rise again before rolling the dough out on a floured board. Butter it well and sprinkle it with cinnamon. Roll up the dough and cut slices about 1-inch thick. Place them on buttered cookie sheets or baking pans, and let them rise until they are light and fluffy before baking them in a 350° oven for 15 to 20 minutes or until golden brown. Frost the rolls when they have cooled.

The rolls may be dipped in melted margarine and rolled in the following mixture:

1½ cups white sugar
1½ cups brown sugar
2 tablespoons cinnamon
½ cup nuts

Place the coated rolls on buttered pans and let them rise. Bake them as above, removing them from the pans while still warm.

RAISIN CINNAMON ROLLS

½ cup milk
1½ teaspoons salt
½ cup sugar
¼ cup shortening
2 tablespoons dry yeast

½ cup lukewarm water
2 teaspoons sugar
2 eggs, beaten
4 cups all-purpose flour
Melted butter

Scald the milk, then add the salt, sugar and shortening. Cool it to lukewarm. Sprinkle the yeast over the ½ cup of lukewarm water to which the 2 teaspoons of sugar have been added. Let this mixture stand for 10 to 15 minutes before stirring it and adding it to the milk. Add the beaten eggs, then work in about 4 cups of flour. Cover the batter and let it rise until double in bulk. Divide the dough in 2 and roll each half into a 9 x 12-inch rectangle. Brush each half with melted butter and sprinkle it with the following mixture:

1 cup brown sugar
2 tablespoons cinnamon
⅔ cup raisins

Roll up the rectangles as you would for jelly rolls. Cut them into 1-inch slices and place them on greased pans. Cover and let them rise until double in bulk, then bake them at 350° for about 35 minutes. Frost the rolls while they are warm with the following icing:

1 cup icing sugar
¼ teaspoon vanilla
Enough milk to make a stiff icing

IDA MAE DOUGHNUTS

Add 1½ packages of yeast to 2 cups of warm water and 1 cup of scalded milk (lukewarm) to which ½ cup of sugar has been added. Let the mixture stand for 15 minutes, then add:

¾ cup cream
5 eggs, beaten
¾ cup raisins, if desired

½ cup margarine or butter
1 cup sugar
½ teaspoon salt

Also add 9 to 10 cups of flour —enough to make a moderately stiff dough. Let it rise, then roll it out, cutting out doughnuts before letting it rise again. Deep fry the doughnuts in lard or cooking oil, first adding several tablespoons of vinegar to keep the grease from soaking into them. This recipe makes about 50 medium-sized doughnuts.

NO-FRY DOUGHNUTS

2 packages active dry yeast
¼ cup warm water
1½ cups lukewarm milk (scalded, then cooled)
½ cup sugar
1 teaspoon salt
1 teaspoon nutmeg

¼ teaspoon cinnamon
2 eggs
⅓ cup shortening
4½ cups all-purpose flour
¼ cup butter or margarine, melted
Cinnamon sugar or sugar

In a large mixing bowl, dissolve the yeast in the warm water. Add the milk, sugar, salt, nutmeg, cinnamon, eggs, shortening and 2 cups of the flour. Blend these ingredients for ½ minute with an egg beater, scraping the bowl constantly, then beat the mixture hard for 2 minutes more, scraping the bowl only occasionally. Stir in the remaining flour until the batter is smooth, scraping the side of the bowl. Cover it and let it rise in a warm place until double in size (50 to 60 minutes).

Turn the dough out onto a well-floured cloth-covered board, and roll it around lightly to coat it with flour. (The dough should be soft to handle.) With a flour-covered rolling pin, gently roll the dough to ½-inch thickness. With a floured 2½-inch doughnut cutter, cut out doughnuts and lift them carefully with a spatula to a greased baking sheet, placing them 2 inches apart. Brush them with melted butter, then cover and let them rise until double in size, for about 20 minutes.

Preheat the oven to 425°, then bake the doughnuts 8 to 10 minutes or until they are golden in color. Immediately brush them with melted butter and shake on cinnamon sugar or sugar. This recipe makes 1½ to 2 dozen doughnuts.

YEAST DOUGHNUTS

6 cups all-purpose flour (or more)
1 cup lukewarm water
2 cakes yeast
1 tablespoon sugar
1 cup scalded milk

2 teaspoons salt
3 tablespoons sugar
¼ pound shortening
3 eggs, beaten

Sift the flour. Pour the water over the yeast, adding the tablespoon of sugar; stir it and let it stand. Meanwhile, pour the scalded milk into a bowl and add the salt, 3 tablespoons of sugar and the shortening. When it cools to lukewarm, add the water/yeast mixture and 3 cups of the flour. Beat the mixture until it is smooth, then add the eggs and the rest of the flour. Let the dough rise in a warm place until it is double in size. Roll it out, cutting out the doughnuts and letting it rise again. Fry the doughnuts in hot grease. This recipe makes about 75 doughnuts.

CREAM STICKS

2 packages yeast
1 cup warm water
6 cups all-purpose flour
1 cup scalded milk
½ cup margarine

⅔ cup sugar
2 eggs
½ teaspoon salt
1 teaspoon vanilla

Dissolve the yeast in the water, then mix it with the rest of the ingredients to form a dough. Let the dough rise until it is double in size; knead and form it into sticks 3½ x 1½-inches. Let it rise again before frying it in deep fat.

Cream Filling;

3 tablespoons flour
1 cup milk
1 cup sugar

1 cup Crisco
1 teaspoon vanilla
2½ cups confectioner's or icing sugar

To make the filling, cook together the flour and milk. Cream the sugar and Crisco, then add the flour/milk mixture and the vanilla. Cream it well and add the powdered sugar. Slit open the top of the cream sticks to fill them. If desired, frost them with the following frosting.

Frosting;

½ cup brown sugar
4 tablespoons butter
2 tablespoons milk

1 teaspoon vanilla
Icing sugar

Mix the first three ingredients and let them come to a boil before allowing them to cool. Add the vanilla and enough icing sugar to make the frosting the right spreading consistency.

PUFFY STICKS

1 cup boiling water
¼ cup shortening
½ cup sugar
1 teaspoon salt
1 cup milk

1 cake yeast
½ cup lukewarm water
2 eggs, beaten
8 cups flour

Pour the boiling water onto the shortening, sugar and salt, then add the milk. When the mixture is lukewarm, add the yeast which has been dissolved in the lukewarm water, then the eggs and about half of the flour. Beat it vigorously, then add the remaining flour to make a soft dough. Place it in a greased bowl and keep it covered in the refrigerator until it is ready to use. Then take part of the dough and roll it out to about ¼-inch thickness. With a knife, cut it into oblong pieces and fry them in deep fat (400° to 425°). Put the rest of the dough into the refrigerator to keep for another day.

RUBY'S LONG JOHNS

1½ packages dry yeast
¼ cup warm water
½ cup boiling water
½ cup shortening
⅓ cup sugar

1 teaspoon salt
½ cup milk
2 eggs, beaten
5 to 6 cups sifted all-purpose flour

Dissolve the yeast in the warm water. Combine the boiling water and the shortening, add the sugar and salt, and stir the mixture until it is lukewarm. Blend in the dissolved yeast, the milk and eggs. Gradually stir in enough flour for easy handling, kneading the dough until it is smooth. Place it in a greased bowl, turning the dough to grease the top. Cover it and let it rise in a warm place until double in size (about 1 hour). Turn the dough onto a floured surface, and roll it to ½-inch thickness. Cut it into strips, any size, before covering it and letting it rise to double in size (about 30 minutes). Deep fry the strips at 375°, drain them on absorbent paper, then dip them into a thin glaze.

DATE AND NUT BREAD

Pour 1½ cups of boiling water over 1 cup of chopped pitted dates or raisins. Let them stand for 10 minutes, then add the following and beat the mixture well:

1½ cups sugar
2¼ cups sifted flour
½ teaspoon salt
2 teaspoons soda
1 tablespoon melted shortening

1 beaten egg
½ teaspoon baking powder
½ teaspoon vanilla
1 cup chopped nuts

Bake it in a greased 9 x 5 x 3-inch loaf pan at 350° for 1¼ hours or until done.

You may like it best after it "ages" for a day or two, or after you take it from the freezer later on.

ORANGE NUT BREAD

Grated rind of 1 orange
½ cup water
1 teaspoon salt
½ cup sugar
Milk
Juice of 1 orange
1 egg, beaten

1 cup sifted all-purpose flour
1 cup whole wheat flour
2 teaspoons baking powder
¼ teaspoon soda
¼ cup shortening
½ cup chopped nuts

Combine the orange rind, water, salt and sugar and boil the mixture for 10 minutes. Allow it to cool. Add milk to the orange juice to make 1 cup, before adding it with the beaten egg to the cooled mixture. Blend the flours with the baking powder and soda, and cut in the shortening until the mixture is of meal-like consistency. Pour the liquids into the dry ingredients and stir vigorously until they are well mixed, then add the nuts and blend the mixture. Bake it in a loaf pan in a moderate oven (350°) for 50 to 60 minutes.

DELICIOUS PUMPKIN BREAD

1⅔ cups sifted all-purpose flour
¼ teaspoon baking powder
1 teaspoon soda
¾ teaspoon salt
½ teaspoon cinnamon
½ teaspoon nutmeg
⅓ cup shortening

1⅓ cups sugar
½ teaspoon vanilla
2 eggs
1 cup mashed pumpkin
⅓ cup water
½ cup chopped walnuts or pecans

Grease a regular (9 x 5 x 3-inch) loaf pan. Sift together the flour, baking powder, soda, salt and spices. Cream the shortening, sugar and vanilla before adding the eggs, one at a time, and beating thoroughly after each addition. Stir in the pumpkin. Then add the previously sifted dry ingredients alternately with the water, beating just until the mixture is smooth. Be careful not to overbeat. Fold in the nuts.

Turn the batter into the prepared pan and bake it at 350° for about 45 to 55 minutes or until done. Turn the bread out onto a wire rack and allow it to cool before storing it in a tight container. Slice and serve this bread with butter.

CREAM PUFFS

½ cup butter
1 cup boiling water
1 cup sifted all-purpose flour

¼ teaspoon salt
4 eggs

Melt the butter in the boiling water and add the flour and salt together, stirring vigorously. Cool the mixture, stirring it constantly until it forms a ball that doesn't separate. Add the eggs, one at a time, beating hard after each addition until the mixture is smooth. Form cream puffs 2½ inches in diameter and place them 2 inches apart on greased cookie sheets. Bake them at 450° for 15 minutes or 325° for 25 minutes. Remove them from the cookie sheets to cool on a wire rack. When the cream puffs are cold, cut a hole in the side of each one, and fill them with sweetened whipped cream or vanilla sauce. This recipe makes 12 cream puffs.

CORNMEAL MUFFINS

1 cup cornmeal
1 cup all-purpose flour
¼ cup sugar
1 teaspoon salt
4 teaspoons baking powder

1 cup milk
2 eggs, beaten
4 tablespoons melted butter or other
   shortening

Sift together the dry ingredients, then add the milk, eggs and melted shortening. Stir the mixture quickly until the dry ingredients are just moistened. Bake the batter in greased muffin tins for about 20 minutes at 400°.

SIX-WEEK MUFFINS

2 cups boiling water
6 cups bran (or all-bran cereal)
1 cup shortening
3 cups sugar (scant)
4 eggs, beaten

1 quart buttermilk
5 cups all-purpose flour
5 teaspoons soda
2 teaspoons salt

Pour the boiling water over 2 cups of the bran and let it stand. Mix in the melted shortening. Mix the rest of the bran with the sugar, eggs and buttermilk. Sift the flour with the soda and salt. Then combine all the ingredients and bake the batter as needed at 400° for 20 minutes. Dates, raisins or chopped apples may be added at baking time.

This batter will keep for up to 6 weeks in the refrigerator.

BLUEBERRY MUFFINS

2 tablespoons shortening
2 tablespoons sugar
1 egg
2 cups all-purpose flour

3 teaspoons baking powder
¼ teaspoon salt
1 cup milk
1¼ cups floured blueberries

Cream together the shortening and sugar before adding the egg, flour, baking powder, salt and milk. Mix it thoroughly, then fold in the blueberries. Bake the batter in greased muffin tins at 400° for 20 minutes.

WHOLE WHEAT MUFFINS

2 cups whole wheat flour
4 teaspoons baking powder
1 teaspoon salt

2 tablespoons sugar
1 cup milk
2 tablespoons lard

Mix together the flour, baking powder, salt and sugar, then stir in the milk. Mix in the melted lard and beat the batter well. Bake it in greased muffin pans in a moderate oven (425°) for 20 to 25 minutes. This recipe makes 18 muffins.

Chopped figs or dates may be added if desired.

BISCUITS SUPREME

2 cups all-purpose flour
½ teaspoon salt
2 teaspoons sugar
4 teaspoons baking powder

½ teaspoon cream of tartar
½ cup shortening
⅔ cup milk

Sift together the dry ingredients, then cut in the shortening until the mixture resembles coarse crumbs. Add the milk all at once and stir it just until the dough follows the fork around the bowl. Roll out the dough to ½-inch thickness. Cut it with a biscuit cutter and place the dough pieces on an ungreased cookie sheet. Bake them in a hot oven (450°) for 10 to 12 minutes.

SOUTHERN BISCUITS

2 cups all-purpose flour
¾ teaspoon salt
3 teaspoons baking powder

1 teaspoon soda
4 tablespoons shortening
1 cup buttermilk

Sift together all the dry ingredients, and work in the shortening. Add the liquid to make a soft dough, then roll it out on a slightly floured board to a thickness of ½-inch. With a biscuit cutter, cut the dough before putting it into a greased pan and baking it in a hot oven (425°) for 15 minutes.

For cheese biscuits, add 1 cup of grated cheese to the mixture.

SOUPS

AMISH BEAN SOUP

2 to 3 tablespoons butter	Salt
1 cup cooked navy beans	Pepper
¼ cup water	Allspice
3 quarts milk (approximate)	2 quarts (approximate) stale bread, thinly sliced

Brown the butter in a saucepan, then add the beans and water. Bring them to the boiling point before adding the milk, salt and pepper to taste, and allspice if desired. Boil the mixture then remove it from the stove, and add enough of the bread to thicken it. Cover it and let it stand for about ½ hour before serving. Serve the soup with pickled red beets or pickles.

Variations: Instead of beans, try diced potatoes.

For Egg Soup, add about 6 or 8 diced hardcooked eggs with the bread, omitting the beans.

BACON BEAN SOUP

1 pound bacon ends, cut into small
   pieces (do not fry)
1 pound navy beans
1 chopped onion
4 quarts water (approximate)
Salt and pepper to taste

Boil the ingredients slowly for about 2 hours. Serve the soup with crackers.

Bacon ends are inexpensive and have lots of smoke flavor and meat. This soup is excellent for those very cold winter evenings.

DELICIOUS BEAN SOUP

1 pound (2 cups) navy beans, dried
2½ quarts water
1 meaty ham bone (1½ pounds)
1 clove garlic, minced
1 small bay leaf
1 cup cubed potatoes

1 cup celery, thinly sliced
1 cup onion, finely chopped
1 cup carrots, cubed
Salt
Pepper

Boil the beans in the water for 2 minutes before removing them from the heat to let stand for 1 hour. Then add the ham bone, garlic and bay leaf to the beans, and cover and simmer them for 2 hours or until the ingredients are almost tender. Add the vegetables and salt and pepper to taste, and simmer them for 1 hour longer. Remove the ham bone, cut off the meat and dice it to add to the beans. Reheat the soup almost to boiling, then remove the bay leaf.

OLD-FASHIONED BEAN SOUP AND HAM

1 pound navy beans
1 ham bone (or bacon)
3 quarts water
½ cup chopped green pepper
1 cup celery, chopped
2 cups diced potatoes

1 medium onion, chopped
3 carrots, sliced
1 tablespoon salt
¼ teaspoon pepper
1 cup tomato juice

Simmer the beans and the ham bone in the water for 2 hours. Add the rest of the ingredients and simmer them for 2 hours longer, or until the beans are tender. (Cut down the cooking time of the beans by soaking them before boiling.)

YANKEE BEAN SOUP

1¼ cups dried navy beans
5 cups water
½ teaspoon salt
1 teaspoon molasses
½ cup salt pork, cut into ¼-inch cubes
⅓ cup onion rings
3 slices bacon, cut into pieces

¼ cup chopped onion
½ cup diced cooked carrots
⅓ cup finely chopped celery leaves
1 teaspoon molasses
2 cups milk
Salt to taste

Place the beans in a 3 to 4 quart sauce pan and add the water. Bring them to a boil before removing them from the heat to stand for 2 hours or overnight. Add the salt, 1 teaspoon of molasses, pork and onions, then cover and simmer them for 2 hours or until the beans are tender. Shake the pan occasionally to prevent sticking. Cook the bacon and chopped onion until the bacon is lightly browned. Mash the beans mixture slightly then add the bacon and the remaining ingredients. Simmer them for 10 minutes.

CABBAGE CHOWDER

3 cups water
4 cups coarsely shredded cabbage
2 cups sliced carrots
3 cups diced potatoes
1 tablespoon salt

½ teaspoon sugar
¼ teaspoon pepper
4 cups scalded milk
2 tablespoons butter

Cook the vegetables and the seasonings in water until they are tender. Add the scalded milk and butter. Serve it with crackers.

CHILLY DAY STEW

1 large carrot, chopped
3 onions
1 quart potatoes, peeled and diced
2 tablespoons rice

2 tablespoons macaroni
1 teaspoon salt
1 pint cream

In a kettle of rapidly boiling water, cook the carrot while you are cleaning and chopping the onions. Add them to the stew kettle, along with the potatoes, rice, macaroni, salt and enough water to cover the ingredients. Cook them slowly until they are tender. When ready to serve, add the cream, or substitute butter and milk. Let it mix thoroughly, but do not boil the stew again. Serve it with crackers or hot toast.

CORN SOUP

3 pints milk
1½ cups creamed corn
1 teaspoon salt

1 tablespoon sugar
2 eggs, well-beaten
2 tablespoons butter

Combine the milk, corn, salt and sugar, and boil the mixture for a few minutes. Add the eggs but do not stir them in. Boil the soup a little longer, then beat it lightly before adding the butter. Serve it with crackers.

CREAM OF CORN SOUP

2 cups boiling water
2 cups canned corn
½ cup celery, chopped
1 tablespoon onion, chopped
½ cup parsley, chopped

2 cups milk
2 tablespoons butter
2 tablespoons flour
1 teaspoon salt
⅛ teaspoon pepper

Add the corn, celery, onion and parsley to the boiling water, cover and simmer for 20 minutes, then strain. Scald the milk and add it to the strained corn stock. Melt the butter and add it to the flour before adding this to the combined liquids. Season and heat the mixture to the boiling point.

FRENCH ONION SOUP

¼ cup butter or margarine
3 large onions, sliced
1 quart beef broth

1 quart water
1 teaspoon Worcestershire sauce
Salt and pepper

Melt the butter or margarine in a large pan. Add the onions and fry them slowly, stirring occasionally until they are soft and golden. Then add the beef broth, water and Worcestershire sauce, and season with salt and pepper. This recipe serves 6 to 8.

Variations: Just before serving, slice in a couple of wieners.

Serve it with cheese crackers.

For a richer soup, add a couple of beef bouillon cubes.

ONION TOMATO SOUP

½ medium-sized onion, cut up
Celery leaves, dried or fresh
4 tablespoons margarine
½ cup flour (approximate)
Tomato juice (about 4 cups)

Water
Sugar
Salt
Red pepper or paprika
Cream or milk

Sauté in the margarine the onion and some celery leaves. When the onion is tender, stir in the flour until it is slightly browned, then slowly add tomato juice. Stir the mixture to smooth the lumps until it becomes the thickness of gravy. Add some water, sugar, salt and red pepper or paprika to suit your taste. Before serving this soup add some cream or milk.

CREAM OF PEA SOUP

1 quart fresh peas
1 cup cubed ham
½ cup ham broth

3 cups milk
1 teaspoon salt
1 tablespoon sugar

Cook the peas and put them through a strainer, reserving the water in which they were cooked. Brown and cook the ham until it is tender. Combine all the ingredients with the reserved water and bring it to a boil. If desired, add ½ cup of cream before serving. Serve this soup with crackers.

SPLIT PEA SOUP

1 cup dried split peas
3 quarts water
1 ham bone
1 tablespoon minced onion
3 tablespoons butter

3 tablespoons flour
1 teaspoon salt
Pepper
2 cups milk

Soak the peas overnight in water, drain them in the morning and cover them with 3 quarts of water. Add the ham bone and onion and cook them until they are soft. Melt the butter and stir in the flour until they are well blended and smooth. Add the salt, some pepper and the milk and cook, stirring constantly until the mixture thickens. Combine it with the peas and ham bone and cook it until the soup is rather thick.

WINTER VEGETABLE SOUP

1 pint celery
1 pint carrots
1 pint cabbage
1 pint green beans
1 quart beef broth, OR
1 soup bone
1 pint peas

2 tablespoons salt
1 pint corn
1 cup soup beans
1 pint lima beans
1 pint tomatoes
Water
½ cup rice

Chop finely the celery, carrots, cabbage and green beans. Combine them with the rest of the ingredients in water to cover (except the rice), and cook them for 2½ to 3 hours. Add the rice 15 minutes before serving.

POTATO CREAM SOUP

2 cups raw potatoes, diced
2 onions, minced
2 stalks celery, diced, OR
2 tablespoons dried celery leaves
2½ cups boiling water

1 tablespoon butter
3½ tablespoons flour
2 cups milk
1½ teaspoons salt
¼ teaspoon pepper

Cook the potatoes, onions and celery in the boiling water. Melt the butter in a double boiler, then add the flour, milk and seasoning to make a basic white sauce (see page 49). Cook it until it is thick and smooth. Rub the potato mixture through a sieve, add the white sauce and garnish it with parsley before serving. Serve the soup with crackers.

Variations: This soup may also be made with milk instead of white sauce.

One cup of noodles may be used instead of the potatoes and white sauce. Bring the milk to a boil and cook the noodles until they are soft. Combine all the ingredients, and let the soup stand a short while before serving.

Chopped hardboiled eggs may also be added.

POTATO RIVVEL SOUP

1 medium-sized onion, chopped
5 medium potatoes, diced
Salt and pepper
2 eggs, beaten
1 teaspoon salt

Flour
½ cup butter
⅛ teaspoon celery seed
1 to 1½ quarts milk
Parsley

Cook the first 3 ingredients in water until the potatoes are soft. To make rivvels, add flour to the eggs and salt, and toss and stir them until the mixture is lumpy and almost dry. Sift out the excess flour, then dump the rivvels into the potato mixture and boil them for 15 minutes. Add the butter, celery seed, milk and a pinch of parsley. Heat the soup and serve it.

This is another dish great for those cold winter evenings.

RIVVEL SOUP

½ teaspoon salt
1 cup flour
1 egg
1 quart whole milk

Mix the salt with the flour, then toss the egg lightly through it with a fork until small crumbs form. Stir this into the scalding milk, bring it to a boil, and serve it at once.

When making a small amount of this soup, use only the yolk of the egg to make extra fine rivvels.

VEGETABLE SOUP

1 large soup bone, OR
Ribs of beef
2 cups diced potatoes
2 large onions
1 cup shredded cabbage
4 ripe tomatoes
3 large carrots
½ stalk celery
½ can whole corn, OR

4 ears of corn
½ pint string beans, cut finely
1 green pepper, diced
1 red pepper, diced
1 cup lima beans
⅛ cup rice
¼ cup barley
Parsley leaves

Cook the soup bone or meat in water to cover until it is half done. Add the raw vegetables and cook them for ½ hour, then add the cooked vegetables and cook them until all the ingredients are well done. Cook the rice and barley separately or put it into the kettle with the meat when it is placed on the stove. Add chili powder to make the soup more tasty.

SUCCOTASH CHOWDER

1 large onion, chopped
3 tablespoons butter
1 cup fresh or canned corn
1 cup fresh or canned lima beans
2 cups potatoes, diced
1 cup water

1 teaspoon salt
¼ teaspoon pepper
1 teaspoon parsley, chopped
3 cups milk
2 tablespoons flour
¼ cup water

Sauté the onion in the butter in a pressure cooker until the onion is slightly browned. Add the vegetables, 1 cup of water, and the salt and pepper, cover, and set the control. After the control jiggles, cook the mixture for 2 minutes, then reduce the pressure immediately. Add the milk and heat it to boiling. Blend the flour with the water to make a smooth paste, and add it to the soup, cooking it for 1 minute while stirring constantly. Garnish the servings with chopped parsley.

VEGETABLE OYSTER SOUP (SALSIFY)

Scrape the salsify clean and slice it thinly (about 1 or 2 cups, according to family size). Cook it in water until it is tender, then add milk, salt and pepper to taste, and a chunk of butter. Bring the soup to the boiling point, then serve it over crackers. A few dried parsley or celery leaves may be added.

OYSTER STEW

3 pints milk
1 pint water
1 tablespoon salt (scant)

10-ounce can oysters (or amount
    desired)
3 tablespoons butter

Bring the milk, water and salt to a boil, letting it boil for a few minutes. Add the oysters and keep it over the heat for a few minutes but do not let it boil. Reduce the heat and let the mixture stand until the oysters come to the surface. Then use low heat for 5 to 10 minutes longer, or until the oysters disappear from the top. Add the butter. Serve the stew with crackers.

SALMON SOUP

2 to 3 tablespoons butter
3 quarts milk (approximate)

Salt and pepper
1 can salmon, chopped

Brown the butter in a saucepan, then add the milk, and salt and pepper to taste. When it begins to boil, add the salmon, and heat it. Serve this soup with crackers or toasted bread cubes.

CREAM OF CHICKEN SOUP

Make a medium white sauce. Add a little bit of chopped onion, some peas, diced, cooked carrots, diced cooked potatoes, chopped chicken meat, a pinch of sugar, and salt and pepper to taste.

This recipe may be used as a casserole. Just add more vegetables, a thicker sauce and top it with biscuits. Then bake it.

HAM SOUP

4 cups cubed ham
¾ cup chopped onion
4 medium-sized potatoes

Large handful of noodles
3 quarts milk

Combine the ham and onions and cook them until the ham is soft and brown. Cut the potatoes into small cubes, add a little salt and cook them until they are soft, before adding them to the ham. Cook the noodles in salt water until they are soft, drain, and add them to the ham too, along with the milk. Bring the mixture to a boil, add salt and pepper, and it's ready to serve with crackers.

CHILI SOUP

1 pound ground beef
2 tablespoons shortening
2 onions, minced
½ green pepper, diced
1 quart tomato juice or soup (diluted if
desired)

1 small can kidney beans plus liquid
2 teaspoons salt
1 teaspoon chili powder

Brown the beef in the shortening and add the onions and pepper. Brown them lightly. Stir in the tomatoes, kidney beans, salt and chili powder, and simmer the soup for 1 hour.

WIENER SOUP

Noodles, a handful
1½ quarts milk
½ pound wieners, sliced

1 teaspoon salt
2 tablespoons butter

Cook the noodles until they are tender. Heat the milk, add the wieners, salt and noodles, and boil them together. Then add the butter. Serve the soup with crackers.

HEARTY HAMBURGER SOUP

2 tablespoons butter
1 pound ground beef
1 cup chopped onions
1 cup sliced carrots
½ cup chopped green peppers
2 cups tomato juice

1 cup diced potatoes
1½ teaspoons salt
1 teaspoon seasoned salt
⅛ teaspoon pepper
⅓ cup flour
4 cups milk

Melt the butter in a saucepan and brown the meat. Then add the onions and cook them until they are transparent. Stir in the remaining ingredients except the flour and milk. Cover and cook the mixture over low heat until the vegetables are tender, about 20 to 25 minutes. Combine the flour with 1 cup of the milk, and stir it into the soup mixture. Boil it, add the remaining milk, and heat it, stirring frequently. Do not boil the soup after the remaining milk has been added. This recipe makes quite a large amount.

Hearty Hamburger Soup can be adapted to your family's taste; for example, you can substitute celery for the green pepper, and instead of the 4 cups of milk, use 1 to 1½ cups of skim milk powder and less flour.

VEGETABLES AND SAUCES

HINTS FOR VEGETABLES AND SAUCES

For more economical, nutritious and tasteful mashed potatoes, cook the potatoes with the skins on. When they are soft, push them through a ricer or Foley mill. Immediately stir in hot milk and add salt. They are also good without the milk.

In grandmother's day lard was often used on vegetables instead of butter. It is surprisingly good on cooked cabbage and on cooked navy or snap beans.

To get youngsters to eat more of the healthful salads, give them a serving when they are hungry and impatiently waiting for dinner to be ready.

Vegetables retain their flavor and value more when cooked with very little water, in a pan with a tight-fitting lid. When they begin to boil, lower the heat and allow them to simmer.

Add butter to your red beets and they will not be so apt to boil over.

For something different, put the potatoes through the cole slaw cutter. Add a finely cut red pepper, then fry them.

New potatoes are delicious when washed (unpeeled), grated, then fried in oil, with or without onions. Add salt and pepper.

Add herbs, Italian seasoning, fried chicken seasoning or other seasonings to string beans for a delightful new flavor.

Cut all asparagus tops off beneath the ground, not above. When the stalk is cut, the stump bleeds, and bleeding takes the strength out of the roots. When loose dirt covers the stump it can't bleed.

Put extra value into your cooking by adding herbs. Add parsley to creamed potatoes, chives to cottage cheese, mint to meats, sage and thyme to dressings, dill to pickles, and caraway seeds to rye bread. Herbs are easily grown and make nice shrubs or can be raised in flower boxes.

ASPARAGUS AND KNEPP

6 eggs
2 cups all-purpose flour
1 teaspoon baking powder
¾ teaspoon salt

Boiling water
Asparagus
Butter

Mix together the first four ingredients. Bring some water to a boil. To make the knepp, dip a spoon into the boiling water each time, then put the mixture by spoonfuls into the water. Cook it for 15 to 20 minutes, then drain off the water and put the knepp in a dish. Top it with cooked, well-buttered asparagus.

The knepp are also good topped with peas.

CREAMED ASPARAGUS

Cook asparagus until it is soft, then remove it from the water. Make a gravy from the asparagus water—it is also good when made with whole wheat flour. Butter, salt and pepper it to taste. Put the asparagus with large broken pieces of toast into a dish. Pour the hot sauce over them and serve. Diced hardboiled eggs may be added.

BAKED BEANS

2 pounds navy beans
1 pound bacon, cut into pieces
Salt and pepper to taste

1 cup brown sugar
1 quart tomato juice

Soak the beans in water overnight. Cook them until they are almost soft, drain them, and add the rest of the ingredients. If more liquid is needed, add some water. Bake the beans at 325° for 3 or 4 hours.

BOSTON BAKED BEANS

2 cups small dried beans
2 teaspoons salt
1/8 teaspoon pepper
1/2 cup brown sugar
1/2 cup minced onion

3 tablespoons good brown bacon
   drippings
1 teaspoon prepared mustard
2 cups tomato juice
2 cups water, OR
2 cups juice from cooking beans

Soak the beans overnight, then cook them until tender. Cubed ham may be added if desired. Combine the beans with the rest of the ingredients. Bake them in a slow oven (325°) for 6 to 8 hours or longer until the beans have colored and become tender. Add more water as necessary.

Variations: *Try 1/4 cup brown sugar and 1/2 cup molasses instead of the 1/2 cup brown sugar.*

INDIANA BAKED BEANS

2 1/2 quarts dried navy beans (4 pounds)
4 quarts water
3/4 cup brown sugar
2 tablespoons salt

2 cups ketchup
1 cup molasses
3 1/2 teaspoons prepared mustard
1 large onion (2 1/2 to 3-inch diameter)

Soak the beans overnight in a large kettle of water. Simmer them for about 1 hour in the water in which they were soaked. Mix together the sugar, salt, ketchup, molasses and mustard, and add this mixture to the beans. Lay the onion on top and bake them, covered, in a slow oven (300°) for 5 hours. Add boiling water during cooking if necessary to keep the beans from becoming dry. Remove the onion before serving or canning the beans.

CANNED STRING BEAN DISHES

Make layers of string beans and onion rings. Add mushroom soup (which may be diluted with a little milk). Top them with bread crumbs and bake. (Toasted bread crumbs may be substituted for onion rings.)

Put the string beans in layers in a baking dish with 5 or 6 cut up wieners. Add 1 can of mushroom soup, and bake them at 350° until the soup bubbles.

Add fried or cooked cut up raw onions to the beans, and sprinkle the top with bacon chips.

Dried bread crumbs browned in butter may be added to cooked green beans just before serving. This adds a delicious touch to an ordinary dish.

Fry the beans with flour, minus the liquid. Before serving add a bit of celery seasoning and fried chicken seasoning, or any other seasoning with herbs. Adding leftover meat, finely cut, is also a good idea.

HARVARD BEETS

4 cups cooked diced beets
½ cup sugar
1 teaspoon salt
1 tablespoon cornstarch

¼ cup vinegar
¼ cup water
2 tablespoons butter

Mix the sugar, salt and cornstarch. Add the vinegar and water and stir the mixture until it is smooth. Cook it for 5 minutes, then add the beets and let it stand for 30 minutes. Just before serving, bring the beets to a boil and add the butter. (Omit the salt when using canned beets which have been salted.)

Variations: Harvard Beets can also be made with canned pickled red beets by omitting the vinegar, sugar and salt. Use the beet water to make the sauce.

BROCCOLI WITH SAUCE

Broccoli
2 cups chopped onions
4 tablespoons flour

1 teaspoon salt
2 cups milk
¼ pound mild Cheddar cheese

Cook broccoli in a small amount of water, then drain it. Put half of the broccoli in a buttered casserole, and add the onions. Make a cheese sauce by cooking the flour, salt and milk until it is thick, then adding the cheese and stirring until it melts. Pour ½ of the sauce on top of the broccoli in the casserole. Add the remainder of the broccoli, then the rest of the cheese sauce. Bake it at 375° for about 45 minutes.

BROCCOLI AND BRUSSELS SPROUTS

Cover the vegetables with water and bring them to a good boil. Drain them and add butter and a small amount of water. Then simmer them until tender.

Variations: Place several slices of processed cheese on top of the vegetables. Or sprinkle them with flour and stir, then add a bit of cream.

SOUR CREAM CABBAGE

4 cups very finely grated cabbage
1 tablespoon flour

2 tablespoons sour cream
Salt and pepper

Simmer the cabbage until it is soft in a tightly covered saucepan with very little water. With a flour shaker, sprinkle approximately 1 tablespoon of flour over the cabbage, add the sour cream, and salt and pepper to taste.

BAKED CARROTS

2½ cups cooked, mashed carrots
1 tablespoon onions, minced
2 tablespoons butter
3 eggs, separated
2 cups milk

½ cup minced celery
1 teaspoon salt
Dash of pepper
1 cup bread crumbs

Cook the onions in the butter until they are soft, and add them to the carrots. Add the beaten egg yolks, milk, celery, seasoning and bread crumbs. Then beat the egg whites and fold them in. Place the mixture in a greased baking dish and bake it at 350° for 40 minutes.

Most youngsters who turn up their noses at carrots will love this dish.

SCALLOPED CARROTS

12 carrots
4 tablespoons butter
4 tablespoons flour
2 cups milk
1 diced onion
¼ teaspoon salt

⅛ teaspoon pepper
1 teaspoon mustard
½ cup diced Velveeta cheese
¼ teaspoon celery salt
Crushed potato chips

Slice the carrots and cook them until they are tender but not too soft. Make a basic white sauce (see page 49) with the butter, flour and milk, and add it to the carrots. Also add the onion, salt, pepper, mustard and cheese, then pour this carrot mixture into a casserole. Top it with the potato chips, and bake it at 350° for 45 minutes.

CREAMED CAULIFLOWER

Cook cauliflower in salted water until it is soft. Make a basic white sauce (see page 49) and add cheese (Velveeta is best). Pour the sauce over the cauliflower and serve it hot.

Cheese sauce is good with different vegetables, such as asparagus (with toast).

CREAMED CELERY

1 quart finely cut celery
½ teaspoon salt
2 tablespoons sugar
2 tablespoons vinegar

1 tablespoon flour
Milk
2 tablespoons salad dressing or
    mayonnaise

Cook together the celery, salt, sugar and vinegar until the celery is tender, not using more water than necessary. Add a sauce made with the flour and a little milk. Bring everything to a boil, then stir in the salad dressing or mayonnaise.

CORN FRITTERS

6 big ears of corn
2 eggs
½ teaspoon salt

Pepper to taste
1 cup flour
1 cup milk

Cut the corn with a salad cutter and add the rest of the ingredients. Mix it well and drop it by tablespoons into a frying pan with melted butter or lard.

CRUSHED CORN FRITTERS

1 pint crushed corn
2 eggs
1 cup flour or cracker crumbs
2 tablespoons sugar

2 teaspoons baking powder
Milk to moisten
Salt and pepper to taste

Combine all the ingredients and mix them well. Form the mixture into balls the size of a walnut, and fry them in deep fat.

SCALLOPED CORN

1 quart canned corn
1 cup cracker crumbs
2 eggs, beaten

½ cup milk
Salt and pepper to taste

Place the corn and cracker crumbs in layers in a casserole, keeping a few cracker crumbs for the top. Mix the eggs, milk and seasoning and pour it over the corn. Add more milk until the corn is covered and top it with the reserved crumbs. Bake it at 350° for 20 minutes or until brown. For a taste variation, try adding chopped onions.

This Scalloped Corn recipe may be made on the burner on top of the stove. Simply put all the ingredients into a heavy saucepan and stir them briskly with a fork, heating them on low heat until the corn mixture thickens. Do not stir it while it is heating, as the corn tends to become watery when cooked on the burner.

BAKED CORN

2 tablespoons lard
2 tablespoons flour
1½ cups milk
1 teaspoon salt
¼ teaspoon mustard

Paprika
2 cups corn pulp
1 egg, slightly beaten
1 tablespoon Worcestershire sauce
Buttered crumbs

Make a sauce with the lard, flour, milk and seasonings. Add the corn, egg and Worcestershire sauce. Pour the mixture into a baking dish and cover it with buttered crumbs. Bake it in a moderate oven (350° to 400°) for 15 to 20 minutes.

FRIED CUCUMBERS

1 egg
1 cup milk
2 or 3 cucumbers

2 cups cracker crumbs (approximate),
    finely crushed
Butter or vegetable oil
Salt

Beat the egg and add the milk. Peel and slice the cucumbers, and dip them into the cracker crumbs. Lay the cucumbers out to dry a little, then dip them into the egg/milk mixture and then again into the cracker crumbs. Fry them in butter or vegetable oil, and sprinkle them with salt to taste.

DANDELIONS AND EGGS

Fry dandelion greens in butter until they are crisp. They will turn black but they are not burned, as long as you continue to add butter while frying. Also add salt. If you can still see some green, then they need more frying. When they are done, put eggs on top, cover the pan and turn the burner off. Let them set until the eggs are done.

These greens taste like bacon and eggs, but it takes a little practice to cook them just right. If the dandelion stalk is too mature and bitter, try fixing the flowers in the same manner described above.

FRIED EGGPLANT

½ eggplant
1 egg
¼ cup milk

Cracker crumbs, finely crushed
Crisco
Butter

Pare the eggplant and slice it into ½-inch thicknesses. Dip it into the egg which has been beaten with the milk, then into the cracker crumbs. Fry the eggplant in the Crisco and butter (half and half) until it is nicely browned, but do not fry it too fast.

ONION PATTIES

¾ cup flour
1 tablespoon sugar
1 tablespoon cornmeal
2 teaspoons baking powder

1 teaspoon salt
¾ cup milk
2½ cups finely chopped onions

Mix together the dry ingredients then add the milk. This should make a fairly thick batter. Add the onions and mix it thoroughly. Drop the batter by spoonfuls into deep fat. Flatten them into patties when you turn them.

ONION RINGS

Onions
½ cup flour
¼ teaspoon salt
½ teaspoon baking powder

1 egg, lightly beaten
⅛ cup corn oil
¼ cup milk

Cut onions into rings, dip them into a mixture of the above ingredients, and fry them in deep fat or oil.

FRIED OYSTER PLANT

1 oyster plant
Salt water
Eggs, beaten

Cracker crumbs
Butter

Clean the oyster plant and cook it in salt water until it is soft. Dip it in beaten eggs, roll it in fine cracker crumbs and fry it in butter until it is nicely browned on both sides.

PATCHES

6 medium-sized potatoes, raw
2 tablespoons flour
Milk

Salt and pepper
Parsley (optional)
Onions (optional)

Peel the potatoes, grind or grate them, and drain them in a colander. Stir in the flour and milk to make a thin batter, and add salt and pepper to taste. Parsley and onion may be added. Fry them in a well-oiled, hot skillet.

CRUSTY BAKED POTATOES

6 medium potatoes
4 tablespoons melted butter

½ cup fine cracker crumbs
1 teaspoon salt

Pare the potatoes, wash them and wipe them dry. Cut them in halves and roll them in the melted butter, then in the crumbs to which the salt has been added. Place the potatoes in a greased pan and bake them at 350° for 1 hour.

BASQUE POTATOES

½ cup finely chopped onions
½ cup chopped celery
½ cup shredded carrots
1 clove garlic, minced
Butter

2 cups chicken broth
4 cups potatoes, pared and cubed
Salt and pepper
Parsley, chopped

In a 10-inch skillet, sauté the onions, celery, carrots and garlic in the melted butter until they are tender. Add the chicken broth, potatoes, salt and pepper to the sautéed vegetables, cover them, and simmer for 10 minutes. Then remove the cover, and continue to simmer the vegetables, stirring them occasionally, for 20 minutes more or until the broth thickens. Sprinkle them with parsley. This recipe makes 4 to 6 servings.

FRIED NEW POTATOES

1 quart new potatoes
1 onion
2 tablespoons oil

Grate the unpeeled potatoes, slice in the onion, and fry them together in the oil.

POT LUCK POTATO CASSEROLE

2 pounds jacket-boiled potatoes,
  peeled and chopped
4 tablespoons melted butter
1 teaspoon salt
¼ teaspoon pepper
½ cup chopped onions

1 can cream of chicken soup,
  undiluted
1 pint sour cream
2 cups grated, sharp Cheddar cheese
2 cups crushed cornflakes mixed with
  ¼ cup melted butter

Combine the potatoes and butter in a large mixing bowl. Add the salt, pepper, onions, cream of chicken soup, sour cream and cheese. Blend this mixture thoroughly and pour it into a greased 9 x 13-inch casserole. Cover it with the crushed cornflakes mixed with melted butter. Bake it at 350° for 45 minutes.

SCALLOPED POTATOES

6 cups medium-sized potatoes
3 tablespoons butter
2 tablespoons flour
3 cups top milk or half-and-half
1 teaspoon salt

Pepper to taste
1 teaspoon parsley (optional)
2 tablespoons chopped onions
  (optional)

Slice the potatoes. Make a basic white sauce (see page 49) of the butter, flour and milk. Place half of the potatoes in a greased casserole and cover them with half of the sauce and seasonings. Add the remaining potatoes and seasonings, then the remaining sauce. Cover the casserole and bake it in a moderately hot oven (400°) for about 1 hour. Uncover it and continue baking it until the top forms a brown crust and the potatoes are done.

Variations: To shorten the baking time, potatoes may be boiled for 10 minutes.

Add 5 wieners or 1 cup of diced ham, or 2 to 3 slices of bacon pieces for extra flavor.

Bake the potatoes with 1½ cups of diced Velveeta cheese.

Raw sliced potatoes do not require a sauce when top milk is used.

POTATOES WITH CHEESE SAUCE

Dice a dish of potatoes and cook them in salt water until they are soft. While they are cooking, make a sauce by melting butter in a skillet and adding flour, as for any basic white sauce (see page 49). Next add milk, and when the sauce thickens slightly, add cheese. (Onion may also be added.) Pour the sauce over the hot potatoes and serve.

BAKED SWEET POTATOES

4 cups sweet potatoes, cooked, salted
   and diced
1 cup brown sugar

1 teaspoon flour
½ cup cream
Marshmallow bits

Put the sweet potatoes into a greased casserole, and add the sugar, flour and cream. Bake them at 350° for 20 to 30 minutes or until they are sticky. Cover the top with small marshmallow bits and brown them lightly until they begin to melt.

SPINACH OMELET

Melt butter in a hot skillet. Add spinach, and heat it until it is wilted (about 2 to 3 minutes). Pour 3 or 4 beaten eggs over the spinach. Sprinkle it with salt. Cover it and cook until done.

SQUASH DISHES AND COOKING HINTS

- *When cooking corn on the cob, lay slices of peeled squash on top of the corn. Brush the squash with butter and sprinkle it with salt and pepper. By the time the corn is ready, the squash will be soft.*

- *When baking squash, scoop out the center but don't peel it. Prepare hamburger with your favorite seasoning, and fill the center of the squash with the meat. Cover it with foil and bake it at 350° until the squash is soft.*

- *If you don't have hamburger, peel and finely grate raw potatoes. Put them into the center of the squash, and add butter, milk, salt and pepper.*

- *Add leftover squash to caramel pudding.*

- *Use squash instead of pumpkin for pie.*

- *To make baked squash, brush squash slices with soft butter. Season them with salt and pepper and with brown sugar if desired. Bake them at 375° until they are brown. Turn the squash slices once to brown both sides.*

COCONUT SQUASH

2 cups mashed squash (or pumpkin)
1 cup fine biscuit crumbs, or bread
   crumbs
1½ cups milk
1 cup sugar
½ cup grated coconut

2 egg yolks, well-beaten
3 tablespoons melted butter
1½ grated orange peels (optional)
½ teaspoon nutmeg
¾ teaspoon salt

Mix together all the ingredients thoroughly. In a casserole, bake the mixture at 350° until it thickens and browns slightly. Make a meringue of the egg whites and 2 tablespoons of sugar. Spread it over the squash and brown it.

TOMATO BREAD

1 quart tomato juice, or whole
   tomatoes
Sugar
Pepper
Butter

Heat the tomato juice, and add sugar and pepper to taste, and a lump of butter. Pour it over broken toast or soda crackers just before serving.

TOMATO CASSEROLE

Raw tomatoes, peeled
Green pepper rings
Onion rings
Sugar

Salt
Pepper
Bread crumbs
Butter

Slice the tomatoes and place them in a cake pan. Arrange the pepper rings and onion rings over the tomatoes, and season them with sugar, salt and pepper. Prepare the bread crumbs as you would for filling, seasoning them with salt, pepper and butter. Bake the casserole in a moderate oven (350°) for 1 to 1½ hours.

BAKED TURNIP

1 medium turnip (1½ pounds)	2 tablespoons chopped parsley
¾ teaspoon salt	¼ cup water
1 tablespoon sugar	3 tablespoons butter
⅛ teaspoon ginger	

Peel the turnip and cut it into ½-inch thick slices. Put it into a buttered 1-quart baking dish. Combine the seasonings and sprinkle them over the turnip. Pour the water over all and dot it with the butter. Cover the dish tightly and bake it at 425° for 50 minutes or until done. Stir the ingredients with a fork at least once.

AMISH DRESSING

4 eggs	3 stems celery, finely chopped
½ teaspoon salt	¾ cup diced, cooked potatoes
⅛ teaspoon pepper	2 cups, more or less, diced chicken
½ teaspoon sage	½ cup shredded or diced cooked
½ teaspoon thyme	carrots (for color)
3½ or 4 cups milk as needed	1 loaf bread, diced and toasted
1 medium-sized onion, finely chopped	

Put the eggs into a bowl and beat them. Mix in the salt, pepper, sage and thyme. Add 2 cups of the milk, the onion, celery, potatoes, diced chicken and carrots. Add the bread crumbs with enough milk to moisten them well. (Substitute 1 cup of chicken broth for the milk to give it a different flavor.) Bake this mixture in a well-greased casserole at 350° for 1½ hours or until the liquid is of omelet-like texture.

Variations: Try 2 cups of finely cut cooked ham, instead of the chicken. Also try adding 1 large pepper, cut into short narrow strips. Parsley may be added too.

DRESSING FOR GREENS

Bacon	Vinegar
1 tablespoon flour	Sour cream or buttermilk
1 cup water	2 hardcooked eggs, diced
1 tablespoon sugar	Greens
Salt	

Cut up a few strips of bacon into a pan and fry them. Use part of the drippings to make a pan gravy with the flour. When it is brown, stir in the water and let it boil before adding the sugar, salt and vinegar to taste. A bit of sour cream or buttermilk may be added. Fold in the hardcooked eggs. Add the greens just before serving. This dressing is good with dandelions, lettuce, endive and other greens.

TOMATO GRAVY

1 cup tomato juice
½ cup water
3 tablespoons flour

½ teaspoon salt
½ cup cream
2 cups milk

Place the juice and water in a saucepan and bring it to a boil. Meanwhile, blend the flour and salt with the cream. (Add 2 tablespoons of sugar if desired.) Add the milk and mix it well. Pour the flour mixture into the hot juice, stirring it constantly until it boils and thickens.

This gravy may be served with bread, toast, crackers or fried potatoes.

LEAH'S TOMATO SAUCE

Butter
1 rounded tablespoon flour

Pure tomato juice
Sugar

Melt butter, the size of a walnut, in a pan. Add the flour, stirring it into the melted butter before adding enough tomato juice to make a slightly thickened sauce. Add sugar to taste. Serve this sauce hot with crackers or over toasted bread.

POTATO GRAVY

Pour the water from boiled potatoes into a saucepan. While it is heating, make a thickening of 1 rounded tablespoon of flour, dampen it with milk, then stir in 1 egg yolk. Mix it well, then add about ½ cup of milk. Add the thickening to the potato water, stirring it constantly. Add enough milk for the right consistency. Add salt and pepper to taste and 1 tablespoon of butter. Serve as any other gravy.

When using the white of an egg instead of the yolk, add about 1 tablespoon of cold water to the yolk to keep it from drying out.

BASIC WHITE SAUCE

2 tablespoons melted butter
2 tablespoons flour
2 cups milk

½ teaspoon salt
⅛ teaspoon pepper (optional)

Melt the butter in a saucepan. Stir in the flour, then add half of the milk. Stir it rapidly to remove all lumps, then add the remainder of the milk, and the salt. Cook it for about 1 minute, stirring constantly.

Variations: Add chopped dried celery leaves to the sauce. Cook it a few minutes, then serve it on boiled potatoes or toast.

Fry small pieces of bacon, then make a white sauce from the bacon grease, or brown a diced onion before making the sauce.

Add parsley or celery leaves and 4 or 5 chopped hardcooked eggs.

CHEESE SAUCE

Make the Basic White Sauce above (but slightly thinner) and add 1 cup of diced cheese. Stir it until the cheese is melted.

Cheese sauce is good with many different vegetables. Pour it over them just before serving.

WHOLE WHEAT SAUCE

3 to 4 tablespoons butter, or oil
2 rounded tablespoons whole wheat
   flour
2 cups milk (approximate)

Herbs
Dash of red pepper
$\frac{1}{8}$ to $\frac{1}{4}$ teaspoon basil

Melt the butter (or use oil) and add the flour. Brown it lightly, then add milk (about 2 cups) until the sauce is of the right consistency. Add herb seasonings, the red pepper and basil. This sauce is good over steamed asparagus tips and broken toast, or over string beans, peas, and other vegetables.

ONE DISH MEALS AND CASSEROLES

CHICKEN AND DRESSING

1 chicken, boned and sliced
1 loaf of bread, broken up and toasted
1 large or 2 small onions, chopped
1 cup celery, diced

2 hardcooked eggs, sliced
Salt and pepper to taste
Butter

Make a thin gravy with the chicken broth. Then mix together all the ingredients and put the mixture into a loaf pan or baking dish. Dot the top with butter and bake it at 350° for ¾ to 1 hour.

CHICKEN AND DUMPLINGS

Cook and debone the meat of 2½ pounds of chicken. Put this meat with the broth into a large kettle with a tight-fitting lid.

Dumplings:

1 egg
2 tablespoons milk
½ teaspoon salt

3 teaspoons baking powder
Flour

Beat the above ingredients with enough flour to make a good stiff dough. Drop it by spoonfuls into the boiling broth. Cook the dumplings, covered, for 5 to 8 minutes. It is important that the lid not be removed during this time. Remove the kettle from the stove, take the lid off and serve the chicken and dumplings at once. The dumplings should be light and fluffy.

CHICKEN LOAF

1 cup soft bread crumbs
½ cup sweet milk
3 cups diced cooked chicken
1 teaspoon salt

½ teaspoon pepper
3 eggs, separated
2 tablespoons melted butter
¼ cup chopped pimentos

Let the crumbs stand in the milk for 10 minutes. Then add the chicken, salt, pepper, egg yolks, butter and pimentos. Beat the egg whites until they are stiff and add them to the chicken. Place the mixture in a buttered pan and bake it for 45 minutes at 350°.

51

CHICKEN AND RICE CASSEROLE

In a flat baking dish, place chicken or hamburger. Add chopped celery or other vegetables, and uncooked rice. Add a can each of cream of celery and cream of chicken soup, or substitute a white sauce. Bake it at 350° until the rice is tender.

VEGETABLE CHICKEN CASSEROLE

According to family size, have on hand enough potatoes, carrots (cut into small pieces) and peas. Cook each vegetable separately until it is almost soft. From a canned chicken, drain off the liquid to make a thin gravy. Cut the chicken off the bone and pour the potatoes, carrots, peas and cut up chicken into a roaster or casserole, pouring the seasoned gravy on top of it. Mix it slightly. Make a biscuit dough, then drop pieces of the dough on top of the mixture. Put it into the oven at 400° for 15 to 20 minutes or until the biscuits are done.

As a short cut, cook all the vegetables together.

BAKED BEEF STEW

2 pounds beef cut into cubes	6 medium potatoes, thinly sliced
¼ cup flour	2 medium carrots, thinly sliced
¼ teaspoon celery seed	1½ cups hot water
1¼ teaspoons salt	4 teaspoons beef bouillon
⅛ teaspoon pepper	1 teaspoon Worcestershire sauce
4 medium onions, sliced	Butter or margarine

Mix together the flour and seasonings and dredge the meat in the mixture. In a large casserole with a tight-fitting cover, arrange in layers the meat and vegetables. Add the bouillon to the hot water, then add the Worcestershire sauce. Pour it evenly over the casserole. Dot the surface with butter, cover the casserole and bake it at 325° for 3 hours.

Leftover beef broth may be used instead of the water and bouillon.

DRIED BEEF CASSEROLE

¼ pound dried beef	1 cup milk
Butter	8 ounces noodles
1 can (10 ounces) cream of mushroom soup	Buttered bread crumbs

Fry the beef in butter until it is slightly browned. Add the mushroom soup and milk. Cook the noodles in salted water until they are tender. Drain them, and combine them with the beef in a buttered casserole dish. Cover the top with buttered bread crumbs, and bake it in a moderate oven (350°) until brown.

CHOW MEIN

1 heavy chicken
1 stalk celery, chopped
2 onions, chopped
1 tablespoon butter
1 tablespoon soy sauce

1 tablespoon Worcestershire sauce
Salt and pepper to taste
Sugar (optional)
3 tablespoons cornstarch

Cook the chicken until it is tender, then remove the bones. Fry the celery and onions in butter until they are brown. Add them to the chicken and broth, and cook them until the celery is tender. Add the soy and Worcestershire sauce, salt and pepper, and sugar if desired. Make a thickening with the cornstarch and add it to the chow mein. Serve this dish with chow mein noodles.

LITTLE BEEF PIES

1 beef bouillon cube
2 cups boiling water
3½ cups chopped cooked beef
2 teaspoons Worcestershire sauce
1½ teaspoons salt
1 teaspoon sugar

½ teaspoon paprika
¼ teaspoon pepper
1 package (10 ounces) frozen or
    canned mixed vegetables
¼ cup flour

Dissolve the bouillon cube in the boiling water and add the beef, Worcestershire sauce, salt, sugar, paprika and pepper. Add the vegetables, and cook the mixture for 5 minutes. Combine the flour with enough cold water to make a paste, and slowly stir it into the mixture, cooking it until it thickens. Then spoon it into 6 or 8-ounce oven-proof casseroles.

Pastry;

1 cup flour
½ cup cornmeal
¾ teaspoon salt

⅓ cup shortening
4 tablespoons cold water

Make the pastry by sifting together the flour, cornmeal and salt. Cut in the shortening until the mixture resembles coarse crumbs. Sprinkle the water by tablespoons over the mixture. Stir it lightly with a fork until it is just damp. (If necessary, add another tablespoon of cold water to make the dough hold together.) Form the dough into a ball. Divide it into 6 parts and roll each part to form a circle large enough to fit the top of each casserole. Place the pastry circle over the filling, turn the edges under, and flute them. Make several cuts in the pastry to allow steam to escape. Bake the pies in a preheated oven at 450° for 12 to 15 minutes.

MEAT PIES

Grind 3 or 4 cups of cooked meat. Add hardcooked eggs and chopped onions, and salt and pepper to taste. A desired sauce may be added to moisten the meat, such as salad dressing, ketchup or mayonnaise.

Make a dough with the following ingredients. Mix it lightly.

1 cup milk	2 eggs
2 teaspoons baking powder	2 tablespoons lard
1 teaspoon salt	2 cups all-purpose flour

Roll out the dough and cut it into squares. Put the meat on the squares and fold them over, then press down. Fry them in deep fat.

SUEY STEW

Cut a roast or stewing meat into chunks. Trim off the fat. Cut potatoes into cubes. According to the size of your family, add sufficient carrots and onions, as well as any other vegetable you like. Pour the following ingredients individually over the vegetables and meat;

1 can (10 ounces) cream of celery soup	1 can (10 ounces) cream of chicken soup
½ can water	½ can water

Do not mix the stew. Bake it for 5 hours at 275°.

BEEF AND CHEESE

1½ cups uncooked spaghetti	Seasonings
1 pound ground beef	2 cups milk
1 small onion, chopped	¾ cup grated cheese
2 tablespoons butter	1 cup tomatoes
3 tablespoons flour	

Cook the spaghetti until it is tender, then drain it. In a skillet, brown the beef and onion in the butter. Add the flour, milk and seasonings to taste. Cook it until it is thick. Mix ½ cup of the cheese with the spaghetti, and place ½ of the spaghetti in a baking dish. Add the meat mixture, top it with the tomatoes, and add the rest of the spaghetti. Sprinkle the remaining cheese on top. Bake it at 350° for 25 to 30 minutes.

BUDGET BEEF-NOODLE CASSEROLE

1 pound ground beef
3 tablespoons onions
½ teaspoon salt
½ cup diced cheese
1 egg, beaten

3 cups cooked noodles
1 cup tomato juice
2 teaspoons Worcestershire sauce
¼ cup ketchup

Mix together all the ingredients and pour the mixture into a greased casserole. Top it with ¼ cup of cracker crumbs. Bake the casserole at 350° for 1 hour.

BUSY DAY CASSEROLE

1½ cups cubed ham or hamburger
1 cup diced potatoes
1 cup diced carrots

½ cup peas, canned
½ cup green beans, canned

Brown the ham, then add the potatoes, carrots and water. Cook them until they are tender. Add the peas, beans and enough boiling water to cover them. Stir in 1 tablespoon of flour mixed with a little water. Put this mixture into a large casserole or small cake pan. Top it with your favorite biscuit dough (cheese may be added), dropped by tablespoons into the ham mixture. Bake the casserole at 350° for 20 to 30 minutes, or until done.

CHILI CON CARNE

1 pound ground beef
2 tablespoons shortening
2 onions, minced
½ green pepper

1 small can tomatoes or tomato soup
1 small can kidney beans plus liquid
2 teaspoons salt
1 teaspoon chili powder

Brown the beef in the shortening, and add the onions and diced pepper. Brown these vegetables lightly. Stir in the tomatoes, kidney beans, salt and chili powder. Simmer it for 1 hour, stirring frequently.

DELICIOUS ONE DISH DINNER

Peel potatoes, wash and slice them. Grease a casserole with butter, and put in a layer of potatoes. Add a layer of carrots if you wish, then a layer of sliced onions. Season it with salt and pepper, and put dices of butter on top. Next prepare hamburger patties and put them on top. Add a little water and cover the casserole with aluminum foil. Bake it for 1 hour at 350°.

Variations: Ham may be used instead of hamburger.

Turnips may be added.

Canned tomato soup may be poured over the casserole. Dilute it first with about half water.

FRYING PAN SUPPER

1 pound hamburger
1 small onion, chopped
2 cups potatoes, cut into strips
2 cups shredded cabbage

2 cups finely cut celery
Salt
½ cup water

Fry the hamburger and onion until it changes color, then add the potatoes, cabbage and celery. Sprinkle it with salt and add the water. Cover and simmer it for 20 minutes, or until the vegetables are done.

Canned hamburger or cut up chunk meat may also be used.

GREEN BEAN DISH

4 large potatoes, peeled and sliced
1 pound wieners, cut up, OR
1 pound hamburger, browned
1 quart canned green beans, drained
½ onion, sliced

2 cups milk
½ pound soft cheese
½ cup flour
2 teaspoons salt

Put the first 4 ingredients into a baking dish. Make a sauce by heating the milk enough to melt the cheese, and adding the flour and salt. Pour it over the ingredients in the baking dish, and bake it at 300° for 2 hours.

MEATBALL CHOWDER

2 pounds ground beef
2 teaspoons salt
⅛ teaspoon pepper
2 eggs, beaten
¼ cup chopped parsley
Garlic salt (optional)
½ cup fine cracker or bread crumbs
2 tablespoons milk
3 to 5 tablespoons flour
1 tablespoon salad oil

2 bay leaves (optional)
4 to 6 small onions, cut up
2 or 3 cups diced celery
3 to 4 cups diced potatoes
¼ cup long grain rice
6 cups tomato juice
6 cups water
1 tablespoon sugar
1 teaspoon salt
1½ cups canned corn

Mix thoroughly the meat, salt, pepper, eggs, parsley, garlic salt if desired, crumbs and milk. Form the mixture into balls the size of walnuts. Dip them in flour. In a large kettle, heat the oil, and lightly brown the meatballs on all sides. Add all the remaining ingredients except the corn. Bring the mixture to a boil, cover and cook it slowly until the vegetables are tender. Add the corn last and cook it for 10 minutes more. This recipe serves 12.

Variations: Carrots, peas and celery leaves can be used. Also try V-8 juice with less water.

HAMBURGER CASSEROLE

1 chopped onion
1 pound ground beef, fresh or canned
Salt and pepper
2½ cups canned green beans
1 can (10 ounces) tomato soup

5 potatoes, cooked
½ cup warm milk
1 egg, beaten
Cheese (optional)

Fry the onion and ground beef with salt and pepper to taste until the beef is brown. Mix the beans and soup with the meat. Pour the mixture into a 1½-quart casserole. Mash the potatoes, add the milk and egg, and mix well. Spoon mounds of potatoes onto the meat mixture. Cover it with cheese if desired. Bake the casserole at 350° for 30 minutes.

If leftover mashed potatoes are used, omit the milk.

HANDY CASSEROLE

Put a layer of browned hamburger into a dish. Place over it a layer of sliced potatoes (cooked until almost done), then a layer of canned vegetables. Add 1 can (10 ounces) of mushroom, celery or chicken soup, and top it with a layer of cheese. Cover the casserole with foil and bake it at 350° for 30 minutes.

KINGBURGER KLOPS

1½ pounds hamburger
2 slices bread soaked in water, then
   squeezed dry
3 eggs

1 chopped onion
Salt and pepper to taste
1 bay leaf (optional)

Mix the ingredients together and form the mixture into balls about 2 inches in diameter. Place them in a pan of 1½ quarts of boiling water. Cook them for 10 minutes, then place the balls in a roaster or casserole with 2 quarts of boiled potatoes cut into chunks. Mix together the following ingredients;

1 cup strained water in which the
   meatballs were boiled
1 cup sour cream plus 1 cup cold milk
   OR
2 cups milk

4 tablespoons flour
Salt and pepper to taste

Cook this mixture to make a sauce, then pour it over the meatballs. Bake the casserole at 350° for 45 minutes.

MEATBALL STEW

1½ pounds hamburger
1 cup soft bread crumbs
¼ cup finely chopped onions
1 beaten egg
1 teaspoon salt
½ teaspoon marjoram
¼ teaspoon thyme
2 tablespoons cooking oil

10-ounce can condensed tomato soup
10-ounce can condensed beef broth
4 medium potatoes, pared and
  quartered
4 carrots, scraped and cut into 1-inch
  chunks
8 small white onions, peeled
2 tablespoons chopped parsley

Combine the first 7 ingredients, and shape the mixture into 24 meatballs. Brown them in the oil in a 4-quart pan. Add the condensed soups and vegetables. Bring the mixture to a boil, then cover and simmer it for 30 minutes or until the vegetables are tender. Add the parsley. This makes 6 to 8 servings.

PORCUPINE MEATBALLS

½ cup rice
1 pound ground beef
1 teaspoon salt
½ teaspoon pepper

1 onion, minced
1 small can tomato soup
½ cup water

Wash the rice, then combine it with the meat, salt, pepper and onion. Shape the mixture into small balls. Mix together the soup and water and pour it over the meatballs. Using a pressure cooker if possible, cook the meatballs for 12 minutes. Otherwise, cook them, tightly covered, for 30 minutes.

TAMALE PIE

1 can (1 pint) kernel corn
1 pint tomatoes
½ pound ground beef
¼ pound ground pork
1 small onion, chopped

1½ tablespoons butter
1½ teaspoons salt
½ to 1 tablespoon chili powder
½ garlic bud (optional)

Boil together all the ingredients for 15 minutes. Remove the mixture from the heat and add the following;

¾ cup sweet milk
1 cup granulated cornmeal
1 egg, beaten

Mix it well and pour it into a buttered casserole. Bake it for 1 hour in a moderate oven (325°).

MEXICAN MIX-UP

1½ pounds ground beef
1 cup chopped onions
½ cup chopped green pepper
½ tablespoon chili powder
½ clove garlic
2 cups beef gravy

2 cups kidney beans, drained
2 cups cooked macaroni
¼ teaspoon salt
⅛ teaspoon pepper
½ cup shredded Cheddar cheese

In a skillet, brown the beef and cook the onion and green pepper with the chili powder and garlic until the vegetables are tender. Add the gravy, beans, macaroni, salt and pepper. Pour the mixture into a 2-quart baking dish (12 x 8 x 2 inches) and bake it at 450° for 15 minutes. Stir it, top it with the cheese, and bake it until the cheese melts.

SPAGHETTI DINNER

½ quart canned or fresh hamburger
1 pint pizza sauce (see page 264)

½ pound or more spaghetti
Salted water

Cook the hamburger until the liquid is almost taken up. Add the pizza sauce and simmer it a little longer. Meanwhile, cook in boiling, salted water about ½ pound or more of spaghetti until it is tender. Combine the meat sauce and spaghetti before serving.

SPANISH RICE

1 pound hamburger
1 small onion, chopped (optional)
½ cup diced green pepper
1 cup rice
½ cup cheese, diced

Salt and pepper
½ teaspoon chili powder (optional)
Dash of Italian seasoning (optional)
Tomato juice

Brown the hamburger, adding the onion if desired, and the green pepper. Cook the rice until it is soft, then add it to the hamburger and pepper, followed by the cheese, and salt and pepper to taste. Try adding chili powder and a dash of Italian seasoning for a more zesty flavor. Add the tomato juice (diluted with ⅓ water) to cover the ingredients. Bake it for 1 hour at 350°.

Variations: Peppers may be stuffed with the hamburger, rice, cheese, salt and pepper, and set in diluted tomato juice to bake.

MOCK TURKEY

2 pounds hamburger, browned in
   butter
2 cans (10 ounces each) cream of
   chicken soup
1 can (10 ounces) cream of celery soup

4 cups milk
1 loaf bread, broken
Salt and pepper to taste

Mix together the ingredients. Place the mixture in a pan and bake it at 350° for 45 minutes.

YUMMASETTI

1 large package noodles, cooked in
   salted water
3 pounds hamburger, fried in butter
   with 1 chopped onion
1 pint peas
2 cans (10 ounces each) mushroom
   soup

1 can (10 ounces) cream of chicken or
   cream of celery soup
1 cup sour cream
½ loaf toasted buttered bread crumbs

Mix together all the ingredients (reserving some of the bread crumbs) and pour the mixture into a greased baking dish. Top it with the reserved crumbs. Bake it at 350° for 1 hour.

SAUCY WINTER CASSEROLE

¼ pound bacon, diced
½ cup chopped onions
4 teaspoons Worcestershire sauce, OR
4 teaspoons vinegar
1 cup corn syrup
¾ teaspoon salt
¼ teaspoon paprika

¾ cup water
1½ cups tomato sauce
1 pound wieners, cut up
1 tablespoon cornstarch
2 tablespoons water
Cooked spaghetti or macaroni

Combine the bacon and onions in a skillet and fry them until the bacon is crisp and the onion is soft. Drain off extra fat. Stir in the Worcestershire sauce, corn syrup, salt, paprika, water and tomato sauce. Bring the mixture to a boil. Reduce the heat, cover and simmer it for 10 minutes. Add the wieners and simmer until they are hot. Blend the cornstarch with the 2 tablespoons of water, and stir it into the sauce, boiling it for 1 minute. Serve it on hot spaghetti or any macaroni product.

TEXAS HASH

2 large onions, sliced
2 green peppers, finely cut
3 tablespoons shortening
1 pound hamburger

2 cups tomatoes
1 cup spaghetti or macaroni
2 teaspoons salt
¼ teaspoon pepper

Fry the onions and green peppers slowly in the shortening until the onions become yellow. Add the hamburger and cook the mixture until it falls apart. Then add the tomatoes, spaghetti and seasoning, and mix. Put the mixture into a casserole, cover it and bake it at 375° for 45 minutes.

WIGGLERS

5 slices bacon
1½ pounds hamburger
2 onions
1½ cups diced potatoes
1½ cups celery
2 cups peas

1½ cups carrots, diced
1 can (10 ounces) mushroom soup
¾ quart tomato juice
1½ cups spaghetti, cooked
Velveeta cheese

Cut the bacon into small pieces and fry it with the hamburger and sliced onions until brown. Drain off the fat. Cook the potatoes, celery, peas and carrots before putting them into a roaster with the bacon, hamburger and onions. Add the spaghetti, then stir in the soup and juice. Lay slices of Velveeta cheese on top and bake it for 1 hour at 350°.

SCHNITZ UND KNEPP

1 quart dried apples (schnitz)
3 pounds ham
2 tablespoons brown sugar
2 cups flour
1 teaspoon salt

¼ teaspoon pepper
4 teaspoons baking powder
1 egg, well-beaten
Milk
3 tablespoons melted butter

Wash the dried apples then cover them with water to soak overnight. Cover the ham with boiling water and boil it for 3 hours. Add the apples and the water in which they were soaked, and boil it for 1 hour longer. Add the sugar.

Make the dumplings by sifting together the flour, salt, pepper and baking powder. Stir in the beaten egg, milk (enough to make a fairly moist, stiff batter) and butter. Drop the batter by the tablespoon into the hot ham and apples. Cover it and cook it for 15 minutes. Serve it hot.

BAKED PORK CHOPS

Put a layer of thinly sliced potatoes into a baking dish, and cover them with shredded onions, salt and pepper. Lay over this as many pork chops as needed, seasoned well on both sides. Add enough milk to moisten the ingredients, then bake them at 400° until done.

PORKY PIE

4 medium sweet potatoes
1½ teaspoons salt
2 tablespoons butter
1½ teaspoons cinnamon sugar

1 pound ground pork
1½ cups water
2 tablespoons flour
Dash of pepper

Cook the potatoes in water with 1 teaspoon of the salt, then peel them. Mash them slightly and add the butter, cinnamon sugar and the remaining salt. Add a little milk if necessary. Form the pork into patties, brown them, and drain. (Canned sausage works fine, too.) Make a gravy with the pork broth, water, flour and pepper. Pour it over the patties in a shallow baking pan. Spread the sweet potatoes on top, and bake it at 400° for 20 minutes.

CALIFORNIA RICE

1 pound bulk sausage
1 cup chopped celery
1 cup chopped onion
1 cup raw rice

1 cup cooked, diced chicken
1 can (10 ounces) mushroom soup
1 can (10 ounces) water
Salt and pepper

Brown the sausage, celery, onion and rice. (This step may be ignored if you wish.) Add the chicken, mushroom soup, water and seasonings. Put the mixture into a greased casserole. Bake it for 2 hours at 325°.

LIMA BEAN BARBECUE

2 cups dried lima beans, OR
4 cups cooked or canned lima beans
2 teaspoons salt
1 pound pork sausage links
1 tablespoon prepared horseradish

¼ cup liquid from cooked beans
½ cup chopped onions
1 cup ketchup
1 teaspoon Worcestershire sauce

Add salt to the beans and cook them until tender, then drain them. Fry the sausage until it is brown. Mix together all the ingredients except the sausage, then place ½ of this bean mixture in a 1½-quart casserole dish, and cover it with ½ of the sausages. Make another layer of the remaining bean mixture and sausages. Bake it at 400° for 15 minutes.

WASHDAY DINNER

Melt 1 tablespoon of butter in a large casserole. Line the bottom with a thick layer of onions, then add a generous layer of potatoes. Over the potatoes, sift 2 tablespoons of flour and pour a can (1 pint) of tomato juice. Add thinly sliced sausages to cover the top and add boiling water to cover all the ingredients. Add salt to taste. Bake it at 300° for 3 hours. If the sausages get too brown, turn them over.

BAKED MACARONI AND CHEESE

2 cups macaroni
2 teaspoons salt
2½ cups milk
8 ounces cheese (Velveeta)

Pepper
Butter
Bread crumbs

Cook the macaroni until it is tender in salted water. Put it into a casserole dish, add the milk, cheese, pepper to taste, and dot it with butter. Top the macaroni with bread crumbs, and bake it for about 30 minutes at 325° to 350°, or until brown.

Variations: Try adding chopped peppers, onions, celery or parsley.

MACARONI AND CHEESE

3 tablespoons butter
2½ cups uncooked macaroni
½ pound Velveeta cheese

1 teaspoon salt
¼ teaspoon pepper
1 quart milk

Melt the butter in a baking dish and pour the macaroni into the melted butter, stirring it until the macaroni is coated. Slice the cheese, then cut the slices into 4 pieces. Add it with the salt, pepper and milk to the macaroni. Bake it at 325° for 1½ hours. Do not stir the macaroni while it is baking.

TUNA MACARONI

1 pound elbow macaroni
Tuna chunks
10-ounce can mushroom soup

Milk
Bread crumbs
Cheese slices (optional)

Cook the macaroni according to the directions on the package. Pour part of the macaroni into a greased casserole dish. On top of it, place cut up tuna chunks, then pour ⅓ of the can of mushroom soup over it. Repeat this procedure until the dish is full. Pour milk over all until it covers the macaroni. Top it with bread crumbs and bake it for 1 hour in a moderate oven (350°). Cheese slices instead of bread crumbs may be put on top for the last 10 minutes of baking.

SKILLET SUPPER

1 pound bulk sausage (or 1 quart
   canned)
1 onion, chopped
1 green pepper, chopped
1 quart tomatoes

2 cups uncooked macaroni
2 tablespoons sugar
2 teaspoons chili powder
½ cup water or tomato juice
1 teaspoon salt

Brown the sausage, onion and pepper, pouring off the fat as it collects. Stir in the remaining ingredients. Bring the mixture to a boil, cover it and simmer, stirring often until the macaroni is tender. Two cups of sour cream may be added before serving.

Try substituting hamburger for the sausage.

BAKED SPAGHETTI

2 cups spaghetti
Salted water
Butter
2 slices bacon, cut up
1 slice onion

1 pint tomatoes
Salt and pepper
Bread or cracker crumbs
Grated cheese (optional)

Cook the spaghetti in the salted water. Drain it and pour it into a buttered baking dish. Fry the bacon and onion, and add them to the spaghetti. Season the tomatoes with butter, salt and pepper, and pour them over the above ingredients. Sprinkle them thickly with bread or cracker crumbs, and bake at 350° until brown. Grated cheese may be added if desired.

STARK CHEESE SOUFFLE

1 pint milk
¼ cup quick-cooking tapioca
½ pound cheese, grated

1 teaspoon salt
5 eggs, separated

Scald the milk in a double boiler. Add the tapioca and cook it until it is transparent, stirring frequently. Add the grated cheese and stir it until it is melted. Remove this mixture from the boiler and add the salt. Slowly add the tapioca mixture to the thickly beaten egg yolks. Mix it thoroughly, then fold in the stiffly beaten egg whites. Pour it into a well-greased pan, and set the pan in hot water to bake. Bake it at 350° for 45 minutes, or until a knife comes out clean when inserted.

Variations: Instead of grated cheese, add 1 finely cut green or red pepper.

EGG AND POTATO CASSEROLE

White Sauce
Dash of paprika
6 cups cooked grated potatoes
6 hardcooked eggs, sliced

Grated cheese
Buttered bread crumbs or cracker
  crumbs

Make a basic white sauce (see page 49) and mix in a dash of paprika, the potatoes and hard-cooked eggs. Pour the mixture into a greased baking dish, and sprinkle the top with grated cheese, buttered bread crumbs or cracker crumbs. Bake it at 375° for 30 minutes.

EGG DUTCH (OMELET)

5 eggs
1 teaspoon salt
Pepper to taste

1 heaping tablespoon flour
1 cup milk

Put the ingredients into a bowl in the order given and beat them with a rotary beater. Pour the mixture into a heated greased pan, and cover it tightly with a lid. Place it over medium low heat. Cut and turn the omelet when it is about half done, and continue baking it until done.

QUICK LUNCH

½ onion, diced
Margarine
1 pint sweet corn
1 pint tomato juice

Salt
Pepper
Brown sugar
Eggs (1 for each person)

In some margarine, sauté the onion until it is golden. Add the sweet corn and tomato juice, and salt, pepper, and a small amount of brown sugar to taste. Bring the mixture to a boil then break an egg into it for each person. Cover and cook it for about 3 to 4 minutes, until the eggs are softcooked. When using more than 6 eggs, double the amount of corn, tomatoes and onion.

Children enjoy dipping bread or toast into the egg yolk, then you can cut up the remaining egg white and eat it with the soup. This recipe is also good with crackers.

SCRAMBLED EGGS WITH CHEESE

4 eggs
¼ to ½ cup cheese, diced
Salt and pepper

Break the eggs into a bowl and add the cheese, salt and pepper. Pour the mixture into a hot, greased frying pan. Stir it roughly with a fork, breaking the yolks. Fry it, and serve immediately.

STROGANOFF CASSEROLE

2 cans (6 to 7 ounces each) tuna
1 can (10 ounces) cream of chicken
   soup
½ cup sour cream
¾ cup milk
2 tablespoons chopped parsley

2 cups cooked medium noodles
¼ teaspoon salt
Dash of pepper
2 teaspoons melted butter
3 tablespoons dry bread crumbs

Drain the tuna and break it into bite-sized chunks. Blend the soup and sour cream, and stir in the milk. Add the tuna, parsley, noodles and seasonings. Pour the mixture into a greased baking dish, and top it with buttered crumbs. Bake it at 350° for 20 to 25 minutes, or until it is bubbly.

Variations: *Cheaper canned fish such as mackerel can be used in fish dishes, but in smaller amounts, as they are a little stronger in taste.*

For Sour Cream Substitute, blend cottage cheese by hand or with a blender until it is smooth. Cottage cheese can be used in many recipes instead of sour cream at about half the cost.

VEGETABLE-RICE DISH

Cook together rice, onions to taste, a small amount of carrots and red and green peppers if desired. When the rice is tender and almost dry, add enough milk to make it juicy, then add drained peas, margarine, cubed Velveeta cheese and seasonings to taste. Heat the mixture until the cheese melts, then serve it with fresh bread and butter and a salad or applesauce.

Variations: *For variety, substitute diced potatoes, noodles or macaroni for the rice. Add ham, beef chunks, or almost any kind of meat, and green beans or peas. When potatoes are used, instead of adding plain milk, make a white sauce. The combination of the above ingredients and your imagination will make many nourishing meals.*

MEATS, SAUCES, PIZZA AND MEAT CURING

HINTS FOR MEATS

- *Add vinegar to the water when cold packing meat to keep cans free from grease.*
- *To stretch hamburger, crumble about 5 or more slices of bread into 1 pound of the meat. Add a little milk or tomato juice, or an egg. Mix and form it into patties, then fry them.*
- *Roasting time for beef is approximately 30 to 35 minutes per pound. For a boneless, rolled roast, increase the time by 10 minutes per pound.*
- *Put a handful of soda into scalding water to scald chickens. This will help remove pin feathers.*
- *To make chickens easier to defeather, the water should be heated to 175°.*
- *When dressing a quantity of chickens, place 6 fowls (after scalding, picking and singeing), 3 towels and soap in the washing machine and cover them with warm water. Run the machine for 10 minutes. The chickens come out nice and clean.*
- *When cleaning chickens, use a ball made of nylon netting instead of a knife. Nothing works better.*

CANNED CHICKEN

Cut chicken into bite-sized pieces. Add salt, fry the chicken, then can it. When unexpected company arrives, this can be opened, and a thickening added to provide a meat and gravy dish.

OLD-FASHIONED POULTRY STUFFING

1 cup chopped celery
½ cup chopped onions
½ teaspoon poultry seasoning
¼ cup butter or margarine

1 can (10 ounces) condensed cream of
  chicken soup, OR
1¼ cups chicken gravy
8 cups dry bread cubes

Cook the celery, onions and poultry seasoning in the butter until the vegetables are tender. Add the soup. Mix it lightly, adding the bread cubes. This makes about 4 cups of stuffing, or enough for a 5 to 6 pound bird.

67

CHICKEN COATING MIX

1 cup flour
Pepper (scant)
½ teaspoon salt

2 teaspoons paprika
1 teaspoon baking powder

Mix together the above ingredients. Put the mixture into a plastic bag, then shake it with pieces of chicken to coat them.

BAKED CHICKEN

½ cup flour
2 teaspoons paprika
1 teaspoon pepper
¼ teaspoon dry mustard

3 teaspoons salt
1 cut up broiler or young chicken
¼ pound butter

Mix the dry ingredients well in a plastic bag, then coat the cut up chicken parts with the mixture. In a cake pan, melt the butter. Place the chicken parts in the pan, but do not crowd them. Bake the chicken at 350° for 1½ to 2 hours or until done.

CHICKEN ROLL

Make a biscuit dough. Roll it out, then spread it with cut up cooked chicken. Roll it up as you would to make rolls, then slice it. Place the slices in a greased pan and bake them at 350° until done. Make gravy with the chicken broth, and top the hot slices with it.

Variations: This recipe can be made with ham, using the same method. For the gravy, use a simple white sauce. Stir in cheese spread while it is hot. Serve it hot over the ham rolls.

BARBECUED CHICKEN

Cut fryers into serving pieces. Place them in a shallow baking dish, brush them with oil and bake in a moderate oven at 375° for 45 minutes or until browned. Pour barbecue sauce over the chicken and continue to bake it for 45 minutes longer, basting frequently.

CRUNCHY CHICKEN

Using 3 to 4 pounds of broilers, dip pieces of the raw chicken into melted margarine, then roll them in finely crushed equal parts of cracker and cornflake crumbs. Place the chicken in flat, well-oiled baking pans, laying the pieces side by side but not crowding them. Sprinkle them with salt and your favorite chicken seasoning. Bake them at 375° for 1 hour or until the meat is brown and tender.

CHICKEN SALAD FOR SANDWICHES

1 quart cold, boiled chicken
1 pint celery
4 or 5 hardcooked eggs

Mayonnaise or other dressing
Salt and pepper to taste
¾ cup chopped olives (optional)

Put the chicken, celery and eggs through the coarse blade of a food chopper. Mix in the remaining ingredients.

BARBECUE SAUCE

½ cup ketchup
1 tablespoon vinegar
1 tablespoon sugar

1 tablespoon mustard
1 tablespoon Worcestershire sauce

Mix the ingredients together well. If the sauce is too strong, use less ketchup and add some tomato juice.

CHICKEN BARBECUE SAUCE

¼ cup butter, margarine or oil
1 teaspoon salt
Dash of pepper
1 cup water

2 tablespoons vinegar
2 teaspoons brown sugar
2 tablespoons Worcestershire sauce

Mix together the ingredients, then bring the mixture to a boil. Baste the meat with this sauce.

HOT DOG SAUCE

½ green pepper, chopped
1 medium-sized onion, chopped
2 tablespoons prepared mustard
¾ teaspoon salt

2 tablespoons brown sugar
¾ cup ketchup
1 tablespoon Worcestershire sauce

Mix together all the ingredients, then add 1 pint of water. Cook the sauce for 15 minutes, then add wieners and continue cooking it until the wieners are good and hot.

This sauce is very good on top of mashed potatoes.

SPAGHETTI SAUCE

1 small onion, chopped
1 can (7½ ounces) tomato sauce
1 can (10 ounces) tomato soup
1¼ cups water

½ teaspoon garlic salt
¼ teaspoon pepper
1 tablespoon parsley

Mix the onion, tomato sauce and tomato soup with the water. Simmer it for 10 minutes, then mix in the seasoning and parsley. Place meatballs in the sauce and simmer it uncovered for 25 minutes, turning them occasionally. Mix this sauce with hot, cooked spaghetti and top it with grated cheese.

Variations: This sauce is very good with a cut up stewing hen instead of hamburger. Cook the hen until it is almost done, then finish cooking it in the spaghetti sauce.

BARBECUED HAMBURGER

Brown 1 pound of hamburger with 1 sliced onion. Add 1 teaspoon of salt and a dash of pepper. When the hamburger is brown, add barbecue sauce and steam it for 10 minutes. Serve this dish with buns.

BEEF BARBECUE (LARGE QUANTITY)

1 large bunch celery
1 pound onions
3 bottles (14 ounces each) ketchup
5 teaspoons Worcestershire sauce
1 cup brown sugar

2 tablespoons chili powder
2 tablespoons salt
1 tablespoon pepper
½ cup flour
5 pounds ground beef, browned

Finely mince the celery and onions and simmer them until they are tender. Add the ketchup, Worcestershire sauce, sugar and seasonings. Make a thickening of the flour, and add it to the celery/onion mixture. Cook it on low heat for 10 minutes. (If placed on high heat, it will burn easily.) Add the browned beef and heat it thoroughly to finish the barbecue.

Beef Barbecue may be refrigerated in a closed container and warmed up as needed.

BEEF ROAST

3-pound roast
2 teaspoons salt
Pepper

2 teaspoons brown sugar
3 tablespoons water (approximate)

Mix together the salt, a small amount of pepper, and the brown sugar, and rub it well into all sides of the meat. Place the meat in a casserole and add a small amount of water (approximately 3 tablespoons). Roast it, covered, at 325° for 1 hour or until done.

YORKSHIRE PUDDING

2 eggs
2 cups sour milk
1 cup sweet milk
2 teaspoons baking powder

1 teaspoon salt
1 tablespoon sugar
2 cups sifted all-purpose flour, or
    enough to make a stiff batter

When the beef you are cooking is almost done, pour out the broth (reserving it), leaving about 1 inch in the pan. Mix together the above ingredients to make a batter, and pour it into the broth around the roast. Bake it for 25 minutes with the meat. Thicken the reserved broth to make gravy. Cut the pudding into blocks, pour the gravy over it, and serve it with the beef.

SAUSAGE LOAF

1½ pounds pork sausage meat
1½ cups bread or cracker crumbs
2 tablespoons grated onions
2 tablespoons ketchup

2 tablespoons horseradish
2 teaspoons prepared mustard
1 egg, slightly beaten
½ cup milk

Mix together the sausage and cracker crumbs, then add the onions, ketchup, horseradish, mustard and egg. Moisten the mixture with the milk, and shape it into a loaf. Bake it at 350° for 1 hour.

SAVORY MEAT LOAF

1¼ pounds ground beef, plus
¼ pound ground pork, OR
2 pounds ground beef (omit the pork)
¼ cup minced onions
1 cup oatmeal or crushed crackers
2½ teaspoons salt

1 beaten egg
¼ teaspoon pepper
1 teaspoon mustard
¼ cup ketchup
1 cup tomato juice
Bacon slices

Mix together the ingredients, then form the mixture into a loaf. Put a few bacon slices on top, and pour additional tomato juice over all. Bake the meat loaf at 350° to 375° for 1 hour.

Variations: The mixture may be pressed into a cake pan and topped with ketchup. Bake it for about 1 hour.

Try spreading a glaze over the loaf.

Glaze for Meat Loaf;

½ cup brown sugar
1½ teaspoons prepared mustard
1 tablespoon Worcestershire sauce

Mix together the ingredients and add enough vinegar to make a paste. Spread the glaze over the meat loaf.

HAM LOAF

2 pounds smoked ham (ground)   1½ cups bread crumbs
2 pounds fresh pork (ground)   1 teaspoon salt
2 eggs   1 teaspoon pepper
1½ cups milk

Mix together the ingredients, then form the mixture into a loaf. Pour the following glaze over the top, and bake it at 325° for 2 hours.

Glaze;

Mix together the following ingredients;

1½ cups brown sugar   ½ cup water
1 teaspoon dry mustard   ½ cup vinegar

POOR MAN'S STEAK

1 pound hamburger   1 cup cracker crumbs
1 cup milk   1 teaspoon salt
¼ teaspoon pepper   1 small onion, finely chopped

Mix the ingredients well and shape the mixture into a narrow loaf. Let it set for at least 8 hours, or overnight. Slice it and fry it until brown. Put the slices in layers in a roaster and spread mushroom soup on each piece, using 1 can (10 ounces) of soup. Bake it for 1 hour at 325°. (Pan gravy may be used with the mushroom soup.)

HAMBURGER PUFFS

1 good-sized onion, chopped   ½ green pepper, finely chopped
1 tablespoon butter or oil   1 teaspoon salt
4 large slices bread   ¼ teaspoon pepper
1 cup milk   1 pound ground beef
2 eggs, beaten

Sauté the onions in the butter until they are lightly browned. Crumble the bread into the milk and let it stand until the milk is absorbed. Add the onions and the remaining ingredients to the bread and milk. Mix them well and press them into patties in greased muffin tins. Allow the patties to set for 15 minutes, then bake them for 25 to 30 minutes at 400°. Place the muffin tins on cookie sheets if necessary. Serve the puffs with gravy or ketchup. This recipe makes 8 or 9 puffs.

Variations: *A can of cream soup heated with* ½ *can of milk makes a nice sauce to use with the puffs.*

VEAL LOAF

1 pound beef, finely ground
1 cup bread or cracker crumbs
½ cup cream
1 teaspoon sugar

2 eggs, beaten
1 teaspoon butter
Salt and pepper to taste

Mix the ingredients well. Make a long loaf, and bake it for 1½ to 2 hours at 350°.

CHUNK BEEF PATTIES

1 quart beef chunks
5 double soda crackers, crushed
2 eggs

Parsley
Hamburger seasoning
Milk

Grind the beef chunks. Mix in the cracker crumbs, eggs, a little parsley, hamburger seasoning, or whatever seasoning your family likes. Add enough milk to make soft patties. Fry them.

HAMBURGER-EGG CASSEROLE

6 eggs, beaten
1 pound ground beef, browned
¼ teaspoon pepper
½ teaspoon dry mustard
12 slices bread, cut up

3 cups milk
1 teaspoon salt
1 teaspoon Worcestershire sauce
6 slices cheese, cut up (optional)

Mix together all the ingredients, then put the mixture into a casserole. Place the casserole in a pan of water, and bake it at 350° for 1¼ hours.

BEANBURGERS

2 pounds ground beef
2 tablespoons oil
1 small onion, chopped
½ cup ketchup
1 teaspoon Worcestershire sauce
Water

1 pint kidney beans, cooked and
  drained
Salt and pepper to taste
½ teaspoon garlic powder
½ teaspoon chili powder, OR
1 teaspoon oregano
Cheese slices

Brown the ground beef in the oil. Add the onion, ketchup and Worcestershire sauce. To prevent burning, add sufficient water and simmer for 20 minutes. Add the kidney beans, salt and pepper, garlic powder and chili powder, or oregano. Continue simmering the ingredients for about 30 minutes more. Serve them on buns, using only ½ of the bun. Top each one with a slice of cheese and melt it in a hot oven. Serve them hot.

MEAT PATTIES

2 pounds ground pork or hamburger
2 eggs
1 onion, chopped
1 cup cracker crumbs

1 cup milk
1 teaspoon salt
½ teaspoon pepper

Mix together the ingredients. Form the mixture into patties and fry them.

SOUPERBURGERS

1 pound ground beef
½ cup chopped onions
1 tablespoon shortening
2 tablespoons ketchup

Dash of pepper
1 can (10 ounces) vegetable soup
1 teaspoon prepared mustard
6 buns split and toasted

In a skillet, brown the beef and onions in the shortening. Stir it to separate the meat. Add the remaining ingredients and cook them for 5 minutes, stirring now and then. Serve this on buns or with mashed potatoes.

SOUR CREAM BEEFBURGERS

1½ pounds ground beef
¼ cup Worcestershire sauce
1½ teaspoons salt

1 cup sour cream
1 tablespoon chopped onions
1½ cups cornflakes or bread crumbs

Mix together the first 5 ingredients, then add the crushed cornflakes or bread crumbs. Form the mixture into patties. Broil them for 5 minutes, then turn them over and broil them for 3 minutes more. This recipe makes 10 to 12 burgers.

WAGON WHEEL HAMBURGER

2 pounds hamburger
½ cup barbecue sauce
½ cup dry bread crumbs
2 beaten eggs

¼ cup chopped onion
¼ cup chopped green pepper
1 teaspoon salt

Combine the ingredients, mix them lightly, and put the mixture into an 8-inch, cast-iron skillet. On top make a spoke design with additional barbecue sauce, and sprinkle a little brown sugar over the entire surface. Bake it at 325° for 50 minutes or until done.

LIVER PATTIES

If the beef liver you are using is tough, try grinding it. Season it with salt, and pepper if desired. Chopped onion and beaten egg may be added. Fry the liver like hamburger patties. Add a little flour if necessary, or sprinkle the patties with flour before turning them.

STEAK SUPREME

2 pounds hamburger
2 eggs
½ cup dry bread crumbs

2 teaspoons salt
6 tablespoons onions, finely chopped
Pepper (optional)

Heat lard in a skillet, then press a mixture of the above ingredients into the skillet to about a 1-inch thickness. Brown it on both sides. Add 1 can (10 ounces) of mushroom soup and the same amount of water. Cover the skillet tightly and simmer for 20 minutes.

HAPPY CHANGE MEATBALLS

1 teaspoon salt
1½ pounds ground beef
¼ teaspoon pepper and nutmeg

½ cup cracker crumbs
½ cup milk
2 eggs, slightly beaten

   mixture

Shape the mixture into small balls, and place them in a large shallow baking pan. Bake the meatballs at 350° for 30 minutes, then drain off excess fat.

In a bowl, combine;

2 cups tomato juice
2 tablespoons flour

Mix them well, then add the following;

¾ cup ketchup
½ teaspoon Worcestershire sauce
¼ cup water

Mix these ingredients until blended, then pour the mixture over the meatballs and bake them for 30 minutes longer.

BEGGAR'S DISH

Use 1 pound or more of hamburger with a bit of onion. Fry it until it is well done. Drain off the liquid from a can (16 ounces) of kidney beans, and add the beans to the meat. Mix it well, and fry it again until well done.

This is an economical dish if meat is too expensive.

Variations: A can of condensed tomato soup may be added with the beans. Delicious!

SLOPPY JOES

1 cup water
2 pounds hamburger
½ cup onions, chopped
½ cup celery, chopped
½ cup vinegar

2 tablespoons dry mustard
1 small bottle ketchup
2 tablespoons brown sugar
1 cup tomato paste
Salt and pepper to taste

Add the water to the hamburger and cook it. Add the rest of the ingredients and continue cooking the hamburger until it is done. Serve it on hamburger buns.

SPARERIBS AND SAUERKRAUT

4 pounds or 2 sides spareribs
Salt and pepper
1 quart sauerkraut
1 apple, chopped

2 tablespoons brown sugar
1 tablespoon caraway seeds
1 onion, sliced
2 cups water

Cut the ribs and brown them in a skillet, adding seasonings. Pour off the fat. Place the sauerkraut mixed with the apple, sugar, caraway and onion in a kettle. Place the ribs on top. Pour the water around the meat and sauerkraut. Cover it tightly and simmer it for 1¼ to 1½ hours or until the ribs are very tender.

BARBECUED SPARERIBS

Add canned ribs to Tennessee Barbecue Sauce and simmer them for 15 to 20 minutes. Sausage may be substituted for the ribs.

Tennessee Barbecue Sauce;

1 bottle (15 ounces) chili sauce
⅔ cup brown sugar
2 tablespoons Worcestershire sauce
3 medium-sized onions, chopped

1 bottle (15 ounces) ketchup
3 tablespoons dry mustard
1½ cups water

Mix together all the ingredients and simmer the mixture for 15 minutes.

HAM SALAD FOR SANDWICHES

2 cups cooked ham
3 stalks celery
1 large dill pickle
¼ teaspoon dry mustard

¼ teaspoon onion powder
½ cup mayonnaise
½ teaspoon salt
1 tablespoon lemon juice

Put the ham, celery and pickle through the coarse blade of a food chopper, add the remaining ingredients and mix.

SCALLOPED HAM

1½ cups ham
½ cup ham broth
2 cups cracker crumbs
3 cups milk

2 eggs, beaten
1 teaspoon salt
Dash of pepper
1 tablespoon butter

Brown the ham and cook it until it is tender, then grind it. Line the bottom of a casserole with a layer of cracker crumbs, then a layer of ½ of the ground ham, then the crackers, making 2 layers of each. Mix the milk, seasonings and eggs, and pour the mixture over the meat. Dot the top with the butter. Bake the casserole at 375° for 30 minutes or until done.

HOT HAM AND CHEESE BUNS

½ pound ham
½ pound sharp cheese
⅓ cup sliced onions
2 hardcooked eggs, sliced

½ cup sliced peppers, OR
½ cup stuffed olives, sliced
3 tablespoons salad dressing
½ cup chili sauce

Cut the ham and cheese into ¼-inch cubes. Combine them with the onions, eggs and peppers or olives. Add the salad dressing blended with the chili sauce, mix it well and spread the mixture in 10 split wiener buns. Wrap each one in foil and twist the ends securely. Bake them for 10 minutes at 400° or until the buns are hot.

SCALLOPED WIENERS

1 pound wieners
Water
5 cups coarsely crushed crackers
2 eggs

2 teaspoons salt
Pepper to taste
4½ cups milk
4 brimming tablespoons butter

Add a small amount of water to the wieners and cook them for 10 minutes. Slice the wieners, and make alternate layers of crackers and wieners in a casserole. Beat the egg and add the seasonings and milk. Pour this mixture over the crackers and wieners, and dot the surface with the butter. Bake the casserole at 350° for 30 minutes or until it is done. This will fill a very large casserole or 2 smaller ones.

PIZZA PIE

1 package yeast
¾ cup warm water

2½ cups biscuit mix

Dissolve the yeast in the water, add the biscuit mix, and mix them well. Knead the dough, roll it out, and put it into a greased pan, letting it rise for ½ hour.

1 pound ground beef, cooked
¾ cup chopped onions
½ cup chopped green peppers

1 teaspoon oregano
Salt and pepper to taste
2 cups tomato sauce

To make the topping, cook the ground beef, onions and pepper together. Add the rest of the ingredients and continue cooking them. Spread this mixture over the crust and bake it at 375° for 30 minutes or until it is done. Cheese and/or mushrooms may be put on top.

YEAST PIZZA

1 package dry yeast
1 cup warm water
1 teaspoon sugar
1½ teaspoons salt

¼ cup salad oil
3 cups flour
1 pound cheese
2 cups tomato sauce

Dissolve the yeast in the warm water, add the sugar, salt and oil, and mix it thoroughly. Add ½ the flour and beat it until there are no lumps. Gradually add the remaining flour. Knead the dough for 5 minutes. Take ½ the dough and roll it out to a circle 12 inches in diameter. Place it on a greased cookie sheet, leaving the edges a little thicker than the middle. Repeat this procedure with the other ½ of the dough and put it on a second cookie sheet. Let the dough rise for 20 to 30 minutes. Brush the top with salad oil. Cut the cheese into fine pieces and sprinkle it over the 2 surfaces. Pour the tomato sauce lightly over the cheese. Bake the pizzas at 450° for 15 minutes or until the edges are brown and the cheese is melted.

CRAZY CRUST PIZZA

1 cup flour
1 teaspoon salt
1 teaspoon oregano
⅛ teaspoon pepper
2 eggs
⅔ cup milk

1 quart cooked, drained hamburger
Onions, chopped
Mushrooms, sliced
1 cup pizza sauce
Velveeta cheese slices

Mix together the flour, salt, oregano, pepper, eggs and milk. Grease and flour a pizza pan or cookie sheet with sides. Pour in the batter and tilt the pan so that it covers the bottom. Arrange the hamburger over the batter, and add onions and mushrooms. Bake the pizza at 400° for 20 to 25 minutes. Remove it from the oven, drizzle on the pizza sauce, and lay Velveeta cheese slices on top. Bake the pizza again until the cheese melts.

Variations: Instead of pizza sauce, try tomato sauce, 1½ teaspoons of oregano and pepper.

JIFFY PIZZA

Dough;

2 cups flour
1 tablespoon baking powder
1 teaspoon salt

⅔ cup milk
⅓ cup salad oil

Sauce;

6 ounces tomato paste
¼ cup water
1 teaspoon oregano
¼ teaspoon pepper
½ teaspoon salt

2 tablespoons sugar
1 teaspoon garlic powder (optional)
1 pound browned hamburger
Cheese, finely chopped

Sift together the flour, baking powder and salt, and add the milk and oil to make a dough. Pat it on the bottom of a pizza pan. Mix the first 7 sauce ingredients and spread the mixture over the dough. Spread the chopped meat over the surface and sprinkle it with the cheese. Bake the pizza for 25 to 30 minutes at 425°. It serves 6 or more.

SWISS STEAK

Salt and pepper a 2 or 3-inch steak, and cover both sides with as much flour as it will hold. Sear both sides of the steak, cover it with sliced onions, and pour over it a small bottle of tomato ketchup. Add enough water to cover the steak and bake it for 2 hours at 400°.

If ketchup is not desired, sear the steak and add 1 tablespoon of vinegar, 1 tablespoon of salt and a small amount of pepper. When the steak is browned, cover it with boiling water or cream and simmer it slowly until very tender.

FRIED OYSTERS

3 dozen oysters
½ cup finely crushed cracker crumbs
½ teaspoon salt

2 eggs, beaten
1 tablespoon water
Butter

Drain the oysters. Dip them in the seasoned crumbs, then in the eggs diluted with the water, then again in the crumbs. Fry the oysters with butter until they are golden brown.

SCALLOPED OYSTERS

4 cups crackers, coarsely crushed
1 can (10 ounces) oysters
2 cups milk
1 teaspoon salt

Pepper to taste
1 egg
⅓ cup butter

In a 1½ quart casserole, place a layer of cracker crumbs on the bottom, then a layer of oysters, then crackers, then oysters, making 2 layers of each. Just before baking, add the milk and seasonings to the egg, then pour it over the casserole ingredients. Arrange the butter in thin strips on top. Bake it in a moderate oven (350°) until it is well heated, approximately ¾ to 1 hour.

CANNED FISH

Cut up and pack fish into a jar. Add ½ teaspoon of salt per pint and about ⅓ cup of vinegar to each quart. Seal and cold pack it for 3½ to 4 hours. (The bones will become soft and edible within 4 weeks.) Serve the fish with a little vinegar and pepper.

SALMON LOAF

Fix Amish Dressing (see page 48), omitting the chicken and chicken broth. Add 1 can of salmon, finely cut. Mix it, and form the mixture into a loaf, or press it into a casserole. Bake it at 350° for 1 to 1½ hours.

FRIED SALMON PATTIES

2 cups cracker crumbs
1 cup salmon
1 teaspoon salt (scant)

2 eggs, beaten
1½ cups milk
Pepper to taste

Roll the crackers until they are finely crushed. Mix them with the other ingredients. Drop the mixture by tablespoons and fry it with butter.

SALMON SOUFFLE

1 can salmon, minced
2 egg yolks
1¼ cups milk

1 cup bread crumbs
½ teaspoon vinegar
2 egg whites

Mix together the first five ingredients, then add the beaten egg whites. Put the mixture into a casserole dish, and bake it for 30 to 40 minutes at 400°.

MEAT CURING

Trim the meat, then chill it thoroughly through and through at 40°, being careful that it does not freeze. Never put salt on the meat before it is thoroughly chilled, as salt tends to block the escape of body heat, causing the inside bones to sour before the salt or cure penetrates.

For 100 pounds of meat, use 7 pounds of salt, 2 pounds of brown sugar and 2 ounces of saltpeter. Apply this only once to the meat. For hams, use ½ the required amount and about a week later, the remaining ½. For bacon use ½ of the cure recipe, and apply it only once. Using a cup measure, fill it to slightly rounding with the cure for every 10 pounds of meat (bacon and hams), putting a second cup on the hams a week later.

MEAT CURE

2 pounds brown sugar
4 gallons water
6 pounds salt

2 ounces pepper
1 ounce saltpeter

Bring the ingredients to a boil, then allow the mixture to cool. Pack meat in a tub or crock as tightly as possible with this brine. Put weight on top to keep the meat in the brine. Leave hams in for 4 weeks, bacon only 5 or 6 days. Then smoke the meat, and wrap it in paper or cloth.

CORNED BEEF

50 pounds beef (roasts, steaks, or any
    choice cut)
3 quarts salt

Place the meat in layers in a large crock or similar suitable container. Salt each layer and let it stand overnight. Roughly rinse off the beef and pack it again in a crock.

Make a brine of;

¼ pound baking soda
¼ pound saltpeter

2 pounds brown sugar
2 tablespoons liquid smoke

Place the meat in the brine with enough water to cover the meat well. It will be cured and ready for use in 2 weeks. It can then be cut into suitable pieces and canned (cold pack for 3 hours) or put into the freezer. If the crock is kept in a cool place, the meat may be kept in brine and used any time within 3 months. The flavor of the meat is improved when kept over 6 weeks.

DRIED BEEF

4½ gallons water
Salt enough to float an egg
1 ounce saltpeter

2 pounds brown sugar
20 pounds beef

Combine the water, salt and sugar to make a brine. Put a weight on top of the meat to keep it in the brine. For large pieces of meat, soak them for 60 hours, and for small pieces, 48 hours. Then smoke the meat.

HAM CURING

When curing hams, poke cure around the bones, especially the shank end, with your fingers and finish by patting the remainder on the meat side. Put the meat into a wooden box which has a few drain holes. Place it in a cool cellar or room, keeping the temperature between 45 and 36°, if at all possible, and not below freezing. Two days for every pound of ham are required for curing. A 25 pound ham requires 50 days. The curing time may be shortened somewhat for a very large ham. Bacon curing time is 1½ days for each pound of meat.

After the meat is cured, soak it in cold water for ½ to 1 hour; then scrub it to remove excess salt and mold which forms if your curing room is too warm. This mold won't hurt the meat.

To smoke the meat, pass a twine through the shank of hams or shoulders. For bacon, push a stiff wire through one end to hold it stiff. Put a twine through the meat under the wire to hang it up. Meat will color better when dipped in hot water a few seconds, and scrubbed briskly.

When the meat is cured and smoked, wrap it in a large paper bag. Double the top over and tie it tightly so no flies can enter. The skipper fly which lays eggs to hatch worms, can't be kept out of a room with regular window screens. Hang the meat in a reasonably dry room as this will prevent it from becoming moldy. If it molds, just brush it off. Never wrap your cured meat in plastic.

After you begin cutting a ham, swab some vegetable oil on the cut. This will to some extent prevent mold. This way hams can be kept a long period of time. Some people say it is better the second year than the first. Preferably, it should be aged several months so it will lose its saltiness. If it is still too salty, soak or cook the ham lightly and pour off the first water.

EASY HAM CURING

Add enough salt to water so that an egg floats. In this brine soak the untreated hams for 6 weeks, then smoke them.

To preserve the ham, slice or cut the ham into pieces. Dip each piece into soft, partly melted lard. Place the ham in a jar. Pour the melted lard on top, completely covering the meat. Put lids on the jars and set them on the cellar floor.

MEAT—TO USE NOW OR LATER

Spine, ribs and bacon can be put into salted water (strong enough to float an egg). To use the meat, soak it in clear water overnight so it will not be too salty.

Hams can also be put into salted water and kept there for 6 weeks before smoking.

BARBECUED BONE MEAT

1½ pounds bone meat	½ cup onions, chopped
1 cup celery, chopped	1 cup ketchup
2 tablespoons Worcestershire sauce	1 tablespoon mustard
1 tablespoon brown sugar	¾ teaspoon salt
Tomato juice (optional)	

Mix together the ingredients, then cold pack the mixture for 1 hour. To make a large batch, about 40 pints, use the following quantities;

18 pounds bone meat, ground if desired	1½ cups Worcestershire sauce
12 cups celery, chopped	¾ cup brown sugar
6 cups onions, chopped	3 tablespoons salt
¾ cup mustard	
3 quarts ketchup	

BEEF BARBECUE (FOR CANNING)

10 pounds ground beef	¾ cup prepared mustard
5 cups chopped onions	1½ cups brown sugar
¼ cup salt	⅔ cup Worcestershire sauce
1¼ tablespoons pepper	5 cups ketchup
1 cup vinegar	4 cups beef broth or water

Brown the ground beef and onions. Add the rest of the ingredients with the beef broth or water (using more than 4 cups if necessary). Steam the mixture for 10 minutes. Pack it in jars, seal them, and boil them for 1 to 2 hours. This recipe makes about 9 quarts.

CANNED MEATBALLS

5 pounds hamburger	⅛ teaspoon pepper
3 teaspoons salt	

Mix the ingredients together well, and form the mixture into balls the size of walnuts. Fry them until brown in a skillet. Pack the meatballs in jars. Make a brown gravy and divide it among the jars. If it does not fill the jars, add water. Boil them in a pressure cooker at 10 pounds pressure for 1 hour.

To can meatballs for cooking with spaghetti, put them into cans raw but seasoned, and add water. Cook them for 1 hour and 25 minutes at 10 pounds pressure in a pressure cooker.

CANNED MEAT LOAF

15 pounds ground beef
⅓ cup salt
4 slices bread, crumbled
36 soda crackers, crushed

1 cup oatmeal
3 cups water, milk or tomato juice
4 eggs
Chopped onions (optional)

Mix the ingredients well. Pack the mixture into jars, seal them and process them for 3 hours. Or, form the mixture into balls and fry them. Then pack the meatballs into jars, seal them, and process them for 2 hours.

CANNING BEEFBURGER

Brown hamburger as you would for casseroles, and add salt, pepper and whatever other seasonings you prefer (1 cup of salt and 3 tablespoons of pepper to 25 pounds of meat). Add chopped parsley, diced celery, chopped onions or the vegetables of your choice (or none at all). Put the mixture into jars and cold pack them for 1 hour.

This beefburger is very handy to use in many different dishes.

MINCEMEAT (FOR CANNING)

1 quart ground meat
2 quarts sliced apples
2 quarts cider (or grape juice)
1 quart sour cherries (optional)
5 cups sugar
½ teaspoon cinnamon

¼ teaspoon ground cloves
¼ teaspoon allspice
Juice and rind of 2 oranges (optional)
Salt to taste
2 cups raisins

Mix together all the ingredients and cook the mixture for 15 minutes. Stir it frequently to prevent scorching. Add more cider if necessary. Pour it into hot sterilized jars and seal them at once. Process them for 30 minutes in a hot bath.

BRINE FOR CANNING STUFFED SAUSAGE

2 quarts water
¼ cup salt
¼ cup sugar

½ teaspoon pepper
½ teaspoon saltpeter

Combine the ingredients and bring the mixture to a boil before adding the meat. Boil it for 20 minutes, then pack the meat in jars and cover it with the brine in which it was boiled. Cold pack it for 3 hours.

BEEF AND PORK BOLOGNA

60 pounds beef trimmings
40 pounds pork trimmings
3 pounds tenderizer
3 to 4 ounces black pepper

1½ ounces coriander, OR
1 ounce curry powder
1 ounce mace
Onions if desired

Mix 2 pounds of the tenderizer with the chilled beef trimmings, and grind them using the coarse grinding plate. After grinding, spread the meat in a cool place and let it cure for 48 hours. Grind the chilled pork trimmings with 1 pound of the tenderizer and let it cure. After 48 hours, regrind the cured beef, using a ⅛-inch hole plate. Then add the pork and grind the mixture again. Add the seasonings and mix thoroughly—a small amount of water will help. Thirty to 40 minutes is not too long for thorough mixing.

Stuff the meat tightly into beef or muslin casings and allow it to hang in a cool place overnight. Then hang the bologna in a smoke house, heated 110 to 120°, and smoke it to a rich brown color, for about 2 or 3 hours. Immediately put the hot smoked bologna into water heated 160 to 175° and cook it until it floats or until it squeaks when the pressure of your thumb and fingers on the casing is suddenly released. The cooking time ranges from 20 to 90 minutes, depending on the size of the casing. Plunge the cooked sausage into cold water to chill it. Hang it in a cool, dry place for future use.

LEBANON BOLOGNA

50 pounds beef
1 pound salt
3 tablespoons pepper
2 tablespoons nutmeg
1½ tablespoons saltpeter

2½ pounds sugar
1½ pounds salt
½ pound lard or 9 ounces peanut oil,
    per 25 pounds meat

Salt the beef and let it stand for 4 days. The secret to a good bologna is to let the meat season well before grinding and stuffing it. Cut up the meat in order to grind it, then put it into a large container making alternate layers of the meat and the mixed seasonings. Let it stand in a cold place for 5 to 7 days, turning the meat on top every day or so to prevent drying out. Then grind the meat twice to the desired texture, and add the peanut oil or lard. Mix it well in a wooden or enamel container. Stuff the meat and let it hang for 2 or 3 days to settle, then smoke it, being careful not to overheat it with the fire.

CHICKEN BOLOGNA

25 pounds chicken meat
1 pound tenderizer
1 ounce black pepper
½ cup sugar

2 teaspoons saltpeter
2 teaspoons garlic powder
3 tablespoons liquid smoke

Add the tenderizer to the chicken meat and grind it twice. Let it set for 24 hours, then add the black pepper, sugar, saltpeter, garlic powder and liquid smoke. (The liquid smoke may be omitted and the meat smoked after stuffing.) Mix it well, then grind it again and process it as you would any fresh meat (such as sausage or ground beef), or stuff it into cloth bags and boil it in water for 30 minutes. If you have stuffed the meat, then it may be frozen or canned. To can the bologna, slice it and pack it into jars, adding the broth in which it was cooked. Then cold pack it for 2½ hours.

SUMMER BOLOGNA

60 pounds beef
1 teaspoon saltpeter
⅓ cup pepper (scant)
1 quart molasses

1 pound lard
1 quart salt
3 pounds brown sugar

Let the beef stand until it is just a little old. Soak it in strong salted water for about 30 minutes. Smoke it for ½ day. Grind the beef, add the above mixed ingredients, and mix. Grind it again. Stuff the mixture into bologna-sized bags. Smoke the meat for 7 to 10 days.

This recipe is also very good if you substitute venison for the beef.

SUMMER SAUSAGE

25 pounds beef
10 pounds pork
2 tablespoons garlic powder

1 cup white sugar
2 teaspoons saltpeter
1½ cups warm water

Grind the meat and mix in the rest of the above ingredients.

6 cups salt
5 cups brown sugar

6 heaping teaspoons saltpeter
3 gallons water

To make a brine, mix these ingredients together and bring the mixture to a boil. Let it cool. Stuff the meat into long narrow bags (bologna size) then place them in the brine for 3 weeks. Remove them from the brine and place them in cold water overnight. Hang up the meat and smoke it in the bags. When it is smoked, paraffin the bags well, and hang them in a cool place. The bags may be hung in the cellar stairs but not in the cellar. Slice the meat and eat it cold.

SALADS AND SALAD DRESSINGS

HINTS FOR SALADS

- *Add several handfuls of toasted leftover bread cubes to tossed salads just before serving.*
- *When gelatin is too solid to whip, put the egg beater in hot water before whipping.*

CARROT SALAD

1 package (3 ounces) orange gelatin
   powder
½ cup carrots, finely grated
1 cup crushed pineapple

2 tablespoons sugar (optional)
Raisins (optional)

Prepare the gelatin according to the directions on the box, using slightly more water. When the gelatin starts to thicken, add the carrots and pineapple. If more sweetness is desired, add the sugar, and add raisins according to taste. Stir it and let it set.

CARROT CRACKER SALAD

3 cups carrots, grated
1½ cups soda cracker crumbs
3 hardcooked eggs, chopped
1 small onion, chopped

1 tablespoon sugar
Salt and pepper to taste
1 cup mayonnaise (approximate)

Mix the ingredients together, and serve.

COLESLAW

4 cups cabbage, finely shredded
¾ cup sugar
2 tablespoons water

3 tablespoons vinegar (approximate)
½ teaspoon salt

Mix all the ingredients thoroughly until the sugar is dissolved. If desired, add ½ cup of finely chopped celery or peppers.

Coleslaw Dressing;

1 cup salad dressing
½ cup sugar
1 teaspoon garlic powder

1 tablespoon celery seeds
2 tablespoons vinegar
1 teaspoon salt

Blend the ingredients well before serving this dressing on coleslaw.

CABBAGE SLAW

4 quarts shredded cabbage
2 medium onions, chopped

1 pepper, diced (optional)

Mix these ingredients, then pour over them a mixture of the following ingredients after it has been brought to a boil.

1½ cups sugar
¾ cup salad oil
1 teaspoon celery seeds

¾ cup vinegar
1 tablespoon salt

This salad will last indefinitely in the refrigerator.

DUTCH SLAW

1 large head cabbage, chopped
½ cup vinegar
1 cup celery, diced
2 teaspoons salt
½ teaspoon mustard seeds

½ cup chopped onions
2 cups sugar
1 green pepper, diced
1 teaspoon celery seeds

Mix together all the ingredients and put them into a glass jar. Screw on the lid, and refrigerate it until needed. It is ready to serve.

This salad will last a long time if refrigerated.

HAM-RONI SALAD

1 cup diced ham
2 cups cooked macaroni
¾ cup celery, chopped
1 cup grated carrots
¼ cup green peppers, chopped
¼ cup onions, chopped

3 tablespoons mayonnaise
1½ tablespoons barbecue sauce
  (optional)
Ketchup (optional)
1 teaspoon prepared mustard
Salt and pepper to taste

Combine the ham, macaroni, celery, carrots, peppers and onions. Combine and mix thoroughly the mayonnaise, barbecue sauce, ketchup and mustard. Then combine the two mixtures.

GOLDEN SALAD

1 envelope unflavored gelatin
¼ cup sugar
¼ teaspoon salt
¾ cup pineapple juice
¾ cup orange juice

¼ cup vinegar
1 cup diced pineapple, drained
½ cup orange sections, cut into small
  pieces
½ cup raw carrots, coarsely grated

Mix thoroughly in a saucepan the gelatin, sugar and salt. Add the pineapple juice. Place it over low heat, stirring constantly until the gelatin is dissolved. Stir in the orange juice and vinegar after removing it from the heat. Fold in the pineapple, oranges and carrots. Pour the mixture into a mold and refrigerate it to set.

GREEN BEAN SALAD

1 pound green beans
2 small onions
6 slices bacon

⅓ cup vinegar
2½ tablespoons sugar
½ teaspoon salt

Wash the green beans and cut off and discard the ends. Cut the beans into 1-inch pieces. Cook them for 15 to 20 minutes or until they are tender. Drain them thoroughly and put them into a bowl, keeping them warm. Meanwhile, clean the onions and cut them into ⅛-inch thick slices. Separate the onion rings and put them into the bowl with the beans.

Dice and fry the bacon until it is crisp, without pouring off the drippings. Then add to the bacon the vinegar, sugar and salt. Heat this mixture to boiling, stirring well. Pour the bacon/vinegar mixture over the beans and onions and toss it lightly to coat them thoroughly.

KRAUT SALAD

1 quart sauerkraut, drained
1 cup celery, finely cut
1 small mango, finely cut
1 small onion, finely cut

½ cup cooking oil
1 cup sugar
½ cup vinegar

Mix the ingredients together, and the salad is ready to serve.

MACARONI SALAD

Use well-cooked macaroni instead of potatoes and prepare it the same as you would Potato Salad (see page 93). Macaroni and potatoes may also be combined and used for Macaroni-Potato Salad. Cooked navy beans may also be added.

PEA SALAD

1 cup cooked peas, drained
1 cup celery, finely cut

½ cup sweet pickles, chopped
½ cup diced cheese

Season the ingredients with salt, pepper and sugar, and mix them with a good mayonnaise.

PERFECTION SALAD

1 tablespoon unflavored gelatin
½ cup cold water
1 cup boiling water
½ cup sugar
½ cup mild vinegar
2 tablespoons lemon juice

1 teaspoon salt
1 cup cabbage, finely shredded
2 cups celery, finely cut
2 pimentos, finely cut
¼ cup red or green peppers, finely cut

Soak the gelatin in the cold water for about 5 minutes. Add the boiling water, sugar, vinegar, lemon juice and salt. When the mixture begins to stiffen, add the remaining ingredients. Turn it into a wet mold and chill it. Remove the salad to a bed of lettuce and garnish it with mayonnaise.

QUICK LETTUCE SALAD

Spread lettuce leaves on individual plates. Place a pineapple slice or a spoonful of pineapple chunks on each plate of lettuce, and top it with cottage cheese. On top of the cottage cheese put a spoonful of mayonnaise, and sprinkle it with nutmeats or garnish with a maraschino cherry.

POTATO SALAD

1 quart cooked, salted, diced potatoes
10 (or fewer) hardcooked eggs, sliced
½ cup celery, finely chopped (optional)

2 cups Velvet Salad Dressing
 (see page 101)

1 small onion, minced

Mix the ingredients together, and serve.

SUMMER SALAD

Take several tablespoons of olive oil, cooking oil or sour cream. Add vinegar or lemon juice, then salt to taste. If a sweet salad is desired, honey or sugar may be mixed in with the oil. Add ½ banana, finely diced. Mix these ingredients, then add any of the following vegetables or others of your choice;

Lettuce
Radishes
Cucumber
Celery

Carrots
Tomatoes
Onions
Spinach

Mix them thoroughly then add 1 handful of raisins and a handful of crushed peanuts (optional).

Variations: For a simpler salad, try using only lettuce and onions, or lettuce and diced apples.

THREE-BEAN SALAD

1 cup vinegar
1 cup sugar
2 tablespoons oil
Salt and pepper to taste
1 sweet onion, sliced
1 to 1¼ cups celery, diced

1 quart yellow beans, drained
1 quart green beans, drained
1 small can (1 pint) dark red kidney
 beans, washed and drained
1 green or red sweet pepper, sliced

Mix together the first 4 ingredients, then let the mixture stand while you slice the rest. Mix together all the vegetables, then add the vinegar mixture. Let it stand for 24 hours before serving.

Variations: Salad dressing may be used instead of the vinegar mixture.

TURNIP SALAD

Take 3 cups of finely grated turnips. Add mayonnaise, sugar, salt and pepper to taste. Add enough milk for the right consistency, and mix.

CHRISTMAS SALAD

First Part;

2 packages (3 ounces each) lime gelatin
  powder
3½ cups water

1 medium can crushed pineapple
  (reserve juice)

Prepare the gelatin, using the 3½ cups of water instead of following the package directions. Add the crushed pineapple, and pour it into a 9 x13-inch cake pan. Chill it until firm.

Second Part;

2 packages unflavored gelatin
⅔ cup cold water
1 small package white cream cheese

1 cup whipping cream
Sugar

Bring the reserved pineapple juice to a boil. Soften the gelatin in the cold water and add it to the boiling pineapple juice. Soften the cream cheese and add it to the gelatin mixture. Cool it until it is partially set. Whip the cream and sweeten it to taste. Add it to the pineapple juice/cheese mixture, then pour it over the firm lime gelatin. Refrigerate it until it is firm.

Third Part;

2 packages strawberry gelatin powder
3½ cups water

Mix the gelatin, using the 3½ cups of water instead of following the directions on the package. Chill it until it is partially set. Pour it over the second part and chill the whole salad until it is firm.

Variations: If desired, ½ of the crushed pineapple may be added to the strawberry gelatin instead of putting all of it into the lime gelatin.

COTTAGE CHEESE SALAD

1 small can mandarin oranges
1 small can crushed pineapple
1 package dessert topping mix, OR
1 cup cream, whipped

1 pint creamed cottage cheese
1 package (3 ounces) orange gelatin
  powder

Drain the fruit. Make the dessert topping according to the package directions. Mix the cottage cheese and dry gelatin thoroughly, then add the fruit and whipped topping. Beat the ingredients, then chill. Serve this salad the same day it is prepared.

APRICOT SALAD

Prepare this as you would Three-Layer Salad (see page 94), but use 2 small packages of apricot gelatin powder, 2 diced bananas and 2 cups of mashed apricots for the first layer instead of pineapple.

APPLE SALAD

1 cup white sugar
2 tablespoons flour
1 egg
Cold water
1 cup hot water
Salt
Vinegar

1 tablespoon butter
6 apples, diced
½ cup celery, diced
4 bananas, sliced
½ cup nuts, finely chopped (peanuts
    may be used)

Mix the sugar, flour and egg with enough cold water to make a thickening. Add the hot water and boil it. Add a little salt and vinegar and the butter. Cool the mixture before mixing in the rest of the ingredients.

Variations: Whipped cream, marshmallows and pineapple may also be added.

CROWN JEWEL GELATIN

1 package (3 ounces) raspberry gelatin
    powder
1 package (3 ounces) lime gelatin
    powder
1 package (3 ounces) black cherry
    gelatin powder
1 cup hot water per gelatin package

½ cup cold water per gelatin package
¼ cup sugar
1 cup pineapple juice
1 package strawberry gelatin powder
½ cup cold water
2 cups whipping cream

Prepare separately the first 3 gelatins. For each package, dissolve the gelatin in 1 cup of hot water, then add ½ cup of cold water. Let the gelatin set until it is firm, then cut it into ½-inch cubes.

Heat the sugar and pineapple juice to boiling. Dissolve the strawberry gelatin in the hot liquid, and add the cold water. Chill it until it is syrupy. Whip the cream and fold it into the syrupy gelatin. When this is well mixed, fold in the gelatin cubes. Pour the mixture into a dish and chill it.

FRUIT SALAD

3 pounds sugar
3 cups water
Yellow food coloring
2 packages gelatin soaked in 1 cup
   water
1 quart crushed pineapple
3 pounds bananas, sliced

1 medium jar maraschino cherries
2 quarts peaches
10 oranges
2 pounds red grapes
2 pounds green grapes

Boil the sugar and water for 2 to 3 minutes. Add a few drops of yellow food coloring and the gelatin soaked in the water. Pour the crushed pineapple over the sliced bananas. Stir it gently so the pineapple juice coats the bananas well—this will keep them from turning brown (lemon juice will do the same). Add the bananas and pineapple to the gelatin mixture. Add the other fruit, then mix and chill the salad.

MARY'S LIME SALAD

16 marshmallows
1 cup milk
1 package (3 ounces) lime gelatin
   powder
2 packages (4-ounce size) cream
   cheese

1 medium can crushed pineapple
1 cup cream, whipped
⅔ cup salad dressing

Melt the marshmallows and milk in a double boiler. Pour this hot mixture over the lime gelatin, stirring it until the gelatin is dissolved. Stir in the cream cheese until it dissolves. Add the pineapple and cool the mixture until it becomes syrupy. Blend in the whipped cream and salad dressing. Chill it until it is firm.

MONOTONY BREAKER

1¼ cups boiling water
1 package (3 ounces) cherry gelatin
   powder
1 cup ground cranberries
1 cup sugar

¼ cup water
1 cup ground apples
1 cup crushed pineapple
Broken nuts

Mix together the 1¼ cups of boiling water and the gelatin. Combine the sugar and ¼ cup of water with the cranberries, and cook this mixture until the cranberries are soft. When it is cool, blend the 2 mixtures and add the apples, pineapple and broken nuts. Spoon it into a prepared 4-cup mold, and chill it until firm.

PINEAPPLE AND CHEESE SALAD

1 package (3 ounces) lime gelatin
  powder
1 small can crushed pineapple, drained

2 cups cottage cheese
½ cup nuts, finely chopped

Prepare the gelatin according to the package instructions. When it begins to set, whip it as you would whipping cream. Fold in the pineapple, cheese and nuts. Chill the salad, and serve.

Variations: Try adding ¼ cup of sugar and 1 can of whipped evaporated milk.

PINEAPPLE FRUIT SALAD

1 tablespoon flour
Cold water
1 egg
½ cup sugar
1 tablespoon butter

1 can (19 ounces) sliced pineapple
  (reserve juice)
6 bananas, sliced
1 dozen marshmallows
1 cup mixed nuts

Mix the flour with the water to make a smooth paste. Stir the egg into the paste. Heat together the reserved pineapple juice, sugar and butter, then mix and boil it until it thickens slightly. Allow it to cool before pouring it over a mixture of the cut up pineapple, bananas, marshmallows and nuts. Serve this salad with whipped cream.

Variations: For Lettuce-Pineapple Salad, follow the above instructions but omit the bananas, nuts and whipped cream. Instead, add cut up lettuce and more marshmallows.

THREE-LAYER SALAD

2 packages (3 ounces each) lime gelatin
  powder
1 cup drained, crushed pineapple
½ cup sugar
2 tablespoons cornstarch
2 egg yolks

½ cup cold water
1½ cups pineapple juice
1 package (8 ounces) white cream
  cheese
1 cup Marvel cheese (see page 289)
1 cup whipping cream, whipped

Fix the gelatin according to the package directions, and add the pineapple. Pour it into an oblong cake pan and let it set until it is firm. Combine the sugar, cornstarch and egg yolks. Blend this mixture with the cold water and pour it into the pineapple juice, which has been heated. Cook it until it is thick. Allow it to cool, then pour it onto the gelatin and chill it. When it is ready to serve, top it with the cream cheese blended with the Marvel cheese and whipped cream. Add sugar to the whipped cream if desired.

RIBBON SALAD

First Layer;

1 package (3 ounces) cherry gelatin
   powder

Prepare the gelatin according to package directions, and pour it into an oblong cake pan. Chill it to set.

Second Layer;

⅔ cup milk
16 marshmallows
1 package (8 ounces) cream cheese
1 package (3 ounces) lemon gelatin
   powder

1 small can crushed pineapple
⅔ cup nuts
1 cup whipping cream, whipped

Heat the milk, marshmallows and cheese in a double boiler until all is melted, then add the lemon gelatin. Let the mixture cool before adding the pineapple, nuts and whipped cream. Pour it over the first layer of cherry gelatin and chill.

Third Layer;

1 package (3 ounces) orange gelatin
   powder

Prepare the orange gelatin according to package directions, then pour it on top of the second layer. Let it set in the refrigerator.

WHITE FRUIT SALAD

2 tablespoons unflavored gelatin
½ cup cold fruit juice (drained from
   canned fruit)
1 cup hot fruit juice (drained from
   canned fruit)
1 cup mayonnaise
1 cup whipping cream, whipped

¼ cup icing sugar
½ cup pineapple slices, cut into small
   pieces
½ can white cherries, cut into small
   pieces
½ cup chopped nuts

Soak the gelatin in the cold fruit juice for about 5 minutes, then dissolve it in the hot fruit juice. When the mixture begins to stiffen, add the mayonnaise and fold in the cream and icing sugar. Add the pineapples, cherries and nuts. Pour the mixture into wet molds, and refrigerate. Serve this salad with lettuce, and mayonnaise mixed with a little whipped cream. It serves 12.

TRIPLE TREAT SALAD

First Layer;

1 package (3 ounces) strawberry
   gelatin powder
2 bananas

Prepare the gelatin according to the package directions, then pour it into a 9 x 9-inch pan. Slice the bananas into the gelatin and let it set until firm.

Second Layer;

1 package (3 ounces) lemon gelatin   4 ounces cream cheese
   powder   ⅓ cup mayonnaise
1 cup hot water

Dissolve the lemon gelatin in the hot water. Add the cream cheese and mayonnaise, then beat the mixture well. When it is partially set, pour it over the first layer.

Third Layer;

1 package (3 ounces) lime gelatin   ½ cup crushed pineapple
   powder
2 cups hot water

Dissolve the lime gelatin in the hot water. When it is cool, add the pineapple. Chill it until it is partially set, then pour it on top of the other two layers.

Slice it into cubes for serving.

FRENCH DRESSING

1 can (10 ounces) condensed tomato   1 teaspoon garlic salt
   soup   1 teaspoon dry mustard
½ cup sugar   1 teaspoon horseradish (optional)
1 teaspoon paprika   1 cup cooking oil
1 teaspoon salt   ¾ cup vinegar
1 teaspoon onion salt
1 teaspoon pepper

Put all the ingredients into a jar and shake it. Keep the dressing cool.

Variations: Try adding 2 tablespoons of Worcestershire sauce and 1 small chopped onion.

HOMEMADE MUSTARD

½ cup vinegar
½ cup sugar
2 tablespoons flour

½ cup sweet cream
2 tablespoons dry mustard
1 egg

Mix together all the ingredients, then boil the mixture in a double boiler until it is thick. To color the mustard, add a shake of turmeric.

ELLA'S SALAD DRESSING

¼ cup vinegar
½ cup oil
1 teaspoon salt

⅓ cup ketchup
½ cup sugar
1 tablespoon creamy salad dressing

Shake the ingredients together well. This dressing will keep quite awhile in the refrigerator.

HOMEMADE SALAD DRESSING

1 egg plus water to make ¾ cup
⅔ cup flour
1 cup water
½ cup vinegar
¾ cup cooking oil

1 tablespoon lemon juice
⅔ cup sugar
½ teaspoon dry mustard
2 teaspoons salt

Beat the egg and water thoroughly with an egg beater. Bring to a boil in a 1 quart saucepan the flour, water and vinegar, then blend in the egg and the rest of the ingredients. Beat the mixture hard until it is smooth.

PERFECT SALAD DRESSING

½ cup sugar
1 teaspoon salt
2 tablespoons vinegar (scant)

2 tablespoons salad dressing
⅓ cup milk or cream

Mix together the first 4 ingredients, then add the milk or cream. Mix it until the sugar dissolves. Serve this dressing on cut up lettuce.

SALAD DRESSING

1 pint milk
½ cup sugar
½ teaspoon salt
5 tablespoons flour

3 tablespoons vinegar
2 teaspoons mustard
½ teaspoon turmeric
Cream

Heat the milk, sugar and salt. Moisten the flour with milk and stir it into the hot milk mixture. Continue to stir it until it boils. Add the vinegar, mustard and turmeric (dissolved in hot water). Let it stand until it is cold, then beat the mixture and add cream to the consistency desired.

SUSAN'S SIMPLE SALAD DRESSING

1 cup white sugar
½ cup vinegar
¾ cup ketchup
1 tablespoon salt
½ teaspoon paprika

1 cup salad oil
¼ cup lemon juice
3 tablespoons grated onion
1 teaspoon celery seed

Mix together well all the ingredients. Keep this dressing refrigerated.

TOSSED SALAD DRESSING

1⅓ cups white sugar
2 teaspoons paprika
2 tablespoons dry mustard
1 teaspoon celery seed

2 teaspoons salt
1 cup vinegar
1 cup salad oil
1 small onion, grated

Mix together the ingredients and serve on tossed salad.

VELVET SALAD DRESSING

1 egg
1 tablespoon flour
½ cup sugar
1 teaspoon salt

1 teaspoon prepared mustard
4 tablespoons vinegar
1 cup cold water
3 tablespoons butter

Beat the egg well, then add the flour, sugar, salt, mustard, vinegar and water. Cook it in a double boiler until it is thick. Remove it from the heat and beat in the butter.

This dressing is good on lettuce or potato salads. Cream or 2 tablespoons of mayonnaise may be added if preferred.

CRANBERRY SAUCE

1 pound cranberries
8 apples
2 oranges

4 cups sugar
1 can crushed pineapple (optional)

Grind together all the ingredients. Do not heat the mixture. Let it stand in a cool place or refrigerate it for a few days to sweeten.

COOKED CRANBERRY SAUCE

1½ cups water
1 pound cranberries
18 apples

4 or 5 cups sugar
2 oranges

Add the water to the cranberries and apples and boil them together. Put them through a ricer or food mill, and add the sugar, adjusting the quantity according to taste. Stir the mixture while it cools. Grate the orange rind, extract the juice from the oranges, and add both to the mixture when it has cooled.

CAKES

HINTS FOR CAKES

- Much less sugar can be used in several of the cake, cookie or dessert recipes, and the food is no less tasty. In many instances, molasses or honey can be substituted for sugar. Someone said we pay twice for sugar or sweets—once when we buy them, and again when we pay the dentist's bill.
- When making a ready-mix cake, add 1 tablespoon of cooking oil. This brings out more of the flavor and will make the cake more moist.
- When baking, measure shortening before molasses and it will not stick to the cup.

TIPS FOR MAKING ANGEL FOOD CAKES

- Have all the ingredients at room temperature.
- Use cake flour only.
- Egg whites must be clean and should not contain a part of the yolks.
- Have the sugar clean if beaten with the egg whites. Even a bit of flour might damage the cake.
- Fold in the flour and sugar mixture gently, using a cake scraper. DO NOT BEAT it.
- Bake the cake in an ungreased tube pan. When it is done, turn it upside down to cool.
- Be careful not to over-bake.

AMISH CAKE

½ cup butter
2 cups brown sugar, packed
2 cups buttermilk or sour milk

2 teaspoons soda
3 cups all-purpose flour
1 teaspoon vanilla

Cream the butter and brown sugar. Add the buttermilk and soda, then the flour and vanilla. Bake the batter in a greased and floured 9 x 13 x 2-inch baking pan at 375°. Spread the following topping over the cake after it is done. Return it to the oven and bake it until bubbly, or for 1 minute.

Topping;

6 tablespoons soft butter
4 tablespoons milk

1 cup brown sugar
½ cup nuts

Combine these ingredients.

BROWN SUGAR ANGEL FOOD CAKE

2 cups egg whites (14 to 16)   1 teaspoon salt
1½ teaspoons cream of tartar   2 cups brown sugar
2 teaspoons vanilla   1½ cups sifted cake flour

Beat the egg whites with the cream of tartar, vanilla and salt until stiff peaks form. Gradually sift 1 cup of the sugar over the beaten egg whites and beat them again. Sift the remaining sugar with the flour, and fold it into the egg whites. Turn the batter into an ungreased 10-inch tube cake pan. Bake it at 350° for 45 to 50 minutes.

CHOCOLATE ANGEL FOOD CAKE

¾ cup cake flour   2 cups egg whites (14 to 16)
¼ cup cocoa   1 teaspoon vanilla
¼ teaspoon salt   1½ cups sugar
1 teaspoon cream of tartar

Sift together the flour, cocoa and salt. Add the cream of tartar to the egg whites and beat them until they will hold peaks. Add the vanilla, then add the sugar gradually, and fold this mixture into the flour mixture. Put the batter into an ungreased tube pan and bake it for 40 to 45 minutes at 350 to 375°.

WHITE ANGEL FOOD CAKE

1½ cups white sugar   ½ teaspoon salt
1 cup cake flour   1½ teaspoons cream of tartar
1½ cups egg whites (11 to 12)   1 teaspoon almond flavoring

Sift together 3 times, ¾ cup of the sugar and the flour. Set it aside. Beat the egg whites until they are frothy, then add the salt and cream of tartar. Beat it until it stands in peaks. Add the rest of the sugar about 3 tablespoons at a time, beating well with an egg beater after each addition. Fold in lightly the sugar/flour mixture about ½ cup at a time, then add the almond flavoring. Bake the batter at 375° for about 35 to 40 minutes or until it is done.

*Variations: To make **Nut Angel Food Cake,** omit the almond extract and add ½ cup of ground walnuts to the flour and sugar mixture.*

*For **Maraschino Cherry Angel Food Cake,** grind the drained contents of 1 small jar of maraschino cherries (about ⅔ cup). Fold it into the batter described above and bake it as directed.*

*For **Butterscotch** or **Chocolate Chip Angel Food Cake,** add ¾ cup butterscotch bits or chocolate chips to the batter.*

*For **Jelly Angel Food Cake,** mix in 2 or 3 tablespoons of any fruit flavored gelatin powder.*

CHOCOLATE TWO-EGG CHIFFON CAKE

2 eggs, separated
1½ cups sugar
1¾ cups sifted cake flour
¾ teaspoon soda
¾ teaspoon salt

⅓ cup cooking oil
1 cup buttermilk, or sweet milk
2 squares (2 ounces) unsweetened
  chocolate, melted

Preheat the oven to 350°. Grease well and dust with flour 2 round layer pans (8-inch diameter by at least 1½ inches deep), or 1 oblong pan (13 x 9½ x 2 inches). Beat the egg whites until they are frothy. Gradually beat in ½ cup of the sugar, and continue beating the whites to make a very stiff and glossy meringue.

Sift the remaining sugar, flour, soda and salt into another bowl. Add the oil and ½ of the buttermilk. Beat these ingredients for 1 minute at medium speed on a mixer or for 150 vigorous strokes by hand, scraping the sides and bottom of the bowl constantly. Add the remaining buttermilk, the egg yolks and chocolate. Beat the mixture for 1 minute more, scraping the bowl constantly. Fold in the meringue. Pour the batter into the prepared pans and bake it for 30 to 35 minutes.

APPLE DAPPLE

2 eggs
2 cups white sugar
1 cup cooking oil
3 cups all-purpose flour (scant)
½ teaspoon salt

1 teaspoon soda
3 cups chopped apples
2 teaspoons vanilla
Chopped nuts (optional)

Mix together the eggs, sugar and oil, and add the flour, salt and soda which have been sifted together. Add the chopped apples, vanilla and nuts. Mix the batter well and pour it into a greased cake pan. Bake it at 350° for 45 minutes or until done.

Icing;

1 cup brown sugar
¼ cup milk
¼ cup butter or margarine

Combine the sugar, milk and butter, and cook the mixture for 2½ minutes. Stir it a little after removing it from the stove, but do not beat it. Dribble it over the cake while it and the cake are still hot. A few chopped nuts may be sprinkled over the icing.

APPLESAUCE CAKE

½ cup shortening
1 cup sugar (white or brown)
1 egg
1 cup applesauce
1 cup sifted cake flour
½ teaspoon salt
½ teaspoon baking powder

1 teaspoon soda
½ teaspoon cloves
1 teaspoon cinnamon
1 teaspoon allspice
1 cup raisins
¼ cup chopped nuts

Cream the shortening and add the sugar, beating it until light. Add the egg and beat it until fluffy, then add the applesauce and mix it well. Sift together the flour, salt, baking powder, soda, cloves, cinnamon and allspice, then add the raisins and chopped nuts. Combine the two mixtures. Bake the batter in a greased 8-inch square pan at 350° for 40 to 45 minutes.

Glaze for Applesauce Cake;

½ cup white sugar
2 tablespoons cornstarch
¼ teaspoon cinnamon

½ cup canned applesauce
½ cup water
1 teaspoon lemon juice

In a small saucepan stir together the sugar, cornstarch and cinnamon. Stir in the applesauce, water and lemon juice. Cook this mixture over moderate heat, stirring it constantly until it is thick. Spread it over the cake when it is lukewarm or cold.

ROMAN APPLE CAKE

1 cup brown sugar
½ cup shortening
1 egg
1 teaspoon vanilla
1½ cups all-purpose flour

¼ teaspoon baking powder
¼ teaspoon soda
¼ teaspoon salt
½ cup milk
4 medium apples, chopped

Mix together well all the ingredients but the apples, then fold them in.

Topping;

1 tablespoon melted butter
½ cup brown sugar
½ cup chopped nuts

2 teaspoons cinnamon
2 teaspoons flour

Mix these ingredients together and sprinkle the mixture as crumbs over the batter. Bake it for 45 minutes at 350°. Serve the cake warm.

ROYAL APPLE CAKE

3 cups all-purpose flour	2 eggs
1 teaspoon soda	2 cups sugar
2 teaspoons cinnamon	1 cup water
1 teaspoon baking powder	1 cup nuts
½ teaspoon salt	1 cup raisins
1 teaspoon nutmeg	2 cups diced apples
1 cup oil	

Sift together and set aside the flour, soda, cinnamon, baking powder, salt and nutmeg. Combine and mix well the oil, eggs and sugar, and add the flour mixture alternately with the water. Then add the nuts, raisins and apples. Spread the batter in a greased 9 x 13-inch pan and bake it at 350° until done.

BANANA NUT CAKE

1 cup white sugar	1 teaspoon soda
½ cup butter	2 teaspoons baking powder
2 eggs, well-beaten	Pinch of salt
4 tablespoons sour milk	1 teaspoon cream of tartar
1 teaspoon vanilla	1 cup mashed bananas
2 cups flour	½ cup chopped nuts

Cream the sugar and butter, then add the eggs, milk and vanilla. Add the sifted dry ingredients, then the bananas, and nuts. Bake the batter in a greased and floured 9 x 13 x 2-inch baking pan at 375° for 40 minutes or until done.

BROWN STONE FRONT CAKE

2½ cups all-purpose flour	2 cups brown sugar
1 teaspoon cinnamon	3 egg yolks
½ teaspoon nutmeg	1 cup sour milk or buttermilk
½ teaspoon allspice	1 cup chopped walnuts
1 teaspoon soda	1 cup stewed raisins
½ cup butter	3 egg whites stiffly beaten

Sift together the flour and spices, then add the soda. Cream the butter and sugar, and add the egg yolks. Add the sifted ingredients and milk alternately to this egg mixture. Then add the nuts and raisins and fold in the egg whites. Bake the batter in a greased 9 x 13-inch pan at 350° until it is done, about 30 minutes.

Frost the cake with Creamy Caramel Frosting (see page 132).

BURNT SUGAR CAKE

2¼ cups sifted cake flour
3 teaspoons baking powder
1 teaspoon salt
1 cup sugar
1 cup milk

⅓ cup Burnt Sugar Syrup
 (see page 298)
1 teaspoon almond extract
½ cup shortening
2 eggs, unbeaten

Sift together the flour, baking powder, salt and sugar. Blend together the milk, Burnt Sugar Syrup and almond extract, then add ⅔ of it to the flour mixture. Add the shortening and beat it until the batter is well blended and glossy, then add the remaining liquid. Add the eggs, and beat the batter again until it is very smooth. Bake it in a moderate oven (350°) until done.

Frost the cake with Burnt Sugar Frosting (see page 131).

CARAMEL CAKE

2 cups brown sugar
½ cup lard
2 eggs, unbeaten
1 teaspoon vanilla
2 cups all-purpose flour

1 teaspoon cocoa
2 teaspoons hot water
Sour milk
1 teaspoon soda

Cream together the sugar and lard. Add the eggs, vanilla and flour. Put the cocoa into a cup and add the hot water. Fill the cup with sour milk, then add the soda. Stir this mixture until the cocoa is well dissolved. The cup will run over so be sure to hold it over the mixing bowl while stirring the contents. When the cocoa is dissolved, pour it in with the other mixture and mix it. Bake the batter at 350° until done.

LEMON CHIFFON CAKE

1½ cups sugar
2¼ cups sifted cake flour
3 teaspoons baking powder
1 teaspoon salt
⅓ cup cooking oil

1 cup milk
2 teaspoons lemon juice
Grated rind of 1 lemon
2 eggs, separated

Sift 1 cup of the sugar with the flour, baking powder and salt. Add the oil, ½ of the milk, the lemon juice and rind. Blend this mixture well, then add the egg yolks and the remaining milk, beating it to make a smooth batter.

Beat the egg whites until they are frothy, then gradually beat in the remaining sugar until the mixture is stiff and glossy. Fold this into the batter and pour it into an ungreased 10-inch tube pan. Bake it at 350° for 40 minutes or until done.

CARROT CAKE

2 cups sugar
1½ cups cooking oil
4 eggs
2 cups all-purpose flour
2 teaspoons soda

2 teaspoons baking powder
1 teaspoon salt
2 teaspoons cinnamon
3 cups raw carrots, shredded
½ cup chopped nuts

Cream together the sugar and cooking oil. Add the eggs and beat the mixture well. Sift together the flour, soda, baking powder, salt and cinnamon, and add it to the creamed mixture. Fold in the carrots and nuts. Bake it in a greased 9 x 13-inch pan in a moderate oven (350°) until done.

Cream Cheese Icing;

4 tablespoons butter
8 ounces cream cheese

2 teaspoons vanilla
1 pound icing sugar

Mix together these ingredients until smooth.

ORANGE CARROT CAKE

2 cups whole wheat flour
1 cup brown sugar
1 cup white sugar
2 teaspoons baking powder
2 teaspoons soda
2 teaspoons cinnamon
1 teaspoon nutmeg

1 teaspoon salt
1¼ cups vegetable oil
1 (12-ounce) can frozen, unsweetened
orange juice (save ¼)
4 eggs
2½ cups grated, raw carrots
½ cup chopped nuts

Sift together the dry ingredients. Add the oil and orange juice (saving ¼ can of the orange juice for the glaze). Mix this well, then add the eggs and beat the mixture well. Stir in the carrots and nuts. Bake the batter at 350° for 1 hour or until it is well done.

Glaze;

6 tablespoons butter
2 cups icing sugar

Brown the butter. Add the juice reserved from the cake recipe, and the icing sugar. Spread this glaze over the cake while it is still warm.

SPICE CHIFFON CAKE

1¾ cups plus 2 tablespoons all-purpose
   flour
1½ cups sugar
3 teaspoons baking powder
1 teaspoon salt
1 teaspoon cinnamon
½ teaspoon nutmeg
½ teaspoon allspice

½ teaspoon cloves
5 egg yolks
¾ cup water
2 teaspoons vanilla
½ cup salad oil
1 cup (7 to 8) egg whites
½ teaspoon cream of tartar

Sift together the flour, sugar, baking powder, salt and spices. Beat well the egg yolks, water and vanilla, then add this mixture with the oil to the sifted dry ingredients. Beat the egg whites with the cream of tartar until they are stiff, and fold them in last. Pour the batter into an ungreased 10-inch tube pan and bake it at 325° for 55 minutes, then at 350° for 10 minutes more.

WHOLE WHEAT COCOA CHIFFON CAKE

½ cup cocoa
¾ cup boiling water
½ teaspoon cream of tartar
7 to 8 eggs, separated
1¾ cups whole wheat flour

1½ cups raw sugar
1 teaspoon salt
3 teaspoons baking powder
½ cup salad oil
1 teaspoon vanilla

Stir together the cocoa and boiling water until smooth, then set it aside to cool. Add the cream of tartar to the egg whites (1 cup) and whip them until they form very stiff peaks.

Blend together the flour, raw sugar, salt and baking powder. Make a well and add in order the oil, egg yolks, cooled cocoa mixture and vanilla, and beat them until the mixture is smooth and creamy. Pour this mixture gradually over the whipped egg whites, folding it in gently with a rubber scraper until it is just blended. Bake the batter in a tube pan at 325° for 55 minutes, then at 350° for 10 to 15 minutes more.

CHOCOLATE MAYONNAISE CAKE

2 cups all-purpose flour
1 cup sugar
½ cup cocoa
2 teaspoons soda

1 cup boiling water
1 teaspoon vanilla
1 cup mayonnaise (or Homemade
   Salad Dressing, see p. 100)

Sift together the flour, sugar, cocoa and soda. Mix this with the rest of the ingredients, and bake the batter in 2 greased and floured 8-inch layer pans at 350° for 30 minutes.

AUNT FRONIE CAKE

2 cups sugar
¼ cup shortening
2 eggs, beaten
2 cups all-purpose flour
1 teaspoon baking powder

½ cup sour milk
4 tablespoons cocoa
½ teaspoon salt
2 teaspoons soda

Cream together the sugar and shortening, then add the rest of the ingredients. Mix them well, then mix in thoroughly 1 cup of boiling water. Bake the batter in a greased 9 x 9-inch pan at 350° for about 30 minutes or until done.

CHOCOLATE MINT DREAM CAKE

2 cups cake flour
¾ teaspoon salt
1½ cups white sugar
3 teaspoons baking powder
½ cup cocoa

⅔ cup shortening
1 cup milk
1 teaspoon vanilla
2 eggs

Sift together the dry ingredients. Add the shortening, milk and vanilla. Mix them, then add the eggs and beat well. Bake the batter in a greased 9-inch spring form pan at 350° for 30 to 35 minutes. Cut off the top of the cake using a thread, and add the following filling, or place the filling on top as icing.

Peppermint Whipped Cream Filling;

1 pint whipping cream
⅓ cup icing sugar

½ teaspoon peppermint flavor
Green food coloring

Beat the whipping cream until it is stiff. Add the icing sugar and peppermint flavoring, and tint it with the food coloring.

COCOA CAKE

6 tablespoons butter or margarine
2 cups sugar
2 cups sour milk or buttermilk
2 teaspoons soda

2 teaspoons vanilla
3 cups cake flour (scant)
½ cup cocoa, or less

Melt the butter and mix it with the sugar. Add the sour milk in which the soda has been dissolved. Add the vanilla, then add the flour and cocoa which have been sifted together. Bake the batter for 40 to 45 minutes at 350°.

EASY CHOCOLATE CAKE

Pan Size;

small (8 x 8 inches)	medium (13 x 9½ inches)	large (14 x 9½ inches)	
1	2	3	Measure and sift together; heaping cups of sifted cake flour
1	2	3	rounded tablespoons of cocoa
1	2	3	teaspoons of soda
⅛	¼	½	teaspoon of baking powder
⅛	¼	½	teaspoon of salt
			Beat;
1	2	3	eggs
			Cream together well and add to the eggs;
¼	½	¾	cup of shortening
1	2	3	cups of sugar
			Add the following mixture alternately with the dry ingredients to the egg mixture, and mix well;
¼	½	¾	cup buttermilk or sour milk
½	1	1½	cups boiling water
1	2	3	teaspoons vanilla

The batter will be thin. Bake it in a hot oven, 375 to 400°.

FIVE STAR FUDGE CAKE

1½ cups butter or margarine	6 cups sifted cake flour
4½ cups sugar	3 teaspoons soda
6 eggs	1 heaping teaspoon baking powder
3 teaspoons vanilla	1½ teaspoons salt
6 (1-ounce) squares unsweetened chocolate, melted	3 cups ice water

Cream together the butter, sugar, eggs and vanilla until they are fluffy. Blend in the melted chocolate. Sift together the dry ingredients, and add this mixture alternately with the water to the chocolate mixture. Pour the batter into three 8-inch layer pans which have been greased and lined with waxed paper. Bake it in a moderate oven (350°) for 30 to 35 minutes.

GERMAN SWEET CHOCOLATE CAKE

1 bar (4 ounces) German sweet
   chocolate
½ cup boiling water
1 cup butter or margarine
2 cups sugar
4 egg yolks, unbeaten

1 teaspoon vanilla
2½ cups sifted cake flour
½ teaspoon salt
1 teaspoon soda
1 cup buttermilk
4 egg whites, stiffly beaten

Melt the chocolate in the boiling water, then let it cool. Cream the butter and sugar until they are fluffy. Add the egg yolks one at a time, beating well after each addition. Then add the melted chocolate and the vanilla.

Sift together the flour, salt and soda. Add this alternately with the buttermilk to the chocolate mixture, beating it well until smooth. Fold in the egg whites. Pour the batter into 3 layer pans (8 or 9-inch) which have been lined on the bottom with waxed paper. Bake it in a moderate oven (350°) for 30 to 40 minutes. Allow the cake to cool, then spread it with Coconut-Pecan Frosting (see page 132).

Variations: Instead of German chocolate you can use 6 tablespoons of cocoa, 2 tablespoons of margarine and an extra ½ cup of flour.

DELUXE CHOCOLATE CAKE

½ cup shortening
½ cup brown sugar, firmly packed
2 cups sifted all-purpose flour
1 teaspoon soda
1 cup granulated sugar
⅔ cup sour milk or buttermilk

1 teaspoon vanilla extract
2 eggs
3 (1-ounce) squares unsweetened
   chocolate, melted in ½ cup boiling
   water

Have the shortening at room temperature, and stir it just enough to soften it. Add the brown sugar, forcing it through a sieve to remove lumps if necessary, and mix it well. Add the flour, soda and granulated sugar, then ½ cup of the sour milk, the vanilla and eggs. Mix them until all the flour is dampened, then continue mixing for 1 minute or 100 strokes. Blend in the remaining sour milk and beat the mixture for 1 minute more. Add the chocolate mixture and beat it for another minute. Scrape the bowl and the spoon often to make sure that all the batter is well mixed. Turn the batter into 2 greased and floured 9-inch layer pans, or one loaf pan. Bake it in a moderate oven (350°) for 30 minutes.

MARBLE CAKE

2½ cups cake flour
1½ teaspoons baking powder
1⅔ cups sugar
1½ teaspoons soda
1 teaspoon salt
¾ cup shortening

¾ cup sour milk
2 eggs, unbeaten
1 square (1 ounce) chocolate, melted
2 tablespoons hot water
¼ teaspoon soda
1 tablespoon sugar

First, sift together the flour, baking powder, 1⅔ cups of sugar, 1½ teaspoons of soda and salt. Then sift this mixture into the shortening alternately with the sour milk. Add the eggs and beat the mixture well.

Mix the chocolate, hot water, ¼ teaspoon of soda and 1 tablespoon of sugar, and add this mixture to ¼ of the batter. Pour the batter by large spoonfuls into 2 greased and floured 9-inch layer pans, alternating the plain and chocolate mixtures. With a knife, cut through the batter in a wide zig-zag pattern. Bake the cake at 350° until done.

SUGARLESS CHOCOLATE CAKE

½ cup cocoa
2 teaspoons soda
2¼ cups cake flour
¼ teaspoon salt

1 cup hot water
1 cup melted lard
1 cup table syrup or honey
2 eggs, beaten

Sift together the dry ingredients. Add the hot water, a little at a time, stirring well after each addition. Add the lard, syrup and eggs, mixing well. Bake the batter in a greased and floured 13 x 9 x 12-inch pan at 350° for 30 to 40 minutes.

VELVET CHOCOLATE CAKE

2 cups cake flour
½ teaspoon salt
½ cup cocoa
½ cup shortening
2 cups brown sugar
1 teaspoon vanilla

2 eggs, well-beaten
1 cup cold water
1 teaspoon soda dissolved in 2
  tablespoons boiling water
1 cup chopped nuts (optional)

Sift the flour once, measure it and mix it with the salt and cocoa, and sift it again. Cream the shortening and add the sugar gradually, beating it thoroughly after each addition. Add the vanilla, then add the well-beaten eggs and beat them until the mixture is fluffy. Beat in the flour mixture alternately with the water, then add the dissolved soda and beat it well. If desired, add chopped nuts. Bake the batter in layer cake pans at 350° for 30 to 35 minutes.

LAZY WIFE CAKE

1½ cups pastry flour
¼ teaspoon salt
2 teaspoons soda
3 tablespoons cocoa
1 cup white sugar

1 teaspoon vanilla
7 tablespoons cooking oil
1 tablespoon vinegar
1 cup cold water

Sift the dry ingredients into a 9 x 9-inch ungreased cake pan. Mix them with a fork. Make three holes in this mixture: into one put the vanilla, into the next the oil, and into the third the vinegar. Pour over all of this the cold water. Mix these ingredients with a fork, but do not beat them. Bake the batter at 350° for 25 to 30 minutes or until done.

FRESH BLUEBERRY CAKE

½ cup butter or margarine
1 cup sugar
2 eggs
2 cups all-purpose flour

½ teaspoon salt
3 teaspoons baking powder
1 cup milk
1 cup blueberries

Cream the butter or margarine, then add the sugar a little at a time, and cream it again. Add the eggs and some of the flour, sifted with the salt and baking powder. Blend this slowly, adding the milk and the rest of the flour. Wash the berries, dry them on a towel, then dust them with some flour. Add them to the batter just before baking. Pour the batter into a greased and floured pan, 9 x 13 x 2 inches. Sprinkle it with cinnamon and sugar, nutmeg, cloves or whatever appeals to you. Bake it at 325° for 45 minutes. Serve the cake with whipped cream or ice cream.

If blueberries are scarce, raisins or currants can be substituted.

FRUIT CAKE

8 ounces mixed fruit peel
2¼ cups nuts
3¾ cups golden raisins
½ cup grape juice
2 cups brown sugar
1 teaspoon almond flavoring

½ cup soft butter
5 eggs
2 cups all-purpose flour
½ teaspoon mace
½ teaspoon cinnamon
¼ teaspoon baking powder

In a bowl, mix together the fruit peel, nuts, raisins and grape juice. Let it stand for 1 hour. Then in a large bowl, mix together the sugar, flavoring, butter and eggs. Add to this mixture the flour, mace, cinnamon and baking powder, which have been sifted together. Combine this with the fruit mixture. Pour it into a greased 10-inch tube pan lined with waxed paper. Bake it at 275° until firm and evenly browned, about 3 hours and 20 minutes. Remove it from the oven and let it cool for ½ hour. Turn the cake onto a cooling rack and let it cool thoroughly. Wrap it in vinegar-soaked cloth and store it in an airtight container for one week.

COCOA CRUMB CAKE

2 cups all-purpose flour
1½ cups brown sugar
½ cup butter or margarine
1 egg, beaten

1 cup buttermilk
2 large tablespoons cocoa (optional)
1 teaspoon soda
1 teaspoon vanilla

Mix together the flour, sugar and butter as for a pie crust, reserving ¾ cup for the topping. To the remainder of the crumbs add the egg, buttermilk, cocoa, soda and vanilla. Pour the batter into a cake or pie pan and sprinkle the reserved crumbs on top. Bake it at 350° for 30 to 40 minutes.

FRUIT COCKTAIL CAKE

2 cups all-purpose flour
1⅓ cups sugar
3 teaspoons soda
1 can (19 ounces) fruit cocktail

2 eggs
1 teaspoon vanilla
½ teaspoon salt

Mix together all the ingredients and blend them well. Pour the batter into a 9 x 13-inch pan. Bake it at 350° for 45 minutes or until it breaks away from the pan.

Boil the following ingredients for 5 minutes before spreading the mixture on the cake as topping.

Topping;

8 tablespoons butter
1 cup brown sugar

½ cup milk
Coconut or nuts (optional)

CREME VELVET CAKE

½ cup margarine or shortening
1½ cups sugar
½ teaspoon salt
1 cup water

2½ cups cake flour
2½ teaspoons baking powder
3 egg whites
1 teaspoon vanilla

Cream the margarine and gradually add the sugar, creaming them well. Add the salt and water alternately with the sifted flour and baking powder. Then fold in the stiffly beaten egg whites and vanilla. Bake the batter in 2 greased 8-inch layer pans at 350° for 35 to 40 minutes.

DATE CAKE

1½ cups whole, pitted dates
2 cups boiling water
2 teaspoons soda
1 cup brown sugar
2 tablespoons butter

1 teaspoon salt
2 eggs, beaten
1¼ cups all-purpose flour
Nut meats (optional)

Put the dates and boiling water into a pan over heat. Cook the dates until they are soft. Add the soda, brown sugar, butter and salt. After this mixture has cooled a little, add the eggs, flour and nuts. Bake the batter at 350° until done.

This is a cake that is good without frosting.

FEATHER CAKE

½ cup shortening
2 cups sugar
1 cup milk

3 cups self-rising flour
1 teaspoon vanilla
3 whole eggs or 5 egg whites

Cream the shortening, add the sugar, and cream it again. Add the milk and flour alternately, then the vanilla. Lastly, add the eggs. Mix the batter and bake it at 350° for 30 to 40 minutes in pans of your choice.

If you use all-purpose flour, add 3 teaspoons of baking powder and ½ teaspoon of salt.

GOLDEN FLUFF CAKE

2 cups sifted cake flour
3½ teaspoons baking powder
1 teaspoon salt
1⅓ cups sugar
⅓ cup shortening

½ teaspoon lemon (optional)
½ teaspoon vanilla flavoring
1 cup milk
⅓ cup (4 medium) egg yolks

Sift together the dry ingredients. Add the shortening (which should be at room temperature), lemon, vanilla and ⅔ of the milk. Beat this mixture for 200 strokes before adding the remaining ⅓ cup of milk and the egg yolks. Beat it again for 200 strokes, then pour the batter into 2 greased and floured 8-inch layer pans or 1 loaf pan. Bake it for 30 to 35 minutes in a moderate (350°) oven.

MIRACLE FRUIT CAKE

1½ cups chopped dates
1½ cups raisins
1½ cups brown sugar
⅔ cup butter or substitute
4 tablespoons molasses or corn syrup
1½ cups hot water
2 eggs
Candied fruit

1 cup chopped nuts
3 cups all-purpose flour
1½ cups whole wheat flour
3 teaspoons soda
1½ teaspoons nutmeg
2 teaspoons cinnamon
2 teaspoons baking powder

Combine the first 6 ingredients in a saucepan and boil the mixture gently for 3 minutes. Let it cool in a large mixing bowl. Beat the eggs and add them to the fruit mixture. Add candied fruit (see recipe following) and the chopped nuts.

Sift together 4 times, the flours, soda, nutmeg, cinnamon and baking powder. Add this to the fruit mixture, stirring it well. Pour the batter into loaf pans or bread pans lined with waxed paper. Bake it in a moderate oven (350°) until a toothpick comes out clean when inserted.

Candied Fruit;

½ cup butter or margarine
1 cup brown sugar

2 cups drained cherries (sweet or sour)
1 medium can crushed pineapple

Melt the butter in a saucepan and add the sugar. To this mixture add the cherries and pineapple. Let it stand for about 15 to 20 minutes.

NUT CAKE

2 cups sugar
½ cup butter
3 eggs
1 teaspoon vanilla
2½ cups cake flour

¾ teaspoon salt
2 teaspoons baking powder
1 cup milk
1 cup nuts

Cream the sugar and butter, then add the eggs and vanilla, beating them together well. Sift together the flour, salt and baking powder, and add it alternately with the milk to the egg mixture. Fold in the nuts. Bake the batter in a greased and floured 9 x 13 x 2-inch baking pan at 350° for 30 minutes.

LEMON LAYER CAKE

⅔ cup butter
1¾ cups sugar
2 eggs
1½ teaspoons vanilla

3 cups sifted cake flour
2½ teaspoons baking powder
½ teaspoon salt
1¼ cups milk

Cream the butter and sugar. Add the eggs and vanilla and beat them until they are fluffy. Sift the flour, baking powder and salt, and add this mixture alternately with the milk to the egg mixture, beating after each addition. Beat the batter thoroughly before pouring it into 2 greased and floured 9-inch round pans. Bake it at 350° for 30 to 35 minutes. Allow the cakes to cool, then remove them from the pans. Fill the cakes with Lemon Filling (following), and top the cake with Fluffy White Frosting (see page 133).

Lemon Filling;

¾ cup sugar
2 tablespoons cornstarch
½ teaspoon salt
¾ cup water

2 egg yolks, slightly beaten
3 tablespoons lemon juice
1 teaspoon grated lemon peel
1 tablespoon butter

Combine in a saucepan the sugar, cornstarch and salt. Add the water, egg yolks and lemon juice. Cook and stir this mixture over medium heat until it is thick. Remove it from the heat, then add the lemon peel and butter.

CRUMB CAKE

2 cups brown sugar
2½ cups all-purpose flour
½ cup shortening
2 teaspoons baking powder

1 teaspoon soda
1 cup thick sour milk
2 eggs
1 teaspoon vanilla

Mix together the sugar, flour, shortening, baking powder and soda. Reserve 1 cup of crumbs from this mixture. Mix together and add the remaining ingredients. Pour the batter into a greased 9 x 13 x 2-inch pan, sprinkle the reserved crumbs over top and bake it at 350° for 30 minutes or until done.

HANDY MADE CAKE

½ cup butter or margarine
2 cups sugar
3 eggs, beaten
2½ cups bread flour

3 teaspoons baking powder
1 teaspoon salt
1 cup milk
1 teaspoon vanilla

Cream the butter and sugar. Add the eggs. Sift together the flour, baking powder and salt, then add this alternately with the milk to the egg mixture. Add the vanilla. Bake the batter at 350° for 35 to 40 minutes.

OATMEAL CAKE

1¼ cups boiling water
1 cup instant oatmeal
½ cup shortening
1 cup brown sugar
1 cup white sugar
2 eggs

1½ cups cake flour
1 teaspoon nutmeg, if desired
1 teaspoon cinnamon
1 teaspoon soda
½ teaspoon salt
1 teaspoon vanilla

Pour the boiling water over the oatmeal and let it set for 20 minutes. Cream the shortening and sugars well. Add the unbeaten eggs, one at a time, beating well after each addition. Blend in the oatmeal mixture. Sift together the flour, spices, soda and salt, and fold this mixture in. Add the vanilla. Bake the batter in a greased and floured 9 x 13 x 2-inch pan at 350° for 30 to 35 minutes.

While the cake is still hot from the oven, spread on the following topping and put it under the broiler for about 2 minutes or until it is brown.

⅔ cup brown sugar
1 cup chopped nuts
1 cup coconut

6 tablespoons melted butter
¼ cup cream
1 teaspoon vanilla

Mix these ingredients together well.

OLD TIME MOLASSES CAKE

2 cups all-purpose flour
¾ cup molasses
¼ cup sugar
2 teaspoons soda

1 egg
½ cup buttermilk or sour milk
½ cup hot water

Mix the ingredients thoroughly. Bake the batter at 325 to 350° for 30 to 40 minutes.

SORGHUM MOLASSES CAKE

2 cups sorghum molasses
2 eggs
3 cups self-rising flour
½ teaspoon salt
½ teaspoon allspice
1 teaspoon cinnamon

1 cup cooking oil
1½ cups milk
½ teaspoon cloves
1 teaspoon nutmeg
Raisins or nuts (optional)

Mix together the above ingredients, then bake the batter at 350° for 30 to 35 minutes until done.

CAROB OATMEAL CAKE

1½ cups boiling water
1 cup quick rolled oats
¼ cup carob powder (available in
  health food stores), or cocoa
1 teaspoon soda
¼ teaspoon salt
1 cup flour (½ cup unbleached, ½ cup
  whole wheat, if desired)

⅓ cup cooking oil
1½ cups raw sugar
2 eggs, beaten
1 teaspoon vanilla
Shredded coconut and sunflower
  seeds

Pour the boiling water over the oats and carob powder, stirring it until smooth. Allow it to cool. Sift together the soda, salt and flour. Cream the oil and sugar and add the beaten eggs and vanilla. Then add the carob and flour mixtures to the eggs. Pour the batter into an 8 x 12-inch greased pan, and top it with shredded coconut and sunflower seeds instead of frosting. Bake it at 350° for about 45 minutes.

This cake will stay nice and moist for a week.

PINEAPPLE UPSIDE DOWN CAKE

3 tablespoons brown sugar
3 tablespoons butter
5 slices pineapple

Spread the sugar and butter in a skillet, then heat and melt them. Arrange the pineapple on top, and cover it with the sponge cake batter as follows.

3 egg yolks
½ cup sugar
¼ cup boiling water
½ teaspoon lemon flavoring

¾ cup cake flour
1 teaspoon baking powder
¼ teaspoon salt

Beat the egg yolks thoroughly. Add the sugar, boiling water and lemon flavoring. Mix them for 1 minute. Sift together and add the flour, baking powder and salt. Beat this mixture quickly for about ½ minute before pouring it over the pineapple as instructed above. Bake it for 25 to 30 minutes at 350°. Turn the cake upside down on a plate to serve it.

Variations: Try substituting other fruit for the pineapple.

ORANGE COCONUT CAKE

¾ cup shortening
2 cups sugar
1½ teaspoons grated orange rind
2 egg yolks
½ cup orange juice
¾ cup water

3¼ cups cake flour
½ teaspoon salt
4 teaspoons baking powder
½ cup coconut
4 egg whites

Cream the shortening and add the sugar gradually. Beat it until it is fluffy. Add the orange rind and beaten egg yolks, then beat the mixture again. Mix in the orange juice and water. Sift the flour, salt and baking powder twice, then add these dry ingredients to the mixture. Fold in the coconut and stiffly beaten egg whites. Pour the batter into 9-inch layer pans and bake it at 350° for 30 to 35 minutes.

PENNSYLVANIA DUTCH HUSTLE CAKE

⅓ cup milk
¼ cup sugar
½ teaspoon salt
¼ cup butter or margarine
¼ cup lukewarm water
1 package dry yeast

1 egg, beaten
1⅓ cups sifted all-purpose flour
1½ cups apple slices
2 tablespoons brown sugar
¼ teaspoon cinnamon
¼ teaspoon nutmeg

Scald the milk, then stir in the sugar, salt and half of the butter or margarine. Cool the mixture to lukewarm. In a mixing bowl dissolve the yeast in the lukewarm water, then stir in the lukewarm milk mixture. Add the egg and flour, and beat the dough until it is smooth. Spread it evenly in a greased 9 x 9-inch pan. Arrange the apple slices on top, and sprinkle it with a mixture of the sugar, cinnamon and nutmeg. Dot the top with the remaining butter or margarine. Cover the dough and let it rise in a warm draft-free place for 40 minutes or longer, until it is double in bulk. Bake it at 400° for 25 minutes.

SHOO-FLY CAKE

4 cups all-purpose flour
¾ cup shortening
2 cups brown sugar

2 cups boiling water
1 cup molasses
1 tablespoon soda

Mix thoroughly the flour, shortening and sugar. Reserve 1 cup of the crumbs for the topping. Add to the remaining crumbs the boiling water, molasses and soda. Mix these ingredients well, then pour the batter into a greased cake pan. Sprinkle the reserved crumbs over the batter, then bake it at 350° until done.

PRALINE CAKE

1 cup butter or vegetable shortening
2 cups sugar
4 eggs, separated
3 cups sifted cake flour

1 teaspoon soda
1 cup buttermilk
1 teaspoon cream of tartar

Cream the shortening and sugar until light. Add the egg yolks, one at a time, and beat them until they are fluffy. Sift together the flour and soda, and add it alternately with the buttermilk and cream of tartar. Fold in the stiffly beaten egg whites. Pour the batter into a 9 x 13 x 2-inch greased and floured cake pan, and bake it at 350° for 50 minutes. Remove the cake from the oven and spread it with Praline Topping (see page 134). Place it under the broiler or in a hot oven for 1 or 2 minutes.

RAISIN NUT LOAF

1 cup cooked raisins
1½ cups warm raisin juice
1½ cups white sugar
1½ cups brown sugar
½ cup shortening
2 eggs

¼ teaspoon salt
½ teaspoon nutmeg
½ teaspoon cinnamon
1 teaspoon soda
3 cups all-purpose flour
1 cup chopped nuts

Cook raisins, using enough water to make 1½ cups of juice when they are done. Cream the sugars and shortening. Add the eggs and beat the mixture well. Add the sifted dry ingredients and warm raisin juice to the egg mixture, then stir in the raisins and nuts. Bake the batter in a greased loaf pan at 350° for 1 hour or until done.

NUT SPICE CAKE

3 cups cake flour
1½ teaspoons soda
¾ teaspoon salt
¾ teaspoon allspice
¾ teaspoon cloves
1½ teaspoons cinnamon

⅔ cup shortening
1 cup granulated sugar
1 cup brown sugar
3 eggs
1½ cups buttermilk
½ cup chopped nuts

Sift the flour, soda, salt and spices together. Cream the shortening and add the sugars gradually. Cream them well. Add the eggs one at a time, and beat the mixture well after each addition. Add the sifted dry ingredients alternately with the buttermilk. Add the nuts with the final addition of the dry ingredients. Pour the batter into 2 greased paper-lined 9-inch layer pans. Bake it at 350° for 35 to 40 minutes.

OLD SPICE CAKE

1 tablespoon or 1 cake yeast	1 cup sugar
1 cup warm water	1 teaspoon soda
1 teaspoon sugar	1 teaspoon salt
2 eggs, beaten	½ teaspoon cinnamon
½ cup lard, softened	½ teaspoon nutmeg
1 cup raisins	½ teaspoon cloves
2½ cups all-purpose flour	½ teaspoon allspice

Dissolve the yeast in the warm water and teaspoon of sugar. Mix together the eggs, lard and raisins, and stir in the yeast. Sift together the rest of the ingredients and add them to the first mixture. Let the batter set in a warm place for about 25 to 30 minutes, then bake it in a greased 9-inch round cake pan at 350° for 30 minutes.

SOUR CREAM SPICE CAKE

½ cup shortening	2 teaspoons cinnamon
2 cups brown sugar	1 teaspoon cloves
3 eggs, separated	1 teaspoon allspice
1¾ cups cake flour sifted with	1 cup sour cream
½ teaspoon salt	1 teaspoon vanilla
1 teaspoon soda	

Cream the shortening and sugar, and add the egg yolks. Add the flour, soda and spices, then add the sour cream and beat the mixture well. Add the vanilla and fold in the stiffly beaten egg whites. Bake the batter in greased 8-inch layer pans for 25 minutes at 350°.

SUGARLESS SPICE CAKE

2¼ cups sifted cake flour	½ cup shortening
2¼ teaspoons baking powder	1 cup corn syrup
1¼ teaspoons cinnamon	2 eggs, unbeaten
¼ teaspoon nutmeg	½ cup milk
¼ teaspoon cloves	1 teaspoon lemon rind
¼ teaspoon salt	1 teaspoon vanilla

Sift together the flour, baking powder, spices and salt. Cream the shortening and add a little of the flour mixture at a time until all of it has been stirred in. Add the syrup and eggs and beat the mixture well. Then add the milk, lemon rind and vanilla. Bake the batter for 30 minutes at 350°.

PUMPKIN SPICE CAKE

½ cup shortening
1¼ cups sugar
2 eggs, beaten
2¼ cups sifted cake flour
2½ teaspoons baking powder
½ teaspoon soda
1 teaspoon salt

2 teaspoons cinnamon
½ teaspoon ginger
½ teaspoon nutmeg
1 cup pumpkin
¾ cup milk
½ cup chopped nuts

Cream the shortening, then add the sugar gradually and continue creaming it until it is light and fluffy. Blend in the eggs. Sift together the dry ingredients. Combine the pumpkin and milk. Add the dry ingredients alternately with the pumpkin mixture to the egg mixture, beginning and ending with the dry ingredients. Stir in the chopped nuts. Bake the batter in 2 greased 9-inch layer pans at 350° for about 30 minutes.

Frost the cake with your favorite butter cream icing, using orange juice for the liquid and grated orange rind for added zest.

LEMON SPONGE CAKE

1 cup sifted cake flour
1 teaspoon baking powder
½ teaspoon salt
½ cup cold water
2 teaspoons grated lemon rind

2 egg yolks, beaten
¾ cup plus 2 tablespoons sugar
2 egg whites
1 teaspoon lemon juice

Sift together 4 times, the flour, baking powder and salt. Add the water and lemon rind to the egg yolks and beat them until they are lemon-colored. Add the ¾ cup of sugar (2 tablespoons at a time), beating after each addition. Then add the sifted ingredients, slowly stirring to blend them. Beat the egg whites until they peak, and add the lemon juice and 2 tablespoons of the sugar, beating until they are well blended. Fold this mixture into the rest of the batter, and pour it into a tube pan. Bake it for 1 hour at 350°.

SPONGE CAKE

1½ cups sugar
1½ cups cake flour
1 teaspoon baking powder
¼ teaspoon salt

½ cup cold water
5 eggs, separated, and beaten well
¾ teaspoon cream of tartar

Sift together the first 4 ingredients. Beat the water with the egg yolks until they are thick, then fold them into the dry ingredients. Beat the egg whites with the cream of tartar until they stand in peaks, then fold them into the other mixture. Bake the batter in a tube pan for 1 hour at 350°.

YELLOW SPONGE CAKE

1½ cups sifted cake flour
1½ cups sugar
6 eggs, separated
1 teaspoon vanilla

½ teaspoon baking powder
¼ teaspoon salt
½ cup cold water

Sift together the flour and 1 cup of the sugar. Beat the egg yolks with the rest of the sugar, the vanilla, baking powder and salt until they are fluffy. Then add alternately the flour/sugar mixture and ½ cup of cold water. Fold in the stiffly beaten egg whites. Pour the batter into a tube pan and bake it approximately 1 hour at 350°.

Cooked Icing;

¾ cup milk
⅓ cup flour
½ cup butter or margarine
¾ cup sugar

1 teaspoon vanilla
Coconut, shredded, or ground
    nutmeats

Combine the milk and flour and cook the mixture until it is very thick. Let it cool before beating in the butter, sugar and vanilla. Continue to beat the mixture until it is fluffy like whipped cream. Ice the cake with it and cover it with coconut or nutmeats.

TOASTED SPICE CAKE

½ cup shortening
2 cups brown sugar
2 egg yolks
2½ cups cake flour
½ teaspoon salt
1 teaspoon soda

1 teaspoon baking powder
1½ teaspoons cinnamon
1 teaspoon cloves
1¼ cups sour milk
1 teaspoon vanilla

Cream together the shortening and sugar. Add the egg yolks and beat the mixture well. Sift the flour once, then measure and add the salt, soda, baking powder and spices. Sift these again before adding them to the first mixture alternately with the milk and vanilla. Beat the mixture well after each addition. Pour the batter into a greased flat pan (8 x 12 x 1¼ inches).

2 egg whites
1 cup light brown sugar

½ cup nuts, finely chopped, OR
½ cup shredded coconut

Beat the egg whites until they are stiff enough to hold peaks. Slowly add the sugar, beating the mixture until it is smooth. Spread it over the cake batter and sprinkle it with the nuts or coconut before baking it at 350° for 40 minutes.

WHITE AS SNOW CAKE

2½ cups sifted cake flour
4½ teaspoons baking powder
1½ cups sugar
1 teaspoon salt
½ cup shortening

1 cup milk
4 egg whites to make ½ cup, unbeaten
1 teaspoon vanilla extract
Nuts, chopped (optional)

Sift all the dry ingredients into a mixing bowl. Add the shortening (soft but not melted) and ⅔ of the milk. Beat these ingredients 150 strokes by hand to make a well blended and glossy batter. Add the remaining milk, the egg whites and vanilla, and nuts if desired. Beat the batter again until it is smooth, about 150 strokes. Pour it into 2 well-greased and floured 8-inch layer cake pans or 1 loaf pan, and bake it in a moderate oven (350°) for 30 minutes.

ZUCCHINI SQUASH CAKE

1 cup oil
2 cups sugar
3 eggs
3 cups all-purpose flour
1 teaspoon baking powder
1 teaspoon soda

1 teaspoon salt
2 cups peeled, drained zucchini,
   mashed
½ cup raisins
2 teaspoons vanilla
Chopped nuts (optional)

Prepare this recipe the same as you would Pumpkin Spice Cake (see page 125). Pour the batter into 2 small loaf pans or 1 large one, and bake it for 1 hour at 350°.

ANGEL GINGERBREAD

1 cup white sugar
½ cup shortening
½ cup baking molasses
2 eggs
2 cups sifted cake flour
½ teaspoon salt

½ teaspoon ginger
½ teaspoon cinnamon
½ teaspoon nutmeg
¾ cup boiling water
1 teaspoon soda

Mix together the first 9 ingredients, beating them well. Then add the boiling water in which the soda has been dissolved. Bake the batter in a moderate oven (350°) for 25 to 30 minutes or until it is done. Serve the cake with whipped cream.

VELVET CRUMB CAKE

1⅓ cups biscuit mix
¾ cup sugar
3 tablespoons soft shortening

1 egg
¾ cup milk
1 teaspoon vanilla

Preheat the oven to 350°. Grease and flour a square pan (9 x 9 x 1½ inches). Mix the biscuit mix and sugar. Add the shortening, egg and ¼ cup of the milk. Beat these ingredients for 1 minute. Gradually stir in the rest of the milk, then add the vanilla and beat them for ½ minute longer. Pour the batter into the prepared pan and bake it for 35 to 40 minutes. Cover the cake with Broiled Topping while it is warm.

Broiled Topping;

3 tablespoons soft butter
⅓ cup brown sugar, packed
2 tablespoons cream

½ cup shredded coconut or Wheaties
¼ cup chopped nuts

Mix together the butter, brown sugar, cream, coconut and nuts. Spread it over the baked cake, then place it under low heat until the topping is bubbly and brown, for 3 to 5 minutes.

SUNSHINE CAKE

8 eggs
½ teaspoon cream of tartar
1½ cups raw sugar
½ teaspoon salt

1½ teaspoons lemon extract
2 tablespoons water
1 cup whole wheat flour
½ cup chopped nuts

Separate the eggs. Beat the egg whites until they are frothy, then add the cream of tartar. Gradually add 1 cup of the sugar. Continue beating the whites until they form very stiff peaks. Beat the egg yolks until they are very thick, then add the salt, lemon extract and the rest of the sugar. Continue to beat the mixture while adding alternately the water and whole wheat flour. Beat it well. Very gently fold the yolks into the whites, then fold in the nuts. Pour the batter into an ungreased angel food cake pan. Bake it at 325 to 350° for 1½ hours. Invert the cake on a funnel and let it cool for 1 hour. Remove it from the pan. This cake may be eaten unfrosted, or frosted with Seafoam Frosting (see page 135).

COCOA ICING

1 cup sugar
4 teaspoons cocoa
2 tablespoons cornstarch

1 cup boiling water
2 tablespoons butter
Vanilla

Boil the sugar, cocoa, cornstarch and water until thick, then add the butter and vanilla.

TROPICAL GINGERBREAD

½ cup shortening
½ cup sugar
1 egg
2½ cups all-purpose flour
1½ teaspoons soda
1 teaspoon cinnamon

1 teaspoon ginger
½ teaspoon cloves
½ teaspoon salt
1 cup baking molasses
1 cup hot water

Melt the shortening and let it cool. Add the sugar and egg, then beat the mixture well. Sift together the flour, soda, spices and salt. Combine the molasses and hot water. Add this alternately with the flour mixture to the egg mixture. Bake the batter in a 9 x 9 x 2-inch pan at 350° for 50 to 60 minutes.

EASY CHOCOLATE ROLL UP

¼ cup butter
1 cup chopped pecans
1⅓ cups flaked coconut
1 can (15½ ounces) sweetened
   condensed milk
3 eggs
1 cup sugar

⅔ cup all-purpose flour
⅓ cup cocoa
¼ teaspoon salt
¼ teaspoon baking powder
⅓ cup water
1 teaspoon vanilla

Line a 15 x 10-inch jelly roll pan with foil. In the pan, melt the butter and sprinkle the nuts and coconut evenly. Drizzle it with the condensed milk. Beat the eggs at high speed for 2 minutes until they are fluffy. Gradually add the sugar and continue beating them for 2 minutes more. It is not necessary to sift the flour—spoon it into a cup, level it, and add the remaining ingredients. Blend this into the egg mixture for 1 minute, beating it lightly.

Pour the batter evenly into the pan. Bake it at 375° for 20 to 25 minutes until the cake springs back when touched in the center. Sprinkle the cake in the pan with icing sugar. Cover it with a towel and put a cookie sheet lightly over the towel. Invert the cake and remove the pan and foil. Using a towel, roll up the cake jelly roll fashion, starting on the 10-inch side.

ICINGS AND FILLINGS

HINTS FOR ICINGS

- A teaspoon of vinegar beaten into a boiled frosting when flavoring is added will keep it from being brittle or breaking when cut.
- To keep icing soft, add a pinch of baking soda to the whites of eggs before beating them. Then beat them in the usual way and pour hot syrup over them. The frosting will be soft and creamy.

BEAT'N'EAT FROSTING

1 egg white, unbeaten
¾ cup sugar
¼ teaspoon cream of tartar

1 teaspoon vanilla
¼ cup boiling water

Mix together well the first 4 ingredients. Add the boiling water and beat the mixture rapidly with an egg beater for 4 to 5 minutes until it is thick. This is delicious as a quick topping.

BURNT SUGAR FROSTING

3 tablespoons soft butter or margarine
1 egg yolk, beaten
5 tablespoons Burnt Sugar Syrup (see page 298)

2 tablespoons cream
4 cups sifted icing sugar
1 teaspoon almond extract

Cream together the butter or margarine and egg yolk. Beat in alternately the syrup, cream, sugar, and extract until the frosting is smooth and creamy enough to spread.

BUTTER-CREAM FROSTING

1 pound icing sugar
¼ teaspoon salt
¼ cup butter or margarine

¼ cup cocoa
1 egg
3 tablespoons hot water

Blend together the ingredients and beat the mixture until it is thick enough to spread. This recipe makes enough to frost the top and sides of an 8-inch layer cake.

131

COCONUT-PECAN FROSTING

1 cup evaporated milk, or cream
½ cup butter or margarine
1 cup sugar
3 egg yolks

1 teaspoon vanilla
1⅓ cups shredded coconut
1 cup chopped pecans

Combine the milk, butter, sugar, egg yolks and vanilla. Cook and stir the mixture over medium heat until it is thick (about 12 minutes). Add the coconut and pecans, then beat the mixture until it is thick enough to spread. This makes 2½ cups.

CREAM CHEESE FROSTING

8 ounces white cream cheese
8 tablespoons margarine

1 pound icing sugar
2 teaspoons vanilla

Cream together the cheese and margarine, then add the sugar and vanilla and stir it until it is creamy.

CREAMY CARAMEL FROSTING

4 tablespoons margarine
1 cup brown sugar, firmly packed
¼ teaspoon salt

¼ cup whole milk
2½ cups icing sugar (approximate)
½ teaspoon vanilla

Melt the margarine in a saucepan. Blend in the brown sugar and salt. Cook it over low heat, stirring it constantly for 2 minutes. Stir in the milk, and continue stirring until the mixture comes to a boil. Remove it from the heat, and gradually blend in the icing sugar. Add the vanilla. Thin the frosting with a small amount of canned milk if necessary.

CREAMY ICING

¼ cup sugar
2 tablespoons water
2⅓ cups icing sugar
1 teaspoon salt

1 egg
½ cup Crisco
1 tablespoon cocoa
1 teaspoon vanilla

Boil the sugar and water together for 1 minute. Mix together the icing sugar, salt and egg, then blend it with the first mixture. Add the Crisco, cocoa and vanilla, and beat it until it is creamy.

CHOCOLATE FUDGE ICING

2 squares (2 ounces) unsweetened
   chocolate
1¼ cups milk
2 cups sugar

Dash of salt
1 tablespoon light corn syrup
3 tablespoons butter
1½ teaspoons vanilla

Add the chocolate to the milk and place it over low heat. Cook it until it is smooth and blended, stirring constantly. Add the sugar, salt and syrup. Stir it until the sugar is dissolved and the mixture boils. Continue boiling it until the mixture forms a very soft ball when tested in water. Cool it to lukewarm, then add the butter and vanilla and beat it until it can be spread. If it hardens too soon, add a small amount of hot water.

FLUFFY WHITE FROSTING

2 egg whites
½ cup sugar
½ cup white corn syrup

Put the egg whites in the top of a double boiler, and add the sugar and white syrup. Beat the mixture over boiling water until it is thick enough to support the egg beater upright. Then spread it over the cake and swirl it. It will stay soft.

GELATIN FROSTING

3 tablespoons fruit flavored gelatin
   powder
¼ cup water

2 small egg whites
1 cup sugar
⅛ teaspoon cream of tartar

Heat the gelatin and water in the top of a double boiler. Beat the egg whites. Mix together the sugar and cream of tartar, then add it to the gelatin mixture with the egg whites. While it is still over boiling water, beat this mixture until it peaks. Remove it from the heat and beat it for 1 minute before spreading.

LEMON FROSTING

½ cup butter or margarine
Dash of salt
1 teaspoon grated lemon rind

4 cups icing sugar
4 teaspoons lemon juice
⅓ cup milk

Cream the butter, salt and rind. Gradually add part of the sugar. Then add the remaining sugar alternately with the lemon juice and milk until the mixture is of the right consistency to spread.

MAPLE CREAM ICING

1 cup brown sugar
¼ cup butter or margarine
3 tablespoons milk

½ teaspoon maple flavoring (optional)
1 cup icing sugar
1 teaspoon vanilla

Mix together the brown sugar, butter and milk and bring the mixture to a full boil. Remove it from the heat and add the icing sugar and vanilla, stirring until it is of spreading consistency.

MARSHMALLOW FROSTING

1 egg white, unbeaten
⅞ cup sugar
3 tablespoons water

1 teaspoon vanilla
12 marshmallows cut into pieces
1 to 2 cups moist coconut

Put the egg white, sugar and water into a double boiler. Beat the mixture constantly with an egg beater for 6 minutes. Remove it from the heat and add the vanilla and marshmallows. Beat it until it is of a consistency to spread. Add the coconut, reserving enough to sprinkle on top.

PRALINE TOPPING

½ cup brown sugar
1 cup chopped nuts, OR
½ cup shredded coconut

¼ cup melted butter
3 tablespoons cream

Mix together the sugar, nuts, butter and cream. Spread the mixture over the cake, then place it under the broiler or in a hot oven for 1 or 2 minutes.

GRANDMA'S CARAMEL FROSTING

2 cups brown sugar
1 cup top milk
¼ teaspoon cream of tartar

Cook the sugar and top milk over medium heat until it reaches the soft ball stage (230°). Remove it from the heat and add the cream of tartar, stirring it very little to blend. Set the frosting aside to cool to lukewarm but do not let it get too cold. Beat it until it thickens enough to spread on cake. Work fast when it is of the right consistency.

MINUTE FUDGE ICING

¼ cup butter
1 cup sugar

¼ cup cocoa (scant)
¼ cup milk

Melt the butter in a saucepan, then add the rest of the ingredients. Stir the mixture over low heat until all the ingredients are dissolved, then bring it to a rolling boil and boil it for 1 minute. Remove the icing from the heat and beat it until it is creamy enough to spread.

NUT ICING

2 cups brown sugar
1 cup sweet cream
½ cup ground hickory nuts

Lump of butter
1 teaspoon vanilla

Boil together the sugar and cream to the soft ball stage. Set it aside until it is cool, then add the nuts, butter and vanilla. Beat it until it thickens enough to spread on cake. Work fast when the icing is of the right consistency.

SEAFOAM FROSTING

1 egg white
¾ cup raw sugar
Pinch of salt

¼ teaspoon cream of tartar
2 teaspoons honey

Beat these ingredients with an egg beater in the top of a double boiler until peaks form (about 7 minutes).

SIMPLE ORANGE ICING

3 cups icing sugar
4 tablespoons orange juice

Grated rind of 1 orange
2 tablespoons melted butter

Combine the sugar, juice and rind. Beat this mixture well, then add the melted butter. Stir it until it is well blended.

ORANGE ICING

¼ cup margarine or butter
¾ cup granulated sugar
¼ cup orange juice

¼ cup orange gelatin powder
¾ cup sifted icing sugar

Melt the margarine, then add the sugar, orange juice and gelatin. Boil the mixture for 1 minute. When it has cooled slightly, beat in the icing sugar until the icing is of spreading consistency.

CARAMEL FILLING FOR SPONGE CAKE

2 tablespoons white sugar
1 cup water
1 tablespoon butter

1 cup white sugar
3 eggs, beaten
2 tablespoons flour

Melt the 2 tablespoons of sugar in a pan without water. Then add the water and boil it to a syrup. Add the butter and the 1 cup of sugar. Pour over this mixture the eggs which have been combined with the flour. Beat the mixture well, then bring it to a boil, stirring constantly. Spread it on sponge cake.

This or any other filling may be used for gelatin rolls.

SOFT ICING

3 tablespoons flour
⅔ cup milk
¾ cup Crisco

Flavoring
¾ cup granulated sugar

In a saucepan, cook the flour and milk until thick, then allow it to cool. Cream together the Crisco, flavoring of your choice and sugar. Combine the 2 mixtures and beat vigorously until the icing is smooth.

SUGARLESS FROSTING

1¼ cups corn syrup
3 egg whites

1 teaspoon baking powder
2 teaspoons vanilla flavoring

Boil the corn syrup in a saucepan over direct heat until it spins a thread when dripped from a spoon. Beat the egg whites until they are foamy, then add the baking powder and beat them again until stiff. Add the corn syrup slowly while beating vigorously. Add the flavoring and continue beating until the frosting is stiff and stands in peaks. This makes frosting for two 9-inch layers, 1 medium loaf cake, or 16 large cup cakes.

CHOCOLATE FILLING

2 squares (2 ounces) chocolate
1 cup rich milk

1½ cups sugar
Butter the size of an egg

Shave the chocolate finely, then add it to a pan with the milk, sugar and butter. Boil these ingredients to the desired thickness.

CLEAR LEMON FILLING

¾ cup sugar
3 tablespoons cornstarch
⅓ teaspoon salt
1½ tablespoons grated lemon rind

6 tablespoons lemon juice
1½ tablespoons butter
¾ cup water

Mix together in a saucepan the above ingredients. Bring the mixture to a boil and boil it for 1 minute, stirring it constantly. Chill the filling before using it.

CREAM FILLING

1 pint milk
1 egg
½ cup sugar

3 tablespoons cornstarch
1 lump butter

Cook the above ingredients until thick. Cool the mixture and spread it between layers of cake.

ORANGE CAKE FILLING

Juice and rind of 1 orange
1 cup cold water
1 cup sugar

2 egg yolks
1 tablespoon corn starch

Cook the ingredients until the mixture is thick and clear.

COOKIES, BARS, FINGERS AND SQUARES

APPLESAUCE DROP COOKIES

2 cups all-purpose flour
1 teaspoon soda
¼ teaspoon salt
1 teaspoon cinnamon
½ teaspoon nutmeg
½ cup butter
½ cup white sugar

½ cup brown sugar, packed
1 egg
1 cup applesauce
1 cup rolled oats
½ cup raisins
½ cup chopped nuts
½ cup chocolate chips

Sift together the first 5 ingredients, then set the mixture aside. Mix the butter and sugar, add the egg, then blend these ingredients. Add the applesauce with the sifted dry ingredients before adding the rest and mixing well. Drop the batter by teaspoonfuls onto an ungreased cookie sheet, and bake it for 8 minutes at 375°.

BUSHEL OF COOKIES

5 pounds sugar
2½ pounds lard
12 eggs
1 pound salted peanuts, ground coarsely with
1 pound raisins
2 pounds quick cooking oats

1 cup maple syrup
2 ounces or 3 tablespoons soda
2 ounces or 3 tablespoons baking powder
1 quart sweet milk
6 pounds flour

Mix together all the ingredients to make a batter. Drop it by spoonfuls onto a cookie sheet, and bake it at 350°.

Half recipe in cup measures;

7 cups sugar
2½ cups lard
½ pound peanuts, ground coarsely with
½ pound raisins
2 tablespoons soda

2 cups milk
6 eggs
4¾ cups oatmeal
½ cup maple syrup
2 tablespoons baking powder
12 cups flour

APPLESAUCE NUT COOKIES

½ cup shortening
1 cup sugar
1 egg
1 cup thick unsweetened applesauce
2 cups all-purpose flour
½ teaspoon cinnamon

¼ teaspoon cloves
3 teaspoons baking powder
½ teaspoon salt
½ cup raisins
½ cup nuts

Cream the shortening, then add the sugar and egg. Add the applesauce and the dry ingredients before folding in the raisins and nuts. Drop the batter by teaspoonfuls 2 inches apart on a cookie sheet and bake them at 350° for 15 to 20 minutes.

CARROT COOKIES

½ cup shortening
1 cup brown sugar
½ cup granulated sugar
1 teaspoon vanilla
1 egg

1 cup cooked carrots, mashed and
  cooled
2 cups all-purpose flour
½ teaspoon baking powder
Pinch of salt
¾ cup raisins

Cream together the shortening and sugar. Add the vanilla, egg, carrots and the remaining ingredients in the order listed. Drop the batter by spoonfuls onto a cookie sheet and bake it at 375° until done.

CHERRY COOKIES

2¼ cups all-purpose flour
1 teaspoon baking powder
½ teaspoon soda
½ teaspoon salt
¾ cup shortening
1 cup sugar
2 eggs

2 tablespoons milk
1 teaspoon almond extract
1 teaspoon vanilla
1 cup chopped pecans
⅓ cup chopped maraschino cherries
1 cup chopped dates
2½ cups cornflakes

Sift together the flour, baking powder, soda and salt. Combine the shortening and sugar, then blend in the eggs. Add to this mixture the milk, almond extract and vanilla. Blend in the sifted dry ingredients and mix it well. Add the pecans, cherries and dates, and mix it well again. Shape the dough into balls, using 1 level tablespoon per cookie. Crush the cornflakes and roll each ball of dough in them. Place the balls on a greased cookie sheet and top each one with ¼ cherry. Bake them at 375° until done. Do not stack them until they are cold.

BUTTERSCOTCH COOKIES

6 cups brown sugar
1½ cups butter
4 eggs, beaten
1 tablespoon vanilla

1½ teaspoons soda
2 teaspoons baking powder
6 to 7 cups all-purpose flour

Cream together the sugar and butter until smooth, then add the eggs and vanilla. Sift the soda and baking powder with the flour, and add it to the first mixture. Shape the dough into rolls and chill them. Slice them and bake the cookies at 350° for 15 to 20 minutes.

CHOCOLATE MACAROONS

2 egg whites
1 cup sugar
⅛ teaspoon salt
½ teaspoon vanilla

1½ cups shredded coconut
1½ squares (1½ ounces) unsweetened
    chocolate

Beat the egg whites until stiff, then gradually beat in the sugar and salt. Beat the mixture well after the sugar has been added. Add the vanilla, and fold in the coconut and the chocolate which has been melted over hot water. Drop the batter by teaspoons onto a greased cookie sheet. Bake it at 275° for about 30 minutes. This recipe makes 1½ dozen cookies.

CHOCOLATE PEANUT BUTTER COOKIES

2 cups sifted all-purpose flour
½ teaspoon double-acting baking
    powder
¼ teaspoon soda
¼ teaspoon salt
½ cup shortening
½ cup peanut butter

½ cup white sugar
½ cup brown sugar, firmly packed
1 egg, well-beaten
½ cup milk
1 cup (6 ounces) semi-sweet chocolate
    chips

Preheat the oven to 375°. Sift together the flour, baking powder, soda and salt. Cream together the shortening and peanut butter, then blend in the sugars. Add the egg and mix it thoroughly before stirring in the sifted flour mixture alternately with the milk. Mix it well again. Fold in the chips. Drop the batter by spoonfuls onto an ungreased baking sheet and bake it for about 12 minutes. This recipe yields about 3 dozen cookies.

CHOCOLATE PINWHEEL

½ cup sugar
½ cup shortening
1 egg yolk
1½ teaspoons vanilla
1½ cups all purpose flour

¼ teaspoon salt
½ teaspoon baking powder
3 teaspoons milk
1 square (1 ounce) unsweetened
   chocolate, melted

Mix together all the ingredients but the chocolate to make a smooth dough. Divide it into 2 equal portions. To 1 portion add the melted chocolate. Roll the white dough ⅓-inch thick on a floured surface. Roll the chocolate dough the same size and place it on top of the first dough. Roll it like you would a jelly roll. Chill the dough, then cut it into slices and bake it at 350° until done.

CHOCOLATE SANDWICH WAFERS

1¼ cups sugar
2 eggs
1 teaspoon vanilla
½ cup butter
3 squares (3 ounces) chocolate,
   melted

2 cups all-purpose flour
½ teaspoon soda
1½ teaspoons baking powder
½ teaspoon salt

Combine the sugar, eggs, vanilla, butter and chocolate. Beat the mixture until it is creamy, then gradually add the flour, soda, baking powder and salt. Chill the dough well, then roll it out ⅛-inch thick and cut it into rounds. Put them onto an ungreased cookie sheet and bake them at 350° for 8 to 10 minutes. Let them cool, then put them together with your favorite filling.

SOFT CHOCOLATE COOKIES

1 teaspoon salt
1 teaspoon soda
2 teaspoons pure vanilla extract
1 cup shortening
2 cups light brown sugar

3 squares (3 ounces) unsweetened
   chocolate
2 eggs, unbeaten
2½ cups sifted all-purpose flour
¾ cup sour milk
1 cup chopped nuts

Blend the first 3 ingredients with the shortening. Gradually mix in the sugar. Melt the chocolate over hot water and add it to the mixture. Beat in the eggs, then add the flour alternately with the milk. Stir in the nuts. Drop heaping teaspoons of the batter, 2 inches apart on a lightly greased cookie sheet. Bake the cookies in a moderate oven (375°) for 10 to 12 minutes or until done. Let them cool and store them in an airtight container. This recipe yields 5 dozen cookies.

SOFT CHOCOLATE CHIP COOKIES

½ cup shortening
1 cup sugar
2 large eggs, or 3 small
½ cup milk
2½ cups all-purpose flour

1 teaspoon baking powder
¾ teaspoon soda (in milk)
1 small package (6 ounces) chocolate
    chips, or butterscotch morsels

Mix the ingredients to make a batter. Drop it by teaspoons onto a greased cookie sheet and bake it at 400°. When slightly brown around the edges, the cookies are done.

SOUR CREAM CHOCOLATE COOKIES

2 cups brown sugar
¾ cup shortening
2 eggs
1 teaspoon vanilla
2 squares (2 ounces) chocolate

2 teaspoons soda
1 cup sour cream
4 or 5 cups all-purpose flour
Pinch of salt

Cream together the sugar, shortening, eggs and vanilla. Melt the chocolate over hot water and add it to the sugar mixture. Put the soda into ½ cup of the sour cream and add it alternately with the flour and salt and the remaining cream. Make the dough as soft as can be handled. Chill it for a few hours. Roll it out ¼-inch thick, cut it and bake it in a moderate oven (350°) until done.

COCONUT OATMEAL GEMS

1 cup raw sugar
1 cup honey or maple syrup
½ cup vegetable oil
3 eggs
½ cup chopped dates or raisins
3 cups whole wheat flour
1 teaspoon soda

½ teaspoon baking powder
1 cup ground oatmeal or wheat germ
3 cups rolled oats
½ teaspoon salt
1 cup unsweetened coconut
½ cup hickory nuts

Cream together the sugar, honey and oil until light and fluffy. Add the beaten eggs and dates, beating the mixture thoroughly. Add the dry ingredients, coconut and nuts, mixing well after each addition. Drop the batter by spoonfuls onto a cookie sheet, then flatten the cookies with a fork. Bake them at 350° until done.

CHURCH COOKIES

3 tablespoons soda
1 teaspoon salt
1 cup hot water
12 to 15 cups all-purpose flour
5 cups sugar
2½ cups lard

1 cup molasses
4 eggs
2 teaspoons vanilla
2 teaspoons ginger
Dash of cinnamon (optional)
1 teaspoon baking powder

Dissolve the soda and salt in the hot water. Add this to the flour, and mix in the rest of the ingredients in the order they are listed. Roll out the dough, cut it with a cookie cutter, and bake it at 375° until done.

COCONUT COOKIES

2 cups all-purpose flour
1 teaspoon salt
2 teaspoons baking powder
¾ cup sugar

½ cup melted shortening
2 eggs
2 teaspoons vanilla
1 cup shredded coconut

Sift together the flour, salt and baking powder. Blend the sugar and shortening, add the eggs, and stir the mixture well. Stir in the vanilla and coconut, then add the sifted dry ingredients. Form the dough into a roll and chill it. Slice the dough and bake it at 375° until done.

DATE COOKIES

8 cups all-purpose flour
4 cups sugar
2 teaspoons soda
2 teaspoons cream of tartar

1 teaspoon salt
2 cups shortening
6 large eggs

Blend together all the ingredients, and drop the batter by spoonfuls onto a cookie sheet. Bake the cookies at 375° until done. When they have cooled, spread the following date filling between pairs of cookies. The cookies may seem a little hard at first, but several hours after the filling has been spread they will be soft and delicious.

Date Filling;

2 tablespoons cornstarch
2 cups water
1 cup cut-up dates

2 cups brown sugar
Juice of 2 lemons, OR
2 tablespoons Realemon

Bring the ingredients to a boil and cook the mixture until it is thick. Cool it and spread it between pairs of cookies.

COCONUT KRISPIES

1 cup butter, or ¾ cup oil
1 cup raw sugar
½ cup honey
2 eggs
1 teaspoon vanilla
2 cups whole wheat flour
½ cup wheat germ

½ teaspoon soda
¼ teaspoon salt
½ teaspoon baking powder
1 cup shredded coconut, unsweetened
2 cups rolled oats
1 cup bran flakes (optional)

Mix together the ingredients in the order given. Form the dough into balls the size of a walnut. Place them on a greased cookie sheet and bake them at 350° for 10 to 12 minutes.

DATE-FILLED OAT COOKIES

3 cups brown sugar
2 cups shortening, half butter
1 teaspoon vanilla
6 cups all-purpose flour

1 teaspoon salt
2 teaspoons soda
4 cups rolled oats
1 cup buttermilk

Cream together the sugar and shortening. Add the vanilla. Sift and measure the flour, then add the salt, soda and rolled oats. Add these dry ingredients alternately with the buttermilk, and mix thoroughly. Chill the dough for several hours. Turn it onto a lightly floured board and roll it to a ⅛-inch thickness. Cut the dough with a round cookie cutter and place the cookies 1 inch apart on a greased baking sheet. Bake them at 375° until they turn golden brown. This recipe makes 8 dozen cookies.

When they are cold, spread them with the following filling;

2 cups finely chopped dates
1 cup sugar

1 cup water
2 tablespoons cornstarch

Combine the ingredients and cook the mixture until it is thick. Let it cool before spreading on the cookies. Top the filling with another cookie.

CREAM WAFERS

1 cup lard plus 1 cup margarine
8 eggs, beaten
4 teaspoons cream
6 teaspoons soda
4 cups brown sugar

10½ cups all-purpose flour
4 teaspoons cinnamon
Vanilla
Salt

Mix together the ingredients to make a dough. Roll it out and cut it with a cookie cutter or put it through a cookie press. Bake the cookies at 350° until done. Spread them with your favorite frosting and place another cookie on top.

DATE PINWHEELS

Filling;

2½ cups dates
1 cup sugar

1 cup water
1 cup chopped nuts

Cook slowly the dates, sugar and water for 15 minutes. Add the nuts, and allow the mixture to cool.

Dough;

1 cup shortening
2 cups brown sugar
4 eggs

4 to 5½ cups all-purpose flour
½ teaspoon salt
½ teaspoon soda

Cream the shortening and gradually add the brown sugar. Add the well-beaten eggs and beat the mixture until it is smooth. Add the dry ingredients which have been sifted together, and mix it well. Chill the dough thoroughly.

Divide it into 2 parts and roll out each one separately into rectangular shape, less than ¼ inch thick. Spread each piece of the dough with the date filling and roll it up into 2 long rolls as for a jelly roll. Chill the rolls overnight. With a sharp knife slice them into ¼-inch thicknesses. Bake them in a moderately hot oven (400°) for 10 to 20 minutes.

EASY FILLED DROPS

1 cup shortening
1 cup brown sugar
2 eggs
½ cup water, sour milk or buttermilk
1 teaspoon vanilla

3½ cups sifted all-purpose flour
1 teaspoon soda
1 teaspoon salt
⅛ teaspoon cinnamon

Preheat the oven to 400°. Mix together well the shortening, sugar and eggs. Stir in the water and vanilla. Sift together and stir in the flour, soda, salt and cinnamon. Drop the dough by teaspoons onto an ungreased baking sheet. Place ½ teaspoon of date filling (see below) on each cookie and cover it with ½ teaspoon of the dough. Bake the cookies for 10 to 12 minutes. This recipe makes 5 to 6 dozen cookies.

Date Filling;

2 cups dates, cut into small pieces
¾ cup sugar

¾ cup water
½ cup chopped nuts

Cook the dates, sugar and water, stirring constantly until the mixture is thick. Add the nuts, and allow the filling to cool.

GINGER CREAMS

⅔ cup shortening
1¼ cups brown sugar
1 cup molasses
1 teaspoon soda
1 cup hot water
5½ cups flour, OR
4½ cups flour plus 1 cup wheat germ

1 teaspoon cinnamon
½ teaspoon cloves
½ teaspoon salt
1 teaspoon ginger
1 cup raisins
Chopped nuts (optional)

Cream together the shortening and sugar. Add the molasses, then the soda dissolved in the hot water. Add the sifted dry ingredients, then the raisins and nuts. Drop the batter by teaspoonfuls onto a greased baking sheet. Bake the cookies at 350° for 15 to 20 minutes or until done.

OLD-FASHIONED GINGER COOKIES

3 cups baking molasses
1 cup sugar
2 cups shortening
10 cups flour (5 cups pastry, 5 cups bread)

1 teaspoon salt
2 tablespoons soda
1 to 2 tablespoons ginger
1 teaspoon cinnamon
2 cups sour milk or buttermilk

Heat together the molasses and sugar, add the shortening and stir the mixture until it is smooth. Remove it from the heat. Sift together the dry ingredients and add this mixture alternately with the sour milk. Stir it to make a smooth dough, then work it with your hands for 5 minutes. Chill the dough and roll it out to ½-inch thickness. Cut it into cookies, and glaze them with a beaten egg. Bake them at 350° for 20 to 25 minutes. This recipe makes 8 dozen cookies.

SOFT GINGER COOKIES

6 to 8 cups all-purpose flour
¾ teaspoon salt
½ teaspoon cinnamon
2 tablespoons ginger
1 cup lard
1 cup sugar

1 egg
2 cups dark baking molasses
2 tablespoons vinegar
4 teaspoons soda
1 cup boiling water

Sift the flour with the salt and spices. Cream the lard and sugar, then add the egg and beat it until light. Add the molasses and vinegar, then the previously sifted dry ingredients, and the soda dissolved in the boiling water. If necessary, add more flour to make a soft dough. Drop it by teaspoons onto a greased cookie sheet. Sprinkle the cookies with sugar, and bake them for 10 minutes in a moderate oven (350°).

GINGER SNAPS

1 cup sugar
1 cup dark baking molasses
1 cup lard
1 egg

1 teaspoon ginger
½ teaspoon cinnamon
1 teaspoon soda
4 to 5 cups all-purpose flour

Heat together the sugar, molasses and lard. Let the mixture cool while stirring frequently. Stir in the egg, then add the combined ginger, cinnamon, soda and flour. Use enough flour to make a stiff dough. Roll it out very thinly, cut it with a cookie cutter and bake the cookies at 400° until done. They will taste like bakery cookies.

GRAHAM GEMS

2 cups dark brown sugar
½ cup butter or lard
2 eggs
4 cups whole wheat flour (or part
   white)

1 teaspoon soda
5 tablespoons sour cream
¼ teaspoon salt
1 teaspoon vanilla
½ cup raisins (optional)

Mix together the above ingredients, then drop the batter by teaspoonfuls onto a greased cookie sheet. Bake the cookies at 400° until done.

The raisins add a better flavor if they are cooked in a little water first for a minutes. Then add the raisins and water to the dough. In this case, more flour may be required.

JUBILEE JUMBLES

½ cup soft shortening
½ cup white sugar
1 cup brown sugar
2 eggs
1 cup undiluted evaporated milk
1 teaspoon vanilla

3 cups all-purpose flour (scant)
½ teaspoon soda
1 teaspoon salt
½ cup nuts
½ cup coconut
1 package (12 ounces) chocolate chips

Mix together thoroughly the shortening, sugar and eggs. Stir in the evaporated milk and vanilla. Sift together the flour, soda and salt, and stir this mixture into the first. Blend in the nuts, coconut and chocolate chips. Chill the batter for 1 hour, then drop it by spoonfuls onto a greased baking sheet and bake it for 8 to 12 minutes at 375°. While they are still warm, frost the cookies with a creamy fudge frosting.

LEMON CRISPS

1¾ cups shortening
1 cup granulated sugar
1 cup brown sugar
2 tablespoons lemon juice
2 eggs

2 teaspoons grated lemon rind
5½ cups all-purpose flour
½ teaspoon salt
½ teaspoon soda

Mix the ingredients together well, then form the dough into small balls. Place them on a cookie sheet and flatten them. Bake the cookies at 350° for 10 to 12 minutes.

ORANGE CRISPS; Substitute orange juice and rind for the lemons.

LITTLE HONEY CAKES

1½ cups lard
2 cups sugar
4 eggs, beaten
1 cup molasses
1 cup honey
1 cup hot water

2 teaspoons cinnamon
1 teaspoon ginger
2 teaspoons soda
2 teaspoons baking powder
5 cups all-purpose flour (approximate),
   to stiffen

Cream together the lard and sugar. Add the eggs. Blend in the molasses, honey and hot water. Add the cinnamon, ginger, soda, baking powder and flour. Chill the dough overnight, then roll it out and cut it into cookie shapes, or drop it by the spoonful onto a cookie sheet. Bake the cookies at 350° until brown.

MINCEMEAT COOKIES

1 cup shortening
1 cup brown sugar
1 cup white sugar
3 eggs
3 cups all-purpose flour
1 teaspoon soda

½ teaspoon salt
1 teaspoon cinnamon
½ teaspoon cloves
½ teaspoon nutmeg
1 cup mincemeat
1 cup chopped nuts

Cream together the shortening and sugar. Add the eggs and beat until fluffy. Sift and measure the flour, add the soda, salt and spices, then sift it again. Add these dry ingredients to the creamed mixture and mix it thoroughly. Add the mincemeat and nuts. Drop the batter by teaspoonfuls onto a greased baking sheet, and bake it at 350° until done.

MARY'S SUGAR COOKIES

2 eggs
1½ cups granulated sugar
1 cup lard
1 teaspoon vanilla
1 cup sweet milk

4 cups all-purpose flour
2 teaspoons baking powder
2 teaspoons cream of tartar
2 teaspoons soda (scant)

Beat the eggs for 1 minute. Add the sugar and lard and beat the mixture for 1 minute more. Add the vanilla and milk. Sift together the dry ingredients and combine this mixture with the first. Drop the batter by spoonfuls onto a cookie sheet and bake the cookies at 400° until they are golden brown. When the cookies have cooled, spread the following icing on top.

6 tablespoons butter (room
    temperature)
2 teaspoons vanilla

⅛ teaspoon salt
1 pound icing sugar
4 to 5 tablespoons milk

Put all the ingredients into a bowl and beat the mixture for 1 minute. Divide the icing into several parts and color each part with a different food coloring. This will add variety to one batch of cookies.

MICHIGAN ROCKS

1½ cups brown sugar
¾ cup shortening
4 eggs
3 cups all-purpose flour (scant)
1 teaspoon soda

1 pound dates, finely chopped
1½ cups nut meats
1 teaspoon vanilla
¼ teaspoon salt

Mix together the ingredients, then drop the batter by teaspoonfuls onto a cookie sheet. Bake it at 350° for 6 to 8 minutes or until done.

MOLASSES DROP COOKIES

1 cup lard
1½ cups brown sugar
2 eggs
1 cup molasses
1 cup table syrup

1½ cups sweet milk
3 teaspoons soda
1 teaspoon ginger
2 teaspoons cinnamon
6 cups all-purpose flour

Mix the ingredients together to make a batter. Drop it by spoonfuls onto a greased cookie sheet. Bake the cookies in a moderate oven (350°) until done.

OATMEAL MOLASSES COOKIES

½ cup sugar
½ cup molasses
¾ cup shortening
2 eggs
¼ cup sweet milk
2 teaspoons cinnamon

1 teaspoon cloves
1 teaspoon soda
2 cups all-purpose flour
1 cup raisins
2 cups oatmeal

Mix together the ingredients in the order given. Drop the batter by teaspoons onto a greased cookie sheet. Bake it at 350° until done.

MOLASSES SUGAR COOKIES

1 cup sugar
¾ cup shortening
¼ cup molasses
1 egg
2 cups sifted all-purpose flour

2 teaspoons soda
1 teaspoon cinnamon
½ teaspoon cloves
½ teaspoon ginger
½ teaspoon salt

Cream together the sugar and shortening. Add the molasses and egg, and beat the mixture well. Sift together the flour, soda, cinnamon, cloves, ginger and salt, and add this mixture to the first. Mix it well and chill. Form the dough into 1-inch balls. Roll them in granulated sugar and place them 2 inches apart on greased cookie sheets. Flatten them with a spoon or fork. Bake the cookies at 350° for 8 to 10 minutes. This recipe makes 4 dozen cookies.

SOFT MOLASSES COOKIES

¾ cup shortening
¾ cup brown sugar
2 eggs
¾ cup molasses
¾ cup sour cream

2¼ cups all-purpose flour
2 teaspoons soda
½ teaspoon salt
½ teaspoon cinnamon
1½ teaspoons ginger (optional)

Cream together the shortening and sugar. Add the well-beaten eggs, molasses and sour cream, and stir the mixture until it is smooth. Mix together the dry ingredients, and add this mixture gradually to the first. Chill the dough, then drop it by spoonfuls onto a greased baking pan. Bake the cookies at 350° for about 10 minutes.

NO-BAKE COOKIES

2 cups white sugar
3 tablespoons cocoa
¼ cup butter
½ cup milk

3 cups oatmeal (finely crumbled)
½ cup peanut butter
1 teaspoon vanilla

Boil together the sugar, cocoa, butter and milk. Remove this mixture from the heat and add the oatmeal, peanut butter and vanilla. Drop the batter quickly by teaspoonfuls onto waxed paper.

Variations: Coconut, nuts or chocolate chips may be used instead of the peanut butter.

SOFT OATMEAL DROP COOKIES

¾ cup melted shortening
2 eggs, beaten
¾ cup buttermilk
4 cups oatmeal
1½ cups raisins, OR
½ cup shredded coconut
¼ cup corn oil

⅛ teaspoon salt
2 teaspoons soda
½ cup brown sugar
½ cup raw sugar
½ cup honey
2 cups all-purpose flour
1 teaspoon baking powder

Mix together all the ingredients to make a batter. Drop it by spoonfuls onto a greased cookie sheet. Grease your fingers to press the cookies flat and to make a nice edge. Bake them at 350° until done. This recipe makes 42 cookies.

BANANA OATMEAL COOKIES

1½ cups sifted all-purpose flour
1 cup sugar
½ teaspoon soda
½ teaspoon nutmeg
¾ teaspoon cinnamon

¾ cup shortening
1 egg, well-beaten
1 cup mashed bananas
1¾ cups rolled oats
Nuts

Sift together the dry ingredients. Cut in the shortening, then add the egg, bananas, oats and nuts. Beat the mixture thoroughly until all the ingredients are blended. Drop the batter by teaspoonfuls about 1½ inches apart onto greased cookie sheets. Bake it at 400° for about 15 minutes. This recipe makes 3½ dozen cookies.

NUT COOKIES

½ cup shortening
1½ cups sugar
4 egg yolks, beaten
1 teaspoon vanilla
1¾ cups flour

½ teaspoon baking powder
¼ teaspoon salt
¾ cup chopped nuts
2 teaspoons cinnamon

Cream together the shortening and sugar, then blend in the eggs and vanilla. Sift together the flour, baking powder and salt, then mix this with the creamed mixture. Form the dough into tiny balls, and dip them in a mixture of the nuts and cinnamon. Bake them in a moderate oven (350°) until done.

PEANUT BUTTER COOKIES

½ cup shortening
½ cup peanut butter
½ cup granulated sugar
½ cup brown sugar
1 egg, well-beaten

1 teaspoon vanilla
1¼ cups all-purpose flour
¼ teaspoon salt
½ teaspoon baking powder
¾ teaspoon soda

Thoroughly cream the shortening, peanut butter and sugars. Add the eggs and vanilla, then beat the mixture well. Add the sifted dry ingredients and mix it thoroughly. Chill the dough well, then form it into small balls on a cookie sheet, and flatten them with a fork. Bake the cookies in a moderate oven (375°) for 10 to 15 minutes. This recipe makes 3 to 4 dozen cookies.

PEANUT SURPRISES

1 cup shortening (part butter for flavor)
2 cups brown sugar, packed
2 eggs
2 cups all-purpose flour
1 teaspoon baking powder

1 cup flaked wheat cereal
½ teaspoon salt
1 teaspoon soda
2 cups quick cooking oatmeal
1 cup coarsely chopped salted nuts

Mix together the ingredients, then drop the batter by teaspoonfuls onto a lightly greased baking sheet. Flatten out each cookie with a fork dipped in flour. Bake them for 10 to 12 minutes in a moderate oven (350°).

PEANUT BUTTER OATMEAL COOKIES

1 cup shortening	2 teaspoons cinnamon
1 cup peanut butter	½ teaspoon cloves
2 teaspoons vanilla	½ teaspoon nutmeg
2 cups sugar	4 cups quick cooking oats, OR
2 eggs	5 cups wheat flake cereal
3 cups all-purpose flour	⅔ cup milk
2 tablespoons baking powder	1 cup chopped nuts (optional)
1 teaspoon salt	

Cream together the shortening, peanut butter and vanilla, and gradually add the sugar. Continue to cream this mixture until it is light and fluffy, then beat in the eggs. Sift together the flour, baking powder, salt, cinnamon, cloves and nutmeg, then add the oats. Stir this into the creamed mixture alternately with the milk, and blend in the nuts. Spoon the batter onto greased cookie sheets and bake it at 375° for 12 to 15 minutes. This recipe makes 6 dozen cookies.

Variations: Substitute 1 cup of molasses or honey for the 1 cup of sugar.

Stir in 2 cups of raisins, or 2 cups of chopped dates, prunes or apricots (uncooked) when adding the nuts.

PUMPKIN COOKIES

1 cup brown sugar	1 teaspoon soda
1 cup lard	½ teaspoon salt
1 egg	1 teaspoon baking powder
1 cup pumpkin	1 teaspoon cinnamon
2 cups all-purpose flour	

Mix together the sugar, lard and egg, then add the pumpkin and mix it well. Sift together the dry ingredients and add them to the mixture, beating it well. Drop the batter by spoonfuls onto a cookie sheet and bake it at 350° for 10 to 20 minutes. When the cookies have cooled slightly, frost them with the following icing. This makes a very delicious and moist cookie.

1 tablespoon butter	¼ cup pumpkin
1 tablespoon milk	Icing sugar

Cream the butter, add the milk and pumpkin, then add enough sugar to bring the icing to spreading consistency.

PUMPKIN NUT COOKIES

½ cup shortening
1 cup sugar
2 eggs, beaten
1 cup pumpkin
2 cups sifted all-purpose flour
4 teaspoons baking powder

1 teaspoon salt
2½ teaspoons cinnamon
¼ teaspoon ginger
½ teaspoon nutmeg
1 cup raisins
1 cup chopped nuts

Cream the shortening and gradually add the sugar. Cream this mixture until it is light and fluffy. Add the eggs and pumpkin, and mix it well. Sift together the flour, baking powder, salt and spices. Stir in these dry ingredients and mix until they are blended. Add the raisins and nuts. Drop the batter by teaspoonfuls onto a greased cookie sheet, and bake it at 350° for about 15 minutes. This recipe makes 4 dozen cookies.

RAISIN DROP COOKIES

1 cup raisins
1 cup water
¾ cup margarine
1 cup sugar
1 egg

1 teaspoon vanilla
1 teaspoon soda
3 cups sifted all-purpose flour
1 teaspoon baking powder
Pinch of salt

Combine the raisins and hot water and boil it down to ½ cup of liquid. Cream together the margarine, sugar and egg, then add the vanilla and the combined soda, flour and salt. Mix this alternately with the raisins and liquid. Drop the batter by the tablespoon onto a greased cookie sheet, and bake it at 375° for about 15 minutes.

PINEAPPLE DROP COOKIES

3½ cups all-purpose flour
1 teaspoon baking powder
1 teaspoon soda
⅛ teaspoon salt
1 cup sugar

¾ cup Crisco
¾ cup butter
1 egg
½ cup pineapple juice
½ cup sour cream

In a bowl, measure and sift together the dry ingredients. Then cut in the Crisco and butter as for a pie crust. Add the beaten egg, pineapple juice and sour cream, and stir the mixture only enough to blend it. Drop the batter by spoonfuls onto a greased cookie sheet. Press a small piece of pineapple into each cookie before baking them at 400° for 12 minutes or until light brown.

PINEAPPLE COOKIES

1 cup brown sugar
1 cup granulated sugar
1 cup shortening
2 eggs
1 cup crushed pineapple
1 teaspoon pineapple flavoring

½ teaspoon salt
1½ teaspoons soda
½ teaspoon baking powder
4 cups all-purpose flour (more if
  pineapple undrained)

Combine the ingredients in the order given. Drop the batter into muffin tins and bake it at 350° for 20 minutes.

SNITZ COOKIES

1 cup lard
2 cups brown sugar
2 eggs
1 cup cooked snitz (dried apple pieces)
4 cups all-purpose flour

2 teaspoons baking powder
2 teaspoons soda
1 teaspoon salt
1 teaspoon cinnamon
½ cup raisins

Mix together the lard and sugar, then add the eggs and snitz. Sift together the dry ingredients and stir them in. Add the raisins. Drop the mixture by spoonfuls onto a greased baking sheet and bake the cookies at 350° for 10 to 15 minutes or until done.

SOUR CREAM COOKIES

1 cup lard or shortening
3 cups brown sugar
4 eggs
2 cups thick sour cream
2 teaspoons vanilla

1 teaspoon salt
2 teaspoons soda
2½ teaspoons nutmeg
1 teaspoon baking powder
6 to 7 cups all-purpose flour

Cream well the lard and sugar, then add the eggs, beating well after each addition. Add the sour cream and vanilla. Sift together the dry ingredients and add them to the mixture, mixing it well. Drop the batter by teaspoonfuls onto a greased baking sheet, then bake the cookies at 375° until done. Let them cool, then spread them with the following icing.

Icing;

¾ cup butter, browned
3 cups icing sugar
2 teaspoons vanilla

Mix the ingredients together and add hot water until the mixture is of spreading consistency.

RAISIN FILLED COOKIES

Filling;

2 cups chopped raisins
2 tablespoons flour
1 cup water

1 cup sugar
1 tablespoon lemon juice (optional)

Combine these ingredients and boil the mixture until it is thick.

Dough;

1 cup shortening
2 cups brown sugar
2 eggs
1 cup sweet milk

2 teaspoons vanilla
7 cups all-purpose flour
2 teaspoons soda
2 teaspoons baking powder

Cream the shortening, then add the sugar gradually. Add the well-beaten eggs and beat the mixture until it is smooth. Mix in the milk and vanilla. Add the dry ingredients which have been sifted together, and mix well. Roll out the dough and cut it with a round cutter.

Put 1 teaspoon of the filling on a cookie. Make a hole (with a thimble) in the middle of another cookie, then place it on top of the filling. Do not press the two together. Continue with this procedure until the cookies and filling are used up. Bake the cookies at 350° for 20 minutes or until done.

SNICKERS

½ cup white sugar
1 cup brown sugar
1 cup shortening
2 eggs
2¾ cups all-purpose flour

1 teaspoon soda
2 teaspoons cream of tartar
¼ teaspoon salt
½ cup brown sugar
1 teaspoon cinnamon

Mix together well the first 8 ingredients. Chill the dough overnight, then form it into balls. Roll the balls in a mixture of the ½ cup of brown sugar and the cinnamon. Bake them at 350° for about 10 minutes or until done. This recipe makes 6 dozen cookies.

FAVORITE SOUR CREAMS

5 cups brown sugar
2 cups shortening (scant)
2 cups thick sour cream
4 eggs, beaten
1 cup sweet milk

3 teaspoons baking powder
3 teaspoons soda
1 teaspoon vanilla
All-purpose flour, enough to make a
　　soft dough

Mix together the ingredients in the order given. Drop the batter by teaspoonfuls onto a greased baking sheet. Bake the cookies at 350° for 20 minutes or until done. This recipe makes 90 to 100 cookies.

TOLL-HOUSE COOKIES

1 cup shortening
¾ cup brown sugar
¾ cup white sugar
2 eggs, beaten
1 teaspoon hot water
1 teaspoon vanilla
1½ cups sifted all-purpose flour

1 teaspoon soda
1 teaspoon salt
2 cups oatmeal
1 cup chopped nuts
1 package chocolate chips or
　　butterscotch chips

Mix together the shortening, sugars, eggs, hot water and vanilla. Sift together and add the flour, soda and salt. Then add the oatmeal, nuts and chocolate chips. Drop the batter by teaspoons onto a greased cookie sheet, and bake the cookies at 350° for 10 to 15 minutes.

WHOLE WHEAT COOKIES

2¼ cups whole wheat flour
1½ cups sifted all-purpose flour
1½ cups brown sugar
1½ teaspoons soda
1½ teaspoons salt
1½ cups sour milk

2 eggs
½ cup melted butter
¼ cup molasses
1½ teaspoons vanilla
1 cup chocolate bits

Measure out the flours, sugar, soda and salt, and mix them together. Make a well and add the milk, eggs, butter, molasses and vanilla. Beat this mixture well and stir in the chocolate bits. Drop the batter by spoonfuls onto a cookie sheet and bake it at 350° for 6 to 8 minutes or until done.

Variations: Omit the vanilla and chocolate bits and add 1½ teaspoons of cinnamon and 1 cup of raisins.

WHOOPIE PIES

2 cups sugar
½ teaspoon salt
1 cup shortening
2 teaspoons vanilla
2 eggs

4 cups all-purpose flour
2 teaspoons soda
1 cup cocoa
1 cup cold water
1 cup thick sour milk

Cream together the sugar, salt, shortening, vanilla and eggs. Sift together the flour, soda and cocoa, and add this to the first mixture alternately with the water and sour milk. Add slightly more flour if the milk is not thick. Drop the batter by teaspoons onto a greased cookie sheet, and bake the cookies at 400° until done. Let them cool, then put them together with the following filling.

Filling;

1 egg white
2 cups icing sugar (as needed)
1 tablespoon vanilla
2 tablespoons flour

2 tablespoons milk
¾ cup Crisco or margarine
Marshmallow Creme (optional—see
    page 228)

Beat the egg white, before adding the remaining ingredients. Beat the mixture well.

A few drops of peppermint flavoring may be used in place of the vanilla.

DATE BARS

1 pound pitted dates
½ cup granulated sugar
¾ cup light corn syrup

¼ cup orange juice
2 teaspoons grated orange rind
¼ teaspoon salt

To make the filling, combine and cook the above ingredients until the dates are softened and the mixture becomes thick. Allow it to cool.

2½ cups all-purpose flour
1 teaspoon soda
1 teaspoon salt
1 cup brown sugar

1 cup soft shortening
½ cup water
2½ cups oatmeal (uncooked)

Sift together into a bowl the flour, soda and salt. Add the brown sugar, shortening and water, and beat the mixture until it is smooth. Fold in the oatmeal. Spread half of the dough over a greased 10 x 15-inch baking sheet. Cover it with the date filling.

Roll out the remaining dough and place it between 2 sheets of waxed paper. Chill it, then remove the top sheet of paper. Place the dough over the filling, and remove the other sheet of waxed paper. Bake it in a moderate oven (350°) for 30 to 35 minutes. Allow it to cool, then cut it into bars.

CHOCOLATE CHIP BARS

2 cups all-purpose flour
2 cups sugar
2 teaspoons baking powder
2 cups chocolate chips

4 eggs
1½ teaspoons salt
½ cup butter, melted
1 teaspoon vanilla

Mix together the ingredients, then spread the batter on a cookie sheet. (If you want a glossy top, beat the eggs first.) Bake it for 25 minutes at 350°, being careful not to overbake. When it has cooled, slice it into bars.

CHOCOLATE REVEL BARS

2½ cups all-purpose flour
2 cups white sugar
1 cup butter or margarine
1 teaspoon salt

2 eggs
2 teaspoons vanilla
1 teaspoon soda
3 cups oatmeal

Mix together the flour, sugar, butter and salt as for pie crumbs. (Reserve some of the crumbs for topping.) Add the eggs, vanilla, soda and oatmeal, and mix the dough until it is smooth. Spread it ⅔-inch thick in a baking pan, and top it with the following filling.

12 ounces chocolate chips
1 can sweetened condensed milk
2 tablespoons butter

½ teaspoon salt
1 cup nuts (optional)

Melt together in a double boiler the chocolate chips, milk, butter, salt and nuts if desired. Spread this over the batter, top it with the reserved crumbs, and bake it at 350° for 25 to 30 minutes.

RAISIN BARS

3½ pounds bread flour
2 pounds white sugar
1 pound shortening
1 teaspoon salt
2 pounds raisins

Water
5 eggs, beaten
1 pint mild molasses
3 tablespoons soda
½ cup boiling water

Mix together the flour, sugar, shortening and salt as for pie crumbs. Cook the raisins in as little water as possible. Allow them to cool before adding them to the crumbs. Then add the eggs, molasses and the soda which has been dissolved in the boiling water.

Mix the dough and let it stand overnight or longer. Form it into long rolls about ½ inch thick. Garnish the top with beaten egg to which a little water has been added. Bake the rolls at 350 to 375°. Let them set a little before slicing them.

LEMON BARS

1 cup sifted all-purpose flour
½ cup butter or margarine

¼ cup icing sugar

Mix together these ingredients and pour the mixture into an 8 x 8-inch pan. Bake it for 15 minutes at 350°.

2 eggs, beaten
2 tablespoons lemon juice
1 cup sugar

2 tablespoons flour
½ teaspoon baking powder
½ teaspoon lemon flavoring

Combine these ingredients in the order given, then pour the mixture over the baked crust. Bake it for 25 minutes at 350°, then cut it into bars when it has cooled.

ORANGE RAISIN BARS

1 cup raisins
1½ cups water
2 tablespoons shortening
1 cup sugar

2 cups all-purpose flour
1 teaspoon baking powder
1 teaspoon soda
½ teaspoon nutmeg

Stew the raisins in the water. If there is not enough juice to fill 1 cup, add water. Add the shortening and allow it to cool. Sift and add the sugar, flour, baking powder, soda and nutmeg. Spread the dough on a large greased pan and bake it for 18 to 20 minutes at 375°.

Icing;

1 cup icing sugar
Orange juice

1 tablespoon butter

Mix together these ingredients. Spread the mixture over the baked dough while it is still hot, then cut it into bars.

KEUFELS

1 cup plus 2 tablespoons all-purpose
   flour
½ cup margarine or butter
3 ounces cream cheese
1 cup brown sugar

2 tablespoons melted butter
1 teaspoon vanilla
1 egg, beaten
¼ teaspoon salt
¾ cup chopped nuts

To make the dough, mix the first 3 ingredients with a fork. Form the dough into 24 small-sized balls, and with your finger press and shape them into small muffin tins. Then mix the rest of the ingredients and fill the muffin tins with this mixture. Bake it at 350° for 20 minutes.

MARSHMALLOW BARS

1 cup brown sugar
½ cup margarine
1 egg
1 teaspoon vanilla
¼ cup cocoa

2 cups flour
½ teaspoon soda
½ teaspoon salt
½ cup milk

Combine the sugar, margarine, egg and vanilla. Add the dry ingredients, then the milk. Spre
the batter on a greased cookie sheet. Bake it at 375° for 8 minutes before removing it from
oven. Sprinkle miniature marshmallows over the top, then return it to the oven for 1 minu

Icing;

⅓ cup butter
1 cup brown sugar
2 tablespoons cocoa

¼ cup milk
Icing sugar

Combine these ingredients and boil the mixture until it forms large bubbles. Allow it to coc
before adding icing sugar to thicken it. Spread the icing thinly over the baked batter, then slic
it into bars.

OLD-FASHIONED RAISIN BARS

1 cup seedless raisins
1 cup water
½ cup salad oil, shortening or
   margarine
1 cup sugar
1 slightly beaten egg
1¾ cups sifted all-purpose flour

1 teaspoon cinnamon
¼ teaspoon salt
1 teaspoon soda
1 teaspoon nutmeg
1 teaspoon allspice
½ teaspoon cloves
½ cup chopped nuts (optional)

Combine the raisins and water and bring the mixture to the boiling point. Remove it from the
heat and stir in the oil. Allow it to cool to lukewarm, then stir in the sugar and egg. Sift together
the dry ingredients and beat them into the raisin mixture. Stir in the nuts. Pour the batter into a
greased 13 x 9 x 2-inch pan, and bake it at 375° for 20 minutes or until done. When it has
cooled, cut it into bars, and dust them with icing sugar.

*Variations: For thin, brownie-sized cookies, bake the batter in a greased 15½-inch jelly roll
pan for 12 minutes, or until done.*

NUTTY FINGERS

½ cup margarine
¼ cup plus 1 tablespoon icing sugar
1 teaspoon vanilla

1 cup all-purpose flour
1 cup finely chopped nuts

Cream the margarine and add the ¼ cup of icing sugar and vanilla. Then gradually add the flour and nuts. Form cookies the size of a little finger. Bake them at 375° for 8 to 10 minutes or until lightly browned. When they have cooled, roll them in the remaining icing sugar.

This is an easy recipe for little girls and boys to try.

SUNNY GRAHAM CHEWIES

1⅔ cups graham cracker crumbs
2 tablespoons flour
½ cup butter or margarine
1½ cups brown sugar, packed
½ cup nuts

½ teaspoon salt
¼ teaspoon baking powder
2 eggs
1 teaspoon vanilla

Combine 1⅓ cups of the crumbs, the flour and butter in a bowl. Blend this mixture until particles like rice form. Pack it into a greased 9-inch square cake pan, and bake it for 20 minutes at 350°. Then combine the sugar, the remaining crumbs, nuts, salt and baking powder, and blend this mixture. Add the beaten eggs and vanilla, and blend it well again. Pour it over the baked crust before returning it to the oven to bake for 20 minutes or more. When it has cooled, cut it into bars.

TOLL-HOUSE MARBLE SQUARES

1 cup plus 2 tablespoons all-purpose
    flour
½ teaspoon soda
½ teaspoon salt
½ cup soft butter
6 tablespoons white sugar

6 tablespoons brown sugar
½ teaspoon vanilla
¼ teaspoon water
1 egg
12 ounces chocolate morsels
½ cup chopped nuts

Sift together the flour, soda and salt. Blend together the butter, sugar, vanilla and water, then beat in the egg. Mix it with the sifted flour mixture, and add the nuts. Spread the dough in a greased 13 x 9 x 2-inch pan. Sprinkle the chocolate morsels over the dough and place it in the oven for 1 minute. Run a knife through the dough to marbleize it. Bake it at 375° for 12 to 14 minutes, then allow it to cool before cutting it into 24 squares.

GRANOLIES

1½ cups granola cereal
¾ cup unsifted all-purpose flour
1 teaspoon baking powder
¼ teaspoon soda
¼ teaspoon salt
½ cup chopped dates

½ cup chopped nuts
½ cup butter, softened
½ cup sugar
¼ cup molasses
1 egg
½ teaspoon vanilla

Measure out onto waxed paper the cereal, flour, baking powder, soda and salt, then stir to blend the mixture thoroughly. Mix in the dates and nuts. Cream the butter, then beat in the sugar, molasses, egg and vanilla. Stir in the cereal/date/nut mixture and mix it well. Spread the dough in an ungreased 9-inch square pan, and bake it in a preheated 350° oven for 25 to 30 minutes or until done. Allow it to cool before cutting it into squares. This recipe makes 16 to 20 squares.

WALNUT SQUARES

1 egg
1 cup brown sugar
½ teaspoon vanilla
½ cup sifted all-purpose flour

½ teaspoon salt
⅛ teaspoon soda
1 cup chopped walnuts

Beat the egg until it is foamy, then beat in the sugar and vanilla. Sift together and stir in the flour, salt and soda, then mix in the nuts. Spread the batter in a well-greased 8-inch square pan. Bake it at 375° until the top has a dull crust. Cut it into squares while it is still warm. Allow the squares to cool, then remove them from the pan.

PEANUT BUTTER BROWNIES

2 cups sugar
½ cup shortening
1 cup peanut butter
6 eggs
1 tablespoon vanilla

1½ cups brown sugar
4 cups pastry flour
1½ tablespoons baking powder
1½ teaspoons salt
½ cup nuts

Cream together the sugar, shortening and peanut butter. Add the eggs and vanilla, then add the dry ingredients and mix them well. Add the nuts before pressing the dough into 2 cookie sheets and baking it at 350° for 30 minutes. Cut it into bars while it is still warm.

BUTTERSCOTCH BROWNIES

¼ cup butter
1 cup brown sugar
1 egg
1 cup all-purpose flour

1 teaspoon vanilla
½ teaspoon salt
1 teaspoon baking powder
½ cup nuts

Melt the butter in a pan, then stir in the sugar. Heat it until the sugar has melted. Allow it to cool, then add the beaten egg, flour, vanilla, salt and baking powder. Add the nuts last. Bake the dough at 350° for 30 minutes, then cut it into squares while it is still hot. Sprinkle it with icing sugar.

YUM YUM BROWNIES

2 cups granulated sugar
¾ cup butter and lard combined
4 eggs, beaten
1 teaspoon vanilla

½ cup chopped nuts
1 cup all-purpose flour
½ teaspoon salt
½ cup cocoa

Cream together well the sugar and shortening. Add the eggs, vanilla and nuts. Sift together the flour, salt and cocoa, and add this to the sugar mixture. Stir it well. Bake the dough in a greased and floured 9 x 13-inch pan at 350° until the dough shrinks from the edges of the pan. Let it cool before cutting it into squares.

PIES AND PASTRIES

HINTS FOR PIES

- *For best results, pie dough should be worked very lightly after the water has been added.*
- Pie crusts will have a browner crust when milk is used in the dough. Milk can also be brushed over the top before baking.
- When making fruit pies, add the sugar when the pan is half full instead of on top—the pastry will then be lighter.
- Do you have trouble baking custard pies? Try heating the milk to the boiling point before mixing it with the eggs. This also helps keep the undercrust crisp.
- For Streusel Pies, mix together ⅓ cup of peanut butter and ¾ cup of powdered sugar. *Spread this on the bottom of a baked pie shell. Cover it with your favorite cream pie recipe and top it with meringue or whipped cream.*
- To glaze pies or cookies, brush the top with beaten egg, or egg white.
- Add a tablespoon of vinegar to the pie dough and a bit of sugar to keep it from drying out when storing it for later use. Store it in a plastic bag or covered dish in a cool place.

PIE CRUST

3 cups sifted pastry flour
1 cup shortening
½ teaspoon salt

1 egg
5 tablespoons water
1 teaspoon vinegar

Mix together the flour, shortening and salt. Beat the egg, add the water and vinegar, then add enough of this to the flour mixture to make a soft dough. This recipe makes 1 double crust pie or 2 single crust pies.

PIE DOUGH

3 quarts flour (11 cups all-purpose
   flour, or 12 cups pastry flour)
2 tablespoons vinegar

4 cups lard
2 cups water (approximate)
2 teaspoons salt

Mix the ingredients together to crumb consistency, using the vinegar and water to wet the mixture. This will be enough for the top and bottom crusts for 6 pies more or less, depending on the size of the pies and how thinly the dough is rolled out. If all the crumbs are not needed at once, they may be stored in a tight container for future use.

PAN PIE DOUGH

1½ cups all-purpose flour
1½ tablespoons granulated sugar
1 teaspoon salt

½ cup cooking oil (scant)
2 tablespoons milk

Mix together in a pan the first 3 ingredients. Add the cooking oil into which the milk has been stirred. Blend the mixture, then press it on the bottom and sides of the pan.

EGG WHITE PIE CRUST

¾ cup graham cracker crumbs
⅓ cup sugar
½ cup pecan pieces

3 egg whites
⅓ cup sugar
1 teaspoon vanilla

Mix together the crumbs, ⅓ cup of the sugar and the pecans. Beat the egg whites until they are stiff, gradually adding the other ⅓ cup of sugar and the vanilla. Add this to the crumb mixture. Pour it into a greased pie pan and bake it at 350° for 30 minutes. When it has cooled, mash it down to the shape of the pan. Fill the crust with ice cream and freeze it. Thaw it slightly before serving, and top it with your favorite fruit.

Variations: *Instead of using ice cream and freezing the pie, just use your favorite filling.*

FLAKY PIE CRUST

2 cups sifted whole wheat flour
1 teaspoon salt
2 tablespoons wheat germ

¾ cup margarine
4 to 5 tablespoons ice water

Combine the flour with the salt in a medium-sized bowl, then add the wheat germ. With a pastry blender, cut in the margarine. Sprinkle the ice water over the pastry and mix it with a fork. The pastry should be just moist enough to hold together.

This dough handles like any other using white flour, but it is far more nutritious.

GRAHAM CRACKER CRUST

1 cup graham crackers
3 tablespoons brown sugar

¼ cup melted butter

Crush the graham crackers into fine crumbs. Add the sugar and melted butter, and mix them thoroughly. Press the mixture firmly in an even layer around the bottom and sides of a 9-inch pie plate. Bake it at 375° for 5 to 8 minutes, then let it cool.

NO-BAKE GRAHAM CRACKER CRUST

1 cup (¼ pound) graham crackers
3 tablespoons icing sugar

¼ teaspoon plain gelatin
¼ cup melted butter

Crush the graham crackers finely. Add the sugar, gelatin and butter and mix it thoroughly. Save 2 tablespoons of the mixture for the topping. Press the rest firmly into a 9-inch pie pan, and chill it for 15 minutes.

NEVER FAIL PIE CRUST

6 cups pastry flour, or 5½ cups all-
purpose flour
2 cups lard

1 teaspoon salt
3 teaspoons baking powder
1 egg in cup, filled with water

Mix together the flour, lard, salt and baking powder until the mixture is crumbly. Add the egg and water, and mix it again. Sometimes more water is required. This dough will keep for awhile.

OATMEAL PIE CRUST

1 cup quick-cooking oats
⅓ cup sifted flour
⅓ cup brown sugar

½ teaspoon salt
⅓ cup butter

Combine the oats, flour, sugar and salt. Cut in the butter until the mixture is crumbly. Press it firmly on the bottom and sides of a 9-inch pie plate. Bake it in a moderate oven (375°) for about 15 minutes. Cool the crust completely and fill it with any desired cream filling.

SPOON PIE DOUGH

½ cup boiling water
1 cup lard
3 cups all-purpose flour

1 teaspoon baking powder
1 teaspoon salt

Add the boiling water to the lard, and stir it until the lard is melted. Then add the flour, baking powder and salt. Stir it with a spoon, then chill the dough in the refrigerator for a few hours.

WHOLE WHEAT PIE CRUST

2 cups whole wheat flour
1 cup ground oatmeal
½ teaspoon salt

⅓ cup vegetable oil
½ cup water

Combine the flour, oatmeal and salt in a bowl. Blend in the oil, then add the water.

MERINGUE FOR PIE

2 egg whites
¼ teaspoon cream of tartar
4 tablespoons granulated sugar

½ teaspoon cornstarch
1 teaspoon vanilla

Beat together the egg whites and cream of tartar until soft peaks are formed. Add the sugar to which the cornstarch has been added, then add the vanilla. Beat the mixture until it is stiff.

APPLE CREAM PIE

3 cups finely cut apples
1 cup brown or white sugar
⅔ cup cream or top milk

¼ teaspoon salt
1 rounded tablespoon flour

Mix together the ingredients, then put the mixture into an unbaked pie shell. Sprinkle the top with cinnamon. Bake the pie in a hot oven (450°) for 15 minutes, then reduce the heat to 325° and bake it for 30 to 40 minutes longer. When the pie is about half done, take a knife and push the top apples down to soften them.

Variations: Elderberries or other fruit may be used instead of apples.

DUTCH APPLE PIE

3 cups sliced apples
1 cup sugar
3 tablespoons flour
½ teaspoon cinnamon
1 beaten egg

1 cup light cream
1 teaspoon vanilla
½ cup chopped nuts
1 tablespoon butter

Place the apples in a 9-inch unbaked pie shell. Mix together the sugar, flour and cinnamon. Combine the egg, cream and vanilla, then add the sugar mixture and mix it well. Pour it over the apples, then sprinkle it with the nuts and dot it with the butter. Bake the pie in a moderate oven (350°) for 45 to 50 minutes until the apples are tender.

PAPER BAG APPLE PIE

6 cups coarsely sliced or chopped
  apples
½ cup sugar

2 tablespoons flour
½ teaspoon nutmeg
2 tablespoons lemon juice

Measure the apples into a bowl, and mix them with the sugar, flour, nutmeg and lemon juice. Turn them into an unbaked pie shell and pat them down evenly.

Topping;

½ cup butter
½ cup flour

½ cup brown or white sugar

Measure out the butter, flour and sugar, cutting in the butter with a pastry blender until crumbs are the size of peas. Sprinkle this evenly over the apples and pat it down around the edges. Slide the pie into a brown paper bag and fold the end under the pie. Put it onto a cookie sheet for easy handling. Bake it at 425° for 50 minutes.

The benefit of this method is a pie with no scorched rim, no under-baked apples, no boiling over in your clean oven, and no grief in general!

PLAIN APPLE PIE

2 tablespoons flour
6 medium apples, sliced
1 cup sugar

¼ teaspoon cinnamon
1 tablespoon water
1 teaspoon butter

Mix together the flour, apples, sugar and cinnamon. Pour this mixture into an unbaked pie shell, add the water, and dot the center with the butter. Place ½-inch strips of dough lattice-style over the apples, connecting the strips to the sides of the pie shell. Bake the pie at 400° until the apples are done.

BUTTERSCOTCH PIE

2 tablespoons butter
1 cup brown sugar

⅔ cup hot water

Brown the butter in a heavy saucepan. Add the sugar and stir it until it is melted. Add the hot water and cook the syrup slowly until all the lumps disappear.

2 tablespoons flour
3 tablespoons cornstarch
½ teaspoon salt

2 egg yolks
2 cups milk
1 teaspoon vanilla

Mix together the flour, cornstarch, salt, eggs and milk, then slowly stir this mixture into the hot syrup. Boil it until it thickens, then add the vanilla. Pour it into a baked pie shell and top it with meringue.

Variations: If you wish to use this as a butterscotch pudding or sauce, add ½ cup more milk.

BASIC CREAM PIE

2 cups milk	½ teaspoon salt
½ cup sugar	2 eggs, separated
2 tablespoons cornstarch	1 tablespoon butter
2 tablespoons flour	1 teaspoon vanilla

Scald 1½ cups of the milk in the top of a double boiler. Make a thickening by combining the sugar, cornstarch, flour and salt, then stir in the remaining ½ cup of milk with the egg yolks. Stir this flour mixture into the hot milk and cook it until it thickens. Remove it from the heat and add the butter and vanilla. Let it cool a little before pouring it into a baked pie shell. Cover the pie with meringue.

Variations:

COCONUT PIE; Add ¾ cup of coconut to the Basic Cream Pie filling. Top it with whipped cream and sprinkle it with coconut.

CHOCOLATE PIE; Add 2 to 4 teaspoons of cocoa to the thickening of the Basic Cream Pie recipe.

BANANA PIE: Cover the bottom of a baked pie shell with sliced bananas before adding the Basic Cream Pie filling.

STREUSEL PIE: Mix ⅓ cup of peanut butter with ¾ cup of powdered sugar. Sprinkle it on the bottom of a baked pie shell, saving some crumbs to put on top. Pour in the Basic Cream Pie filling and top it with whipped cream. Sprinkle the reserved crumbs over the whipped cream.

GRAHAM CRACKER PIE; Pour the cream filling into a graham cracker pie crust.

RAISIN CREAM PIE; Add ⅓ cup of raisins and ½ teaspoon of allspice (optional) to the cream filling.

CHOCOLATE MOCHA PIE

1 tablespoon gelatin	¾ cup sugar
¼ cup cold water	1 teaspoon instant coffee
1 tablespoon cocoa	1 cup whipped cream
⅛ teaspoon salt	1 teaspoon vanilla
1¼ cups milk	Chopped nuts

Soak the gelatin in the water. Combine in a saucepan the cocoa, salt, milk, sugar and coffee, and bring the mixture to a boil, stirring it constantly. Remove it from the heat and stir in the gelatin. Cool it until it has slightly thickened, then fold in the whipped cream and vanilla. Pour the mixture into a baked pie crust and top it with chopped nuts.

Variations: Graham cracker pie crust may be used.

Whipped dessert topping may be substituted for the whipped cream.

CHERRY PIE

2 tablespoons tapioca
1/8 teaspoon salt
1 cup sugar
3 cups drained, pitted sour cherries

1/2 cup cherry juice
1/4 teaspoon almond extract
Red food coloring (optional)

Mix together the ingredients and let the mixture stand for 15 minutes. Pour it into a 9-inch pie shell and dot it with 1 tablespoon of butter. Add a top crust, and bake the pie at 425° for 50 minutes.

CHERRY PIE FILLING

4 cups sweet red cherries, pitted
2 cups sugar
1 1/2 cups water

2 heaping tablespoons cornstarch
1 teaspoon almond flavoring
Red food coloring (optional)

Mix together and bring to a boil the cherries, sugar and water. Then mix the cornstarch with enough water to make a thin paste, and slowly add it to the boiling cherry mixture, stirring constantly until it comes to a boil once more. Add the almond flavoring, a few drops of red coloring if desired, and allow it to cool. This recipe makes enough for 2 pies.

BOB ANDY PIE

2 cups brown or white sugar
4 tablespoons flour
1/2 teaspoon cloves
1 teaspoon cinnamon

1 tablespoon butter
3 eggs, separated
2 cups milk

Mix together the dry ingredients, then add the butter, beaten egg yolks and milk. Fold in the beaten egg whites. Pour the mixture into 2 unbaked pie crusts and bake them at 400° for 10 minutes, then reduce the heat to 350° and continue baking them until done.

COCONUT CUSTARD PIE

2 eggs, beaten
1 cup molasses (white or dark)
1 cup milk
1 teaspoon vanilla

1/2 cup sugar
1 tablespoon flour
2 tablespoons melted butter
1 cup coconut

Mix together all the ingredients and pour the mixture into an unbaked pie shell. Bake the pie at 450° for 15 minutes. Reduce the heat to 350° and bake it for 20 to 30 minutes longer.

RAISIN CUSTARD PIE

3 eggs, beaten
1 cup raisins
1 cup molasses

1 tablespoon butter
1 teaspoon vanilla

Mix together the ingredients, then pour the mixture into an unbaked pie shell and bake it at 400° for 10 minutes. Reduce the heat to 350° and bake it 30 minutes longer.

Variations: Walnuts may be substituted for raisins.

VELVETY CUSTARD PIE

4 eggs, slightly beaten
½ cup sugar
¼ teaspoon salt

1 teaspoon vanilla
2½ cups scalded milk

Thoroughly mix together the eggs, sugar, salt and vanilla. Slowly stir into this mixture the scalded milk, then pour it immediately into an unbaked pastry shell. Bake the pie at 475° for 5 minutes, then reduce the heat to 425° and bake it 30 minutes longer, or until a knife inserted halfway between the center and the edge comes out clean.

ELDERBERRY PIE

2½ cups elderberries
1 cup sugar
3 teaspoons lemon juice or vinegar

⅛ teaspoon salt
2 tablespoons flour

Pour the washed elderberries into an unbaked pie crust. Mix together the other ingredients and pour the mixture over the berries. Cover it with a top crust. Bake the pie at 425° for 10 minutes, then reduce the temperature to 350° and bake it 30 minutes longer.

ELDERBERRY CUSTARD PIE

1 cup elderberry juice
4 tablespoons flour
1 cup sugar

¼ teaspoon salt
1 egg, separated
1 cup milk

Bring the juice to a boil. Combine the flour, sugar and salt, then gradually add the egg yolk and milk. Add this mixture to the boiling juice and stir it until it thickens. Fold in the stiffly beaten egg white. Pour the mixture into an unbaked pie shell, then bake it at 350° for 20 to 30 minutes.

CREAM CUSTARD PIE

3 eggs
1 cup brown sugar

1 cup cream
1 teaspoon vanilla

Beat the eggs, then add the brown sugar, cream and vanilla. Pour the mixture into an unbaked pie shell and bake it in a hot oven (450°) for 15 minutes. Reduce the heat to 300° and bake it for 30 to 35 minutes longer. The filling should appear slightly less set in the center than around the edge.

MOTHER'S ELDERBERRY PIE

1 cup sugar
2 eggs, separated
1 cup sour cream

2 cups uncooked elderberries
2 tablespoons cornstarch

Mix the sugar with the egg yolks, then add the sour cream, elderberries and cornstarch. Cook this mixture until it is thick, and pour it into a baked pie shell. Top it with meringue made with the 2 egg whites, then brown it in the oven.

FRUIT CRUMB PIE

Prepare your favorite fruit pie filling—cherry, blueberry, raspberry, elderberry or raisin. Pour it into an unbaked pie shell and top it with the following crumb mixture.

¾ cup flour
¾ cup oatmeal
⅔ cup brown sugar
½ teaspoon soda

¼ teaspoon salt
1 teaspoon cinnamon
½ cup melted butter

In a bowl, mix together the dry ingredients, then add the melted butter and mix it thoroughly until all the ingredients are moistened.

Bake the pie at 425° for 25 to 30 minutes or until the filling boils and the crumbs are nicely browned. This recipe makes enough crumbs for approximately 3 pies.

HAWAII FOOD PIE

1 cup crushed pineapple
1 cup cold water
½ cup sugar

⅛ teaspoon salt
3 tablespoons cornstarch
2 eggs, separated

Cook together until thick the pineapple, water, sugar, salt, cornstarch and egg yolks. Fold in the beaten egg whites while the mixture is hot, then pour it into a baked pie crust.

LEMON PIE

3 tablespoons cornstarch
1½ cups sugar
Juice and grated rind of 1 lemon

1¼ cups boiling water
3 eggs, separated
6 tablespoons sugar

Mix together the cornstarch, 1½ cups of sugar, and lemon juice. Add the beaten egg yolks, followed by the water in which the lemon rind has been boiled. (Discard the rind.) Cook this in a double boiler, then pour it into a baked pie crust. Beat the egg whites until they are stiff with the 6 tablespoons of sugar before spreading this mixture over the pie. Brown it in the oven.

LEMON SPONGE PIE

2 tablespoons flour
1 cup sugar
1 tablespoon butter

1 cup milk
2 eggs, separated
Juice and grated rind of 1 lemon

Sift together the flour and sugar, then cream in the butter. Add the milk with the egg yolks stirred in, then add the lemon, and the well-beaten egg whites last. Pour the mixture into an unbaked pie crust, and bake it in a moderate oven (375 to 400°) until done. This recipe makes 1 good-sized pie.

Variations: Lemon Sponge may be made without the crust. Set it in a pan of hot water to bake.

MAPLE NUT PIE

½ cup milk
1 cup maple syrup (or maple flavored
   syrup)
2 egg yolks, slightly beaten
1 tablespoon gelatin

Cold water
1 teaspoon maple flavoring
2 egg whites, stiffly beaten
1 cup whipped cream
½ cup chopped nut meats

Heat together the milk and maple syrup. Stir ½ cup of this into the egg yolks and return this mixture gradually to the hot syrup mixture, beating constantly. Cook this mixture a little, then add the gelatin which has been softened in a little cold water. Add the maple flavoring and chill the mixture until it begins to thicken. Fold in the egg whites, then add the whipped cream and chopped nut meats. Pour the mixture into a baked pie shell.

This pie tastes like maple nut ice cream. If you double the recipe, it makes three 8-inch pies.

MONTGOMERY PIE

1 egg	2 cups sugar
1 lemon (juice and rind)	1 cup butter
1 cup sugar	2 eggs
3 tablespoons flour	1 cup milk
1 cup corn syrup	2½ cups flour
1 pint water	2 teaspoons baking powder

Boil the first 6 ingredients until syrupy, then let the syrup cool. Divide it among 3 unbaked pie shells. Cream together the 2 cups of sugar and butter, then beat in the eggs. Sift together the flour and baking powder, and add it alternately with the milk, mixing until well blended. Pour this over the syrup in the pie shells. Bake the pies in a hot oven (450°) for about 10 minutes, then reduce the heat to 350° and bake them until done.

OATMEAL PIE

3 eggs, beaten	⅔ cup oatmeal
⅔ cup white sugar	⅔ cup coconut (optional)
1 cup brown sugar	⅔ cup milk
2 teaspoons margarine, softened	1 teaspoon vanilla

Blend together the ingredients and pour the mixture into an unbaked pie shell. Bake the pie for 30 to 35 minutes at 350°.

Variations: Try adding ½ teaspoon of cinnamon and ½ teaspoon of cloves.

PEACH CRUMB PIE

2½ tablespoons tapioca	⅓ cup packed brown sugar
¾ cup sugar	¼ cup flour
¼ teaspoon salt	½ teaspoon cinnamon
4 cups sliced peaches	2½ tablespoons soft butter

Mix together the first 4 ingredients, then let the mixture set for 5 minutes before pouring it into an unbaked 9-inch pie shell. Mix the rest of the ingredients for the crumb topping, then put it on top of the fruit filling. Bake the pie at 425° for 45 to 50 minutes.

Variations: Other fruit may be used, but this recipe is especially good with apples.

PEACH-PINEAPPLE PIE

1 quart canned sliced peaches
1 small can crushed pineapple
3 tablespoons cornstarch

2 cups sugar
½ teaspoon salt

Cook the ingredients together until the mixture is thick. Bake it between 2 crusts at 400° until the crust is brown. This recipe makes enough for 2 pies.

DOUBLE TREAT PEACH PIE

1 cup sugar
3 tablespoons cornstarch or tapioca
½ cup water

1 tablespoon butter
6 large peaches

Mix together the sugar and cornstarch, then add the water and butter before bringing the mixture to a boil. Dice 3 of the peaches and add them to this syrup, simmering it for 5 minutes or until it thickens. Allow it to cool. Slice the remaining peaches into a baked 9-inch pie shell, and pour the cooled peaches and syrup over it. Top it with whipped cream.

EMMA'S PEACH PIE

½ cup sugar
½ teaspoon salt
2 cups milk
3 tablespoons flour
3 tablespoons cornstarch

1 teaspoon vanilla
½ cup whipping cream, whipped
4 peaches, sliced
¼ cup water
Cornstarch

To make the filling, cook together the first 5 ingredients, then let the mixture cool. Add the vanilla and whipped cream.

To make the glaze, mash half of the peaches and add the water. Boil this for 2 minutes, then strain. Add sugar to taste, and cook it again slightly, thickening it with cornstarch. Put the filling into a baked pie shell. Cover it with the remaining peach slices and top it with the glaze.

FRESH PEACH PIE

Fresh peach halves
1 cup sugar

2 tablespoons butter
3 eggs, partly beaten

Arrange the peaches in an unbaked pie shell. Then mix together the sugar, butter and eggs, and pour this mixture over the peaches. Bake the pie at 350° until the crust is done.

PECAN PIE

2 eggs, beaten
¼ teaspoon salt
½ cup sugar
1 cup molasses (white or dark)
1 tablespoon flour

1 cup milk
1 teaspoon vanilla
2 tablespoons melted butter
1 cup chopped pecans, peanuts or
  coconut

Mix together the above ingredients, then pour the mixture into an unbaked pie shell. Bake the pie for 45 minutes at 350°.

KENTUCKY PECAN PIE

1 cup white corn syrup
½ cup brown sugar
⅓ teaspoon salt
⅓ cup melted butter

1 teaspoon vanilla
3 eggs, slightly beaten
1 cup pecans

Combine the syrup, sugar, salt, butter and vanilla, and mix them well. Add the eggs. Pour the mixture into a 9-inch pie shell, then sprinkle the pecans over all. Bake the pie in a preheated oven at 350° for about 45 minutes.

Variations: This recipe may also be used for tarts.

English walnuts may be used instead of pecans.

OATMEAL PIE; Use ⅔ cup of quick oatmeal instead of nuts.

KRISPIE PIE; Use 1 cup of Rice Krispies instead of nuts.

COCONUT PIE; Use coconut instead of pecans.

The above variations may also be used with Southern Pie (see page 182), omitting the grapenuts.

PINEAPPLE COCONUT PIE

3 eggs
1 cup sugar
1 tablespoon cornstarch
½ cup drained crushed pineapple

½ cup light corn syrup
¼ cup shredded coconut
¼ cup melted butter

Beat the eggs slightly, then add all the remaining ingredients. Blend the mixture well, then pour it into a 9-inch unbaked pie shell. Bake the pie at 350° for 45 to 50 minutes or until it is slightly set.

BETTY'S PUMPKIN PIE

1½ cups brown sugar
1 cup mashed pumpkin
1 tablespoon flour
1 teaspoon cinnamon
3 cups milk

½ teaspoon nutmeg
½ teaspoon allspice
Sprinkle of cloves
5 eggs, separated

Mix the ingredients as you would for a custard pie, beating the egg whites and folding them in last. For an extra rich pie, use part evaporated milk. Bake the pie at 400° for 15 minutes, then reduce the heat to about 350° until done. This recipe makes 2 pies.

MOTHER'S PUMPKIN PIE

⅔ cup sugar
1 tablespoon flour (heaping)
1 tablespoon melted butter
½ cup stewed pumpkin (more for
    stronger flavor)
¼ teaspoon ginger

¼ teaspoon cinnamon
½ teaspoon salt
1 egg, separated
2 or 3 drops vanilla
1½ cups milk

Beat together thoroughly the sugar, flour, butter, spiced pumpkin and egg yolk. Add the vanilla and milk. Beat the egg white and fold it into the mixture. Pour it into an unbaked pie crust and bake it at 400° for 10 minutes, then at 350° until done.

PUMPKIN CHIFFON PIE

1 envelope unflavored gelatin
¼ cup cold water
¾ cup brown sugar
½ teaspoon salt
½ teaspoon nutmeg

1 teaspoon cinnamon
½ cup milk
1 cup cooked pumpkin
3 eggs, separated
¼ cup sugar

Dissolve the gelatin in the water. Mix it in with all the other ingredients except the egg whites and ¼ cup of sugar. Put the mixture into a saucepan over medium heat for 10 minutes, stirring it constantly. Remove it from the heat and let it cool until the mixture is partially set. Then beat the egg whites until stiff, add the ¼ cup of sugar and fold it into the pumpkin mixture. Pour it into a 9-inch baked pie shell. Top the pie with whipped cream before serving.

RHUBARB PIE

2 tablespoons butter
2 cups rhubarb plus ½ cup water, OR
1 pint canned rhubarb (no extra water)
1¼ cups sugar
2 tablespoons cornstarch

⅛ teaspoon salt
2 eggs, separated
¼ cup cream or rich milk

Melt the butter, then add the rhubarb and water (or 1 pint canned rhubarb without water), and 1 cup of the sugar. Cook this mixture slowly until the rhubarb is tender.

Combine ¼ cup of the sugar, the cornstarch, salt, beaten egg yolks and cream. Add this to the rhubarb and cook it until it is thick. Pour this filling into a baked pie crust. Use the egg whites for meringue topping.

Variations: This recipe may be used for pudding. Fold in the beaten egg whites when the rhubarb has finished cooking, then chill it.

RHUBARB CREAM PIE

2½ cups cut up rhubarb
2 tablespoons flour
2 eggs, separated
3 tablespoons water

1 cup sugar
1 tablespoon melted butter
2 tablespoons sugar

Beat the egg yolks with the water. Add the 1 cup of sugar mixed with the flour and melted butter. Stir the mixture until it is smooth. Arrange the rhubarb in an unbaked pie shell, and mix in the sugar mixture. Bake the pie in a hot oven (450°) for 15 minutes. Then reduce the heat to 350° and continue baking it until done. Add meringue made of the beaten egg whites and 2 tablespoons of sugar. Brown it in the oven.

RHUBARB CUSTARD PIE

1¼ cups rhubarb
¾ cup sugar
1 tablespoon flour
¼ teaspoon salt

2 eggs
1 cup milk
1 tablespoon butter

Finely cut the rhubarb and put it into an unbaked pie shell. Mix together the sugar, flour, salt, beaten egg yolks, milk and melted butter. Pour this mixture over the rhubarb. Bake the pie at 400° for 10 minutes, then at 350° for 30 minutes longer. Cover it with a meringue made from the beaten egg whites and 1 tablespoon of sugar. Brown it in the oven.

FRENCH RHUBARB PIE

¾ cup flour
½ cup brown sugar
⅓ cup margarine
1 egg

1 cup sugar
1 teaspoon vanilla
2 cups diced rhubarb
2 tablespoons flour

To make the topping, mix together the flour, ½ cup of brown sugar and margarine. In a separate bowl, mix together the rest of the ingredients, then pour this mixture into an unbaked pie shell. Cover it with the topping, and bake it at 400° for 10 minutes. Continue baking the pie at 350° for 30 minutes longer or until done.

OHIO STATE RHUBARB PIE

1 cup sugar
1 tablespoon flour
½ teaspoon salt

1 egg
2 cups rhubarb
1 teaspoon lemon juice

Mix together the sugar, flour, salt and slightly beaten egg. Add the rhubarb and lemon juice. Bake this mixture between rich crusts, at 425° for 15 minutes, then at 350° for 25 to 30 minutes longer.

SOUTHERN PIE

¾ cup grapenuts cereal
½ cup warm water
3 eggs, well–beaten
¾ cup sugar

3 tablespoons dark corn syrup
3 tablespoons butter, melted
1 teaspoon vanilla
⅛ teaspoon salt

Combine the cereal and water, and let it stand until the water is absorbed. Meanwhile, blend the eggs with the sugar. Add the syrup, butter, vanilla and salt, then fold in the softened cereal. Pour the mixture into a 9-inch unbaked pie shell, and bake it at 350° for 50 minutes or until the filling is puffed completely across the top. Let it cool, then garnish it with whipped topping. Sprinkle the pie with additional cereal, if desired.

Variations: *Omit the grapenuts, and substitute the suggested ingredients shown under Variations on Kentucky Pecan Pie (see page 179).*

SHOO-FLY PIE

2 cups molasses
2 cups hot water
1 cup light brown sugar
1 teaspoon soda (scant)
5 cups all-purpose flour

2 cups light brown sugar
1 cup shortening (scant)
½ teaspoon soda
½ teaspoon cream of tartar

To make the syrup, mix together the first 4 ingredients until they are dissolved. (Use 1 cup or more of syrup per 9-inch pie shell.) Then mix the remaining ingredients to crumb consistency. Pour the syrup into unbaked pie crusts and divide the crumbs over top. Bake them for 10 minutes at 450°, for 30 minutes more at 375°, then for 30 minutes longer at 350°. This recipe makes 4 pies.

Variations: Try adding 2 teaspoons of nutmeg and 3 teaspoons of cinnamon to the crumbs.

Lemon Sauce For Shoo-Fly Pie;

2 tablespoons cornstarch
½ cup sugar
¼ teaspoon salt
2 cups boiling water

¼ cup butter or margarine
3 teaspoons lemon juice
1 tablespoon grated lemon rind

Mix together in a saucepan the cornstarch, sugar and salt. Gradually stir in the boiling water. Cook the mixture, stirring it constantly, until it boils and becomes thick and clear. Remove it from the heat, and stir in the remaining ingredients. Serve this sauce warm over Shoo-Fly Pie. This recipe yields 2¼ cups of sauce.

GOOEY SHOO-FLY PIE

Make crumbs by mixing together the following ingredients.

2 cups flour
¾ cup brown sugar
⅓ cup lard or butter

½ teaspoon nutmeg (optional)
1 teaspoon cinnamon (optional)

To make the syrup, combine the following.

1 cup molasses
½ cup brown sugar
2 eggs

1 cup hot water
1 teaspoon soda, dissolved in hot
    water

Pour ½ of the syrup into a pie crust, then add ½ of the crumbs. Add the remaining syrup and the rest of the crumbs. Bake the pie for 10 minutes at 400°, then reduce the heat to 350° for 50 minutes. This recipe makes enough for 2 pies.

STRAWBERRY PIE

1½ quarts fresh strawberries
2 cups sugar
½ cup cornstarch

Combine the strawberries and sugar and let them stand for 2 hours. Drain off the juice and add water to make 2 cups. Blend in the cornstarch and cook it over low heat until it has thickened. Mix it with the strawberries, then let it cool. Put it into a baked pie crust or graham cracker crust and serve it with whipped cream.

STRAWBERRY CHIFFON PIE

3 eggs, separated
½ cup sugar
1 package gelatin

4 tablespoons cold water
1½ cups crushed fresh strawberries

Beat the egg yolks slightly, then add ¼ cup of the sugar. Put the mixture into the top of a double boiler and cook it, stirring constantly until it thickens. Soak the gelatin in the cold water and add it to the mixture. Remove it from the heat. Stir in the crushed strawberries, mixing well, then chill the mixture until it begins to thicken.

Beat the egg whites until they hold soft peaks. Add the rest of the sugar, beating the mixture until it is stiff. Fold this into the strawberry mixture, then pour it into a baked pie shell. Chill and serve the pie with whipped cream.

Variations: Try substituting ¾ cup of raspberry juice instead of the strawberries.

STRAWBERRY PUDDING PIE

Strawberries
½ small box strawberry gelatin powder

1 cup plus 2 tablespoons boiling water
2 cups Basic Vanilla Pudding (see page 190)

Wash and stem the berries, then slice them into a pie pan. Dissolve the gelatin in the boiling water, and pour it over the strawberries. Let it set until it jells. Make the vanilla pudding, let it cool, then pour it into a baked pie crust. Put the bottom of the pie pan containing the thickened gelatin into a pan of hot water for a moment, until the gelatin loosens. Then slide the gelatin onto the pudding in the crust. Chill the pie. Top it with whipped cream before serving.

Variations: Raspberry or other berry pies may be made with this method, using the same pudding but with gelatin flavors matched accordingly.

FRESH STRAWBERRY CHIFFON PIE

3-ounce package instant vanilla
  pudding or pie filling
1¼ cups crushed strawberries

Prepare the pudding or pie filling according to the package instructions, then blend in the crushed strawberries. Pour the mixture into a graham cracker pie crust and chill it until it is firm. Spread it with whipped cream before serving.

JELLIED STRAWBERRY PIE

2 cups water
1¼ cups sugar
3 tablespoons cornstarch

1 package (3 ounces) strawberry
  gelatin powder
1 pint fresh strawberries, hulled
2 baked pie shells

Cook together the water, sugar and cornstarch until the mixture thickens. Add the dry gelatin powder and let the mixture cool. Pour it over the strawberries in the pie shells, and chill them until firm. Top the pies with whipped cream or your favorite vanilla pudding.

SUSIECUE PIE

1 cup brown sugar
½ cup white sugar
1 tablespoon flour
2 eggs, beaten

1 teaspoon vanilla
2 tablespoons milk
½ cup butter
1 cup pecan or hickory nuts

Mix together the sugars and flour, then add the eggs, vanilla, milk and butter. Beat the mixture until it is thick, then pour it into an unbaked pie crust. Bake it at 375° for 20 minutes, then sprinkle the nuts over the top. Continue baking the pie until the filling has set.

UNION PIE

2 cups sugar (scant)
2 cups sour cream
4 tablespoons flour
1 teaspoon soda

2 cups molasses
2 cups buttermilk
4 eggs, beaten
¾ teaspoon nutmeg

Mix together all the ingredients, then pour the mixture into 4 unbaked pie shells. Bake the pies at 400° for 10 minutes, then at 325° for 20 to 25 minutes or until a knife comes out clean.

FILLED RAISIN PIE

2 cups raisins
4 tablespoons flour
2 cups sugar
2 eggs, separated

2 cups water
1 teaspoon vinegar
1 teaspoon salt

Stew the raisins until they are soft. Add the flour, sugar, egg yolks, water, vinegar and salt. Let the mixture come to a boil while stirring it continuously. Allow it to cool before pouring it into a baked pie crust. Top the pie with meringue.

VANILLA PIE

1 cup molasses or maple syrup
1 cup brown sugar
2 cups hot water
1 egg, beaten
1 cup granulated sugar
½ cup lard

1 egg
1 cup sour milk or cream
2 cups flour
½ teaspoon soda
2 teaspoons baking powder

Cook together the molasses, brown sugar, hot water and beaten egg. Mix together the rest of the ingredients as you would for a cake batter. Divide the batter among 4 unbaked pie shells. Pour the previously prepared syrup over the batter and bake it at 400° for about 10 minutes, then reduce the heat to 350° and bake it until done. The cake will rise to the top during baking.

VANILLA CRUMB PIE

1 cup brown sugar
1 cup maple syrup
2 cups water
2 tablespoons flour

1 egg
1 teaspoon vanilla
½ teaspoon cream of tartar
1 teaspoon soda

Boil together for 1 minute the sugar, syrup, water and flour, then set the mixture aside to cool. In a bowl, beat together the egg, vanilla, cream of tartar and soda, then add this to the syrup mixture. Divide the filling equally into 3 unbaked pie shells. Top the pies with crumbs made from a mixture of the following.

2 cups pastry flour
1 cup brown sugar
½ cup lard

½ teaspoon soda
1 teaspoon cream of tartar

Bake the pies for 45 minutes at 350 to 375°.

GREEN TOMATO PIE

Green tomatoes, peeled, very thinly
  sliced
1½ cups sugar (1 cup white, ½ cup
  brown)

2 tablespoons flour
4 tablespoons vinegar
1 tablespoon butter
1 teaspoon cinnamon

Fill an unbaked pie shell with the tomatoes. (Remove the seeds if you wish.) Mix together the sugar, flour, vinegar, butter and cinnamon, then pour this mixture over the tomatoes. Cover it with a top crust and bake it at 425° for 15 minutes, then at 350° for 30 to 40 minutes.

HALF MOON PIES

1 quart apple snitz (dried pieces)
1½ cups water
1 quart applesauce

1½ cups brown sugar
½ teaspoon cinnamon
½ teaspoon salt

To make the filling, boil the apple snitz in the water until no water remains and the snitz is soft. Drain it in a colander. Add it to the applesauce, sugar, cinnamon and salt.

Make a pie dough (see page 167). For each pie, shape it to the size of a large egg. Roll it out thinly. Fold the dough over to make a crease through the center. Unfold it, and make 2 holes in the top part. On the other half of the dough place ½ cup of the filling. Wet the edges of the dough and fold it over, pressing the edges together. Cut off the remaining dough with a pie crimper. Brush the top with buttermilk or beaten egg, and bake it at 450° until brown.

Snitz Pie;

Put 2 or 2½ cups of this filling into an unbaked pie shell. Place another crust on top and bake it at 400° until the crust is done.

KATIE'S MINCE PIES

6 cups chopped apples
1 pint hamburger
1 cup raisins
3 tablespoons vinegar
1 tablespoon butter, melted

2 cups sugar
1 teaspoon cinnamon
1 teaspoon allspice
Salt to taste

Mix together all the ingredients, then pour the mixture into 2 unbaked pie shells. Bake them at 350° for 25 to 35 minutes.

APPLE FRITTERS

1 cup flour	½ teaspoon salt
2 tablespoons sugar	1 egg
½ cup milk	5 or 6 apples
1½ teaspoons baking powder	Icing sugar, or syrup

Make a batter by combining the flour, sugar, milk, baking powder, salt and egg. Core and peel the apples, then slice them and put them into the batter. Drop them by spoonfuls into 1 inch of fat or oil in a frying pan. Test the apples with a fork—they are done when soft. Drain them on paper towels or in a colander. Sprinkle the fritters with icing sugar or eat them with syrup. This recipe makes about 4 skillets full.

FRIED APPLE TURNOVERS

⅔ cup granulated sugar	1 package refrigerator biscuits, or
½ teaspoon cinnamon	biscuit mix (see page 254)
¼ cup butter or margarine	Icing sugar
2 cups sliced, pared, tart apples	

Combine the granulated sugar, cinnamon, butter and apples in a saucepan. Simmer this mixture, stirring it occasionally until the apples are tender. Separate the biscuits and roll each one to an oval shape, about 5 inches long. Place 1 tablespoon of the apple filling on ½ of the oval, then fold the dough over the filling and seal the edges with a fork. (Be sure they are well sealed or the filling will leak out.) Fry the turnovers in 375° hot deep fat for about 1 minute or until golden brown, turning them once. Drain them and sprinkle them with icing sugar, and serve them warm. This recipe makes 10 turnovers.

DESSERTS AND DESSERT SAUCES

HINTS FOR DESSERTS AND DESSERT SAUCES

- *When cooking tart fruit such as rhubarb, apricots, grapes or red raspberries, add a generous amount of cinnamon. For grapes, add vanilla too, for a different flavor.*

- *In a custard recipe calling for several eggs, 1 or more may be left out if ½ tablespoon of cornstarch is added for each egg omitted.*

- *Commercial whipped cream substitutes make twice as much as the directions say if the amount of milk is doubled. But make sure the bowl, egg beater and milk are very cold before beginning.*

- *Put graham crackers through the meat grinder to keep crumbs on hand for those busy days.*

- *Keep orange drink mix in a salt shaker, then sprinkle it on applesauce for a nice change in taste.*

BASIC CUSTARD RECIPE

1 cup scalded milk
1 tablespoon sugar
¼ teaspoon salt

1 beaten egg
1 teaspoon vanilla
Dash of nutmeg (optional)

Mix together the ingredients, then set the mixture in a pan of hot water to bake at 350° until done. To test if the custard is done, insert a knife in the center, and if it comes out clean, the custard is done. Do not let the custard boil.

This recipe may be expanded to suit one's needs.

Variations: Add chocolate (not cocoa) to the recipe for CHOCOLATE CUSTARD.

For LOW-CALORIE CUSTARD, use a low-calorie artificial sweetener and skimmed milk.

Try lemon flavoring instead of vanilla.

For CARAMEL CUSTARD, try using brown sugar instead of white.

GRAHAM CRACKER CUSTARD

18 graham crackers
½ cup butter
¼ cup sugar

Crush the crackers, then add the butter and sugar. Line a dish with these crumbs, saving a few to put on top.

¾ cup milk
3 eggs, separated
½ cup sugar

1 package (3 ounces) lemon or orange
   gelatin powder
½ to ¾ cup cream, whipped

Bring the milk to a boil and gradually add it to the egg yolks and sugar. Stir the mixture over low heat until the eggs are cooked, then remove it from the heat and add the gelatin. Stir to dissolve. Allow it to cool and partly set, then fold in the stiffly beaten egg whites and whipped cream. Pour this custard into the crumb-lined dish, sprinkle it with the reserved crumbs and chill it.

BASIC VANILLA PUDDING

¾ cup sugar
⅓ cup cornstarch
½ teaspoon salt
2 eggs, separated

½ cup cold milk
3½ cups milk, scalded
1 teaspoon vanilla
1 tablespoon butter

Combine the dry ingredients, then stir in the beaten egg yolks, and cold milk. Beat it into the hot milk and stir it over medium heat until it thickens. Add the vanilla and butter. Fold in the beaten egg whites, or top the pudding with meringue.

Variations: *For COCONUT PUDDING, use the above recipe and add 1 cup of coconut. Top the pudding with meringue and coconut.*

BAKED BERRY PUDDING

1 tablespoon butter
½ cup milk
1 teaspoon baking powder
½ cup sugar

1 cup all-purpose flour
1 cup sweetened berries
1 cup boiling water

Mix together the butter, milk, baking powder, sugar and flour to make a dough, then spread it in a greased, deep baking dish. Pour the berries and boiling water over the dough, and bake it at 400° until the cake part is done.

CHOCOLATE PUDDING

1 cup shortening	3 cups all-purpose flour
2 cups sugar	2 teaspoons soda
2 eggs	1 teaspoon salt
1 teaspoon vanilla	⅔ cup cocoa
1 cup buttermilk or sour milk	1 cup hot water

Mix together the ingredients until smooth, then add 1 cup of hot water. Pour this batter into a 13 x 9-inch pan.

1½ cups sugar	¾ to 1 cup hot water
2 tablespoons cocoa	

Mix together the above 3 ingredients, and pour the mixture over the cake batter. Bake it at 350° for 50 to 60 minutes.

This pudding is great with ice cream.

CHOCOLATE FUDGE PUDDING

3 tablespoons shortening	½ cup nuts, chopped
¾ cup sugar	1 cup brown sugar
1 cup all-purpose flour	¼ cup cocoa
½ teaspoon salt	¼ teaspoon salt
1½ teaspoons baking powder	1¼ cups boiling water
½ cup milk	

Cream together the shortening and ¾ cup of sugar. Sift together the flour, ½ teaspoon of salt and baking powder. Add this alternately with the milk to the creamed mixture. Fold in the nuts and pour the batter into an ungreased pan.

Mix together the brown sugar, cocoa and ¼ teaspoon of salt. Sprinkle this mixture over the top of the batter, but do not stir it in. Pour the boiling water over all, and again do not stir it. Bake the pudding at 350° for 40 to 45 minutes. Serve it with whipped cream.

COTTAGE PUDDING

¼ cup butter	2½ cups all-purpose flour
⅔ cup sugar	4 teaspoons baking powder
1 egg	½ teaspoon salt
1 teaspoon vanilla	1 cup milk

Cream together the butter and sugar and add the well-beaten egg and vanilla. Mix it well. Sift together the dry ingredients, then add them alternately with the milk to the first mixture. Pour it into a well-greased cake pan and bake it in a moderate oven (350°) for 35 minutes. Serve it with fruit and milk.

DATE PUDDING

1 cup chopped dates
1 cup boiling water
1 cup sugar
1½ cups all-purpose flour
½ cup chopped nuts

1 teaspoon butter
1 teaspoon vanilla
1 egg
2 teaspoons soda
½ teaspoon salt

Put the dates into a bowl and pour the boiling water over them. Let them set to cool a little, then add the other ingredients. Bake the pudding at 325° for 30 to 40 minutes, then allow it to cool. Chop it up before serving and mix whipped cream through it.

RICH DATE PUDDING

18 graham crackers, crushed
¾ cup chopped dates
¾ cup chopped nuts

12 marshmallows (chopped)
¼ cup cream

Mix the ingredients together well and pack the mixture in a dish or form it into a roll. Let it set for 12 hours in the refrigerator. Slice it and serve it with whipped cream.

DEPRESSION PUDDING

1 cup brown sugar
1 tablespoon butter or margarine
1½ cups raisins
4 cups boiling water
2 teaspoons vanilla
½ cup nuts (optional)

¼ cup butter or margarine
1 cup sugar
2 cups all-purpose flour
1 cup milk
4 teaspoons baking powder

To make the syrup, combine the first 6 ingredients and boil the mixture for 5 minutes. Pour it into a greased loaf pan. Combine the rest of the ingredients to make a batter, and dab it by tablespoons over the syrup. Bake it for 30 to 35 minutes at 350°, then serve it with whipped cream or milk.

Variations: For CINNAMON PUDDING, prepare the above recipe, but omit the raisins and add 1 teaspoon of cinnamon to the batter. Pour it into a greased pan and pour the syrup on top.

FLUFFY PUDDING

1 egg, separated
⅓ cup sugar
3 tablespoons tapioca

⅛ teaspoon salt
2 cups milk
¾ teaspoon vanilla

Beat the egg white until it is foamy. Gradually add 2 tablespoons of the sugar and beat it into soft peaks. Mix the rest of the sugar with the egg yolk, tapioca, salt and milk, and bring the mixture to a full boil. Very slowly add it to the beaten egg white, stirring rapidly to blend. Then add the vanilla. Let it cool for 20 minutes, then beat it well.

GRAHAM CRACKER PUDDING

Make alternate layers in a serving dish of graham cracker crumbs, Basic Vanilla Pudding (see page 190), and sliced bananas sprinkled with nuts (optional). Top it with whipped cream or sprinkle it with more crumbs.

Variations: Different desserts may be made by adding pineapple chunks, orange slices, strawberries or other fruit, or grapenuts and whipped cream.

STEAMED GRAHAM PUDDING

1 egg
1 cup sugar
1 cup sour milk
1 cup white flour
½ cup raisins

1 cup whole wheat flour
1 teaspoon soda
1 teaspoon cinnamon
2 tablespoons molasses
½ teaspoon salt

Mix together the above ingredients, and steam the mixture on top of the stove, preferably using a greased angel food cake pan covered and set in a large covered kettle. Simmer it for 1 to 1½ hours, then serve it warm with milk.

This is a delicious and economically made pudding.

STEAMED BANANA PUDDING

1¼ cups sugar
1 egg
¼ cup shortening
2 tablespoons molasses
2 cups pastry flour
2 cups mashed bananas

1 teaspoon baking powder
½ teaspoon soda
¼ cup milk
Cloves, cinnamon, ginger and nutmeg
  to taste

Mix together all the ingredients. Put the mixture into a pan and set it in hot water in a covered dish to steam for 2 hours.

CHERRY PUDDING

3 cups all-purpose flour
9 tablespoons butter
9 tablespoons sugar
1 teaspoon salt
3 teaspoons baking powder
1½ cups milk

1 teaspoon vanilla
3 cups pitted cherries
1½ cups water
¼ cup sugar
2 tablespoons flour

Work the first 5 ingredients together as you would for pie crumbs, then add the milk and vanilla. Stir this mixture with a fork until a soft dough is formed. Boil together the remaining ingredients before pouring the mixture into a pan and putting the dough on top. Bake it at 350° for about 1 hour or until done, then serve it hot with milk.

Variations: Other fruit may be used instead of the cherries. And instead of the dough, try using Biscuit Mix (see page 254).

RHUBARB PUDDING

1 egg
1 cup sugar
2 cups all-purpose flour
1 cup milk
2 teaspoons baking powder

1 teaspoon vanilla
4 cups rhubarb
2 cups sugar
2 cups boiling water

Mix together the egg, 1 cup of the sugar, the flour, milk, baking powder and vanilla. Place this dough in the bottom of a cake pan. Then mix together the rhubarb, 2 cups of the sugar and the boiling water. Pour this over the dough and bake it at 350 to 375° for 40 minutes or until done.

SODA CRACKER PUDDING

¼ cup butter
2 tablespoons peanut butter

½ cup brown sugar
18 square soda biscuits, crushed

Melt together the butter and peanut butter, then add it to a mixture of the sugar and cracker crumbs. Mix it well. Wet a bowl and press this mixture around the side and bottom. Reserve ¼ cup of the crumbs for the top.

Filling;

3 cups milk
2 eggs
2 tablespoons cornstarch

1 cup white sugar
1 teaspoon vanilla
½ cup coconut

Boil together until thick the first 4 ingredients, then add the vanilla and coconut. Pour this slowly onto the crumbs. When it has cooled, sprinkle it with the reserved crumbs.

STEAMED CHOCOLATE PUDDING

3 tablespoons melted butter
⅔ cup sugar
1 egg
1⅛ cups cake flour
2 teaspoons baking powder

⅛ teaspoon salt
¾ cup milk
4 tablespoons cocoa
1 teaspoon vanilla

Mix together the ingredients in the order given, then pour the mixture into a buttered double boiler. Cover and steam it for 2 hours.

RAISIN-NUT PUDDING

1 cup brown sugar
2 cups hot water
2 teaspoons butter
1 tablespoon cornstarch
½ cup sugar
2 tablespoons butter

1 cup milk
1 cup all-purpose flour
2 teaspoons baking powder
½ teaspoon salt
½ cup raisins
¼ cup nuts

Boil together for 5 minutes the first 4 ingredients, then pour this syrup into a cake pan. Mix the rest of the ingredients as you would a cake. Pour the batter onto the syrup. Bake it at 350° until a knife inserted comes out clean. Serve this pudding warm with milk or whipped cream.

CROW'S-NEST PUDDING

Make a cake batter with Basic Cake Mix (see page 251) or Handy Made Cake (see page 119). Pour 1 quart of sliced peaches into a buttered baking dish. Sprinkle 1 tablespoon of flour over them. Top this with the cake batter and bake it at 350° for 30 to 40 minutes. Serve it warm with top milk.

Variations: *Try substituting other fruit for the peaches.*

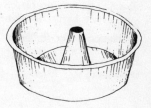

APPLE-CRANBERRY DUMPLINGS

Syrup;

2 cups water
2 cups sugar
½ teaspoon cinnamon

½ teaspoon cloves
½ cup butter

Combine the first 4 ingredients and boil the mixture for 5 minutes. Remove this syrup from the heat and add the butter.

Biscuit Dough;

2 cups all-purpose flour, sifted
1 teaspoon salt
1 tablespoon baking powder

2 tablespoons sugar
½ cup shortening
¾ cup milk

Sift together the dry ingredients and cut in the shortening. Gradually add the milk, tossing the mixture to make a soft dough. Roll it out on a floured board to form an 18 x 12-inch rectangle.

Filling;

4 cups grated, peeled apples
1 cup cooked, drained whole
   cranberries, OR
1 cup whole cranberry sauce

½ cup black walnuts, chopped

Spread the dough with the apples, cranberries and nuts. Roll it up like a jelly roll and cut it into 1-inch slices. Place them in a 13 x 9 x 2-inch pan. Pour the hot syrup over all and bake them in a hot oven (425°) for 40 minutes. Serve the dumplings warm.

APPLE GOODIE

½ cup sugar
2 tablespoons flour
¼ teaspoon salt
1 teaspoon cinnamon
1½ quarts apples, sliced
1 cup oatmeal

1 cup brown sugar
1 cup flour
¼ teaspoon soda
⅓ teaspoon baking powder
⅔ cup butter

Mix together the sugar, flour, salt and cinnamon, then add this mixture to the apples and mix it again. Put it on the bottom of a greased pan. Combine the rest of the ingredients until crumbly, then put this mixture on top of the apple mixture, and pat it firmly. Bake it at 350° until brown and a crust forms. Serve it with milk or cream.

Variations: For Rhubarb Goodie, use the above recipe but substitute 3 cups of diced rhubarb for the apples, and add 1 teaspoon of nutmeg and an extra cup of sugar.

APPLE DUMPLINGS

2 cups all-purpose flour
2½ teaspoons baking powder
½ teaspoon salt
⅔ cup shortening
½ cup milk

6 apples, peeled and halved
2 cups brown sugar
2 cups water
¼ cup butter
½ teaspoon cinnamon

Combine the first 5 ingredients to make a dough. Roll it out and cut it into squares, then place ½ apple on each square. Wet the edges of the dough and press it around the apple to form a ball. Set these dumplings in a pan.

Combine the rest of the ingredients to make the sauce. Pour it over the dumplings and bake them at 350° until the apples are soft and the dough is golden brown.

APPLE RICE BETTY

½ cup honey
¼ teaspoon cloves
1 teaspoon salt
¼ teaspoon cinnamon

1 cup cooked brown rice
4 large apples
½ cup chopped walnuts
2 tablespoons oil

Mix the honey with the spices. Grease a baking dish and place a thin layer of the rice in it. Add a layer of thinly sliced apples, and sprinkle it with the spiced honey and nuts. Repeat the layers until all the ingredients are used, saving some of the honey and nuts for the top. Pour the oil over the surface. Bake it at 350° until the apples are soft. This can be served hot or cold.

APPLE SURPRISE

1 package (3 ounces) gelatin powder
   (any flavor)
½ cup chopped celery
½ cup chopped dates

½ cup diced apples
1 cup drained pineapple
¼ cup chopped nuts
½ cup whipping cream, whipped

Prepare the gelatin according to the package instructions, then let it cool. When it has thickened slightly, fold in the fruit and the rest of the ingredients, adding the whipped cream last. Pour the mixture into a mold and refrigerate it. To serve, garnish it with mayonnaise.

MY OWN APPLE DESSERT

4 quarts washed, sliced cooking apples
1 cup raisins
1 teaspoon cinnamon

1½ cups sugar
2 tablespoons cornstarch
5 or 6 bananas

Put the apples into a large kettle and add the raisins, cinnamon, sugar and enough water to almost cover the fruit. Bring the mixture to a boil.

Mix the cornstarch with a little water, add it to the fruit mixture, then boil it until it thickens. Allow it to cool before slicing in the bananas.

APPLE-RHUBARB CRISP

2 cups finely cut apples
2 cups finely cut rhubarb
1 egg, beaten
¾ cup white sugar

¼ teaspoon nutmeg
½ cup butter or margarine
1 cup flour
1 cup brown sugar

Mix together the apples, rhubarb, egg, white sugar and nutmeg, then place the mixture in a glass baking dish. Combine the butter, flour and brown sugar to crumb consistency. Pack this over the apple/rhubarb mixture and bake it at 375° for 30 minutes. Serve it with sweetened milk or whipped cream.

Variations: Use 4 cups of apples and omit the rhubarb. Add ½ cup of nuts if desired.

SPICED APPLE DESSERT

1 cup brown sugar
1 cup all-purpose flour
½ teaspoon soda
1 teaspoon cinnamon
½ teaspoon baking powder
1 teaspoon nutmeg

1 teaspoon cloves
½ teaspoon salt
4 large apples, cubed or sliced
2 eggs, beaten
4 tablespoons butter

Combine the dry ingredients, then add the apples, egg and butter. Bake this mixture for 45 minutes at 350°. Serve it with milk and sugar when it has cooled.

AUNT CLARA'S DESSERT

1 package (3 ounces) raspberry gelatin
  powder
1 cup boiling water
1 cup pineapple juice
¼ cup butter
1½ cups icing sugar

2 eggs, separated
½ cup melted butter
¼ cup brown sugar
16 graham crackers, crushed
1 cup drained crushed pineapple

Dissolve the gelatin in the boiling water, then add the pineapple juice. Chill the mixture until it is slightly thickened. Cream together the ¼ cup of butter and icing sugar, and blend in the well-beaten egg yolks. Beat the egg whites until they are stiff but not dry, then fold them into the creamed mixture.

Combine the melted butter and brown sugar with the cracker crumbs. Put ½ of the crumb mixture into the bottom of a buttered 9-inch square pan. Spread it evenly with the egg mixture, then spread the pineapple over this filling. Sprinkle on the remaining crumbs, and pour the gelatin over top. Chill it until it is set, then cut it into squares. Top each serving with whipped cream. This recipe serves 9.

RAW APPLE PUDDING

Mix several cups of diced apples, about ¼ cup of chocolate shavings (or chips), nuts and broken homemade graham crackers with whipped cream.

BUTTERSCOTCH NUT TORTE

6 eggs, separated
1½ cups sugar
1 teaspoon baking powder
2 teaspoons vanilla
1 teaspoon almond extract

2 cups graham cracker crumbs
1 cup broken nuts
1 pint whipping cream
3 tablespoons icing sugar

Beat the egg yolks well before adding the 1½ cups of sugar, baking powder, vanilla and almond extract. Then beat the egg whites enough to hold a peak. Fold them into the egg yolk mixture, then add the crumbs and nuts. Line two 9-inch layer pans with waxed paper. Pour in the cake batter and bake it at 325° for 30 to 35 minutes. Allow the cake to cool. Whip the cream and sweeten it with the icing sugar before putting it between layers and on the top and sides. Cover the top with the following sauce.

1 cup brown sugar
¼ cup butter
¼ cup water
1 tablespoon flour

¼ cup orange juice
1 well-beaten egg
½ teaspoon vanilla

Mix the ingredients together well and boil the mixture until it is syrupy. When it has cooled, pour it over the whipped cream on the cake.

CHEESE CAKE

¾ cup graham crackers
½ cup sugar
¼ cup margarine
2 eggs

16 ounces cream cheese
1 teaspoon vanilla
1 cup sugar

Line the bottom of a 9 x 9-inch pan with crumbs made with the graham crackers, ½ cup of sugar and the margarine. Then beat the eggs, add the cream cheese and whip this mixture until it is smooth. Add the vanilla and 1 cup of sugar, then pour it on top of the crumbs. Bake it for 45 to 50 minutes at 300° or until the center is almost set. Top the cake with your favorite fruit pie filling—cherry, blueberry, raspberry, strawberry or any other fruit. Refrigerate it for several hours.

LEMON CHEESE CAKE

1 package (3 ounces) lemon gelatin
   powder
1 cup hot water
30 graham crackers
½ cup margarine

8 ounces cream cheese
1 cup sugar
1 teaspoon vanilla
1 large can evaporated milk, chilled, or
   1 cup whipping cream

Dissolve the gelatin powder in the hot water, then let it stand to thicken. Meanwhile, crush the graham crackers and blend in the butter. Line the bottom of two 8-inch cake pans with the crumbs, saving a few for the top. Soften the cream cheese and add the sugar and vanilla. Whip the cream or evaporated milk until it is thick. Add the cheese mixture and whipped cream to the gelatin which has by this time almost thickened. Beat this mixture until it is fluffy. Pour it into the pans lined with the graham cracker crumbs, and top it with the remaining crumbs. Refrigerate the cakes.

CORN PONE

1 cup corn meal
¼ cup all-purpose flour
1½ teaspoons baking powder
½ teaspoon salt

2 eggs
4 tablespoons sugar
½ cup milk
4 tablespoons shortening, melted

Mix together and sift the dry ingredients, except the sugar. Beat the eggs, then stir in the sugar and milk. Add the sifted dry ingredients and the shortening to the egg mixture. Bake it in a well-greased 9-inch-square pan at 425° for 25 minutes.

WHOLE WHEAT CORN BREAD

Dissolve 1 package or 1 tablespoon of yeast in 1 cup of lukewarm water. Let it set.

3 cups cornmeal
2 cups whole wheat flour
2 cups all-purpose flour
½ teaspoon soda
1 teaspoon salt
1 cup sweet milk

¾ cup soft homemade butter
6 unbeaten eggs
¼ cup baking molasses
¾ cup honey
¾ cup grapefruit juice, OR
¼ cup sweet pickle juice

Mix together the above ingredients and add the yeast. Then pour it into 2 greased 13 x 9 x 2-inch cake pans, let it set until double in size, and bake it at 350° for about 30 minutes or until done. Serve this bread with strawberries or honey. It can be frozen after it has been baked.

Variations: If you use pickle juice in this recipe, add approximately 1½ cups of water instead of milk to make a medium thick cake batter.

CHERRY CRISP

2 tablespoons flour
1 cup sugar
1 teaspoon grated lemon rind
  (optional)

½ cup cherry juice
2 cups drained, unsweetened cherries

Mix together the flour, sugar, lemon rind and juice. Add this to the cherries and put the mixture into a buttered baking dish. Mix lightly into crumbs the following ingredients, and spread it over the cherry mixture.

1 cup sugar
¾ cup flour

7 tablespoons butter
¼ teaspoon nutmeg

Bake this for about 30 minutes in a medium hot oven (375°), and serve it with whipped cream or sweet milk.

Variations: Other fruit besides cherries may be used.

CHERRY ROLLS

1 egg
¾ cup sour cream
2 cups all-purpose flour
¾ teaspoon salt
¼ teaspoon soda

2½ teaspoons baking powder
2 tablespoons butter
2 cups drained cherries
2 tablespoons sugar
1 teaspoon cinnamon

Beat the egg, then add the sour cream. Sift the flour, and add the salt, soda and baking powder before sifting this mixture again. Add it to the egg mixture and stir well. Toss the dough onto a slightly floured board and roll it into an oblong piece ¼ inch thick. Spread it lightly with the soft butter, cover it with the cherries, and sprinkle it with the sugar and cinnamon. Roll it up like a jelly roll and cut it into 1½-inch thick slices. Place them cut side up, close together in a greased 9-inch-square baking pan.

⅓ cup brown sugar
⅓ cup white sugar
1½ tablespoons cornstarch
1½ cups cherry juice

Red coloring, a few drops
½ teaspoon almond flavoring
1½ tablespoons butter

Combine the dry ingredients before adding the liquid, coloring and flavoring. Bring this mixture to a boil, and when it has thickened slightly, add the butter and pour it over the slices in the baking pan. Bake them at 375° for 25 minutes. This recipe makes 12 cherry rolls.

EASY MILK DESSERT

Boil a can of sweetened condensed milk in a kettle of water for 3½ hours. Set it in a cool place to chill, then open both ends and push out the contents. Slice it and put each slice on top of pineapple slices. Add a spoonful of whipped cream, and garnish it with a red maraschino cherry.

This is a handy dessert. You can boil as many as you wish and set them on your pantry shelf for unexpected company.

GRAHAM CRACKER FLUFF

Filling;

1 package gelatin
⅓ cup cold water
½ cup sugar
¾ cup rich milk

2 eggs, separated
1 teaspoon vanilla
1 cup cream, whipped

Soak the gelatin in the cold water. Mix together the sugar, milk and egg yolks. Cook this mixture in a double boiler until the egg yolks are cooked (10 minutes), stirring it constantly. Remove it from the heat, then add the gelatin and vanilla. Chill it until the mixture begins to thicken. Then fold in the egg whites which have been beaten until stiff and the whipped cream.

Crumbs;

1½ tablespoons butter
3 tablespoons brown sugar

12 graham crackers, crushed

Melt together the butter and brown sugar, and mix it with the graham cracker crumbs. Line the bottom of a dish with ½ of the crumbs, then pour in the filling. Put the remaining crumbs on top, and set it in a cool place to chill.

MAPLE SPONGE

2 cups brown sugar
1½ cups hot water
½ teaspoon maple flavoring
1 package gelatin

½ cup cold water
Vanilla pudding
1 cup whipped cream

Boil together for 10 minutes the sugar, hot water and maple flavoring. Soak the gelatin in the cold water for a few minutes, then mix it with the hot syrup. Let it set until it is almost firm, then whip it until it is light and fluffy. Using this sponge, your favorite vanilla pudding, and the whipped cream, put spoonfuls of the three alternately into a serving dish. Nuts or bananas may also be added.

MISSISSIPPI MUD

1 tablespoon butter (heaping)	4 tablespoons flour
1½ cups brown sugar	2½ cups milk
½ cup water	1 teaspoon vanilla
3 eggs, separated	12 graham crackers

Melt the butter and brown it. Add the sugar and water and boil it to make a syrup. Mix the egg yolks, flour and milk. Gradually add ½ cup of hot syrup to the egg mixture and return the whole mixture to the syrup, beating constantly. Bring it to a boil and cook it until thickened. Add the vanilla, then put it into a dish. Roll the graham crackers and spread the crumbs on top. Spread it with the beaten egg whites and a few graham cracker crumbs. Brown it slightly.

OATMEAL BROWN BETTY

1 cup whole wheat flour	½ cup shortening, scant
½ teaspoon salt	2½ cups sliced apples
½ cup brown sugar	¼ cup raisins
½ teaspoon soda	Butter
1 cup rolled oats	½ cup corn syrup or honey

Mix together the dry ingredients, then cut in the shortening until the mixture is crumbly. Spread ½ of it in a baking dish, and cover it with the apples and raisins. Put the remainder of the crumbs on the top to cover the apples and raisins. Dot the top with butter, and drip the corn syrup or honey over it. Bake it in a moderate oven (350°) for 35 minutes or until the apples are soft. Serve it with milk.

Variations: Other fruit may be substituted for the apples.

PEACH PETZ

1 cup all-purpose flour	2 tablespoons butter
½ teaspoon baking powder	¾ cup sugar
¼ teaspoon salt	⅓ cup flour
⅓ cup shortening	14 peach halves (canned)
3 to 5 tablespoons cold water	

Combine the 1 cup of flour, baking powder and salt. Cut the shortening into this mixture, then add the water slowly and mix it, using only enough water to hold the dough together. Chill it, then roll it out a little thicker than pie dough and put it into a large pie plate or cake pan.

Mix together the butter, sugar and ⅓ cup of flour for the filling. Sprinkle ½ of this mixture over the dough. Place the peaches (cut side down) on the dough and cover them with the remaining crumbs. Pour the peach juice over top. Bake it at 375° for 35 minutes or until the crust is brown. Serve it with milk.

TWO-EGG BOSTON CREAM PIE

1 cup sugar	1¾ cups cake flour
1 egg	1 teaspoon soda
½ cup sour cream	2 teaspoons baking powder
½ cup milk	

Mix the ingredients to make a batter, then bake it at 350° in 2 layer cake pans. When the cakes have cooled, split the layers and fill them with the following filling.

¾ cup sugar	1 pint milk
1 egg yolk	1 tablespoon flour
1 tablespoon cornstarch	Vanilla

Mix these ingredients in a saucepan and cook the mixture until it is thick and smooth. Cover the pie with brown sugar frosting.

Variations: Try adding 1½ teaspoons of grated lemon peel, lemon extract or 4½ teaspoons of lemon juice to the filling.

QUICK SYRUP KNEPP

1 cup brown sugar or maple syrup	1 tablespoon butter
2½ cups water	1 teaspoon vanilla

To make the syrup, bring the above ingredients to a boil in a 10-inch-wide cooker.

2 cups all-purpose flour	4 teaspoons baking powder
½ cup brown sugar	½ teaspoon salt
3 tablespoons lard	1 egg
¾ cup milk	

To make the dough, mix the above ingredients as you would for biscuits or pie dough, stirring the mixture lightly. Add it by the spoonful to the boiling syrup. Cover it and let it simmer for 20 minutes. Do not remove the cover at any time during the cooking process. Serve it with milk.

Variations: Cocoa may be added to the syrup or the dough, or both. When you add cocoa to the dough, peaches are especially good in the syrup.

Try adding sliced apples to the syrup.

Make the above dough without the sugar, and drop it onto hot stewed fruit. Follow the cooking directions above.

RASPBERRIES WITH KNEPP

2 cups whole raspberries or juice
¾ cup sugar
2 cups water
3 level tablespoons cornstarch
1 cup all-purpose flour

5 teaspoons baking powder
3 teaspoons sugar
¼ teaspoon salt
1 cup milk

Bring the first 3 ingredients to a boil. Mix the cornstarch with enough water to make a smooth sauce, then stir it into the hot raspberry mixture and bring it to a boil.

Mix together the rest of the ingredients to make a dough, and drop it by spoonfuls into the boiling raspberry mixture. Cover it with a tight lid and let it boil slowly for 20 minutes. Do not uncover it during the boiling period. Serve it with milk.

Variations: Elderberries or other fruit may be used instead of raspberries.

RHUBARB CRUNCH

1 cup whole wheat flour
1 cup brown sugar
1 teaspoon cinnamon

¾ cup oatmeal
½ cup melted butter

Mix together the above ingredients until crumbly, and put ½ of the mixture into a greased 9-inch pan. Cover it with 4 cups of diced rhubarb.

1 cup sugar
2 tablespoons cornstarch

1 cup water
1 teaspoon vanilla

Combine these ingredients and cook the mixture until it is clear. Pour it over the rhubarb. Top it with the remaining crumbs and bake it at 350° for 45 minutes or until the rhubarb is tender.

RHUBARB TAPIOCA

1 cup tapioca (pearl)
2 cups cold water
Cinnamon (optional)
3 cups hot water

2 cups rhubarb
2 cups sugar
1 can (14 ounces) crushed pineapple

Soak the tapioca in the cold water overnight or for a couple of hours. Then add cinnamon if desired, and the remaining ingredients. Cook this mixture, stirring it constantly until the tapioca is clear or nearly clear.

SARAH SCHWARTZ'S RHUBARB ROLLS

2 cups flour
1 teaspoon salt
2 teaspoons baking powder
3 tablespoons lard
⅞ cup sweet milk
Soft butter
Granulated sugar

Rhubarb, finely cut
Dash of nutmeg
1 cup sugar
1 heaping tablespoon flour
¼ teaspoon salt
1 cup hot water
Small lump of butter

Sift together the flour, salt and baking powder. Cut the lard into this mixture, add the milk and mix it well. Roll this dough out ¼ inch thick, spread it thickly with soft butter, granulated sugar and rhubarb, and sprinkle it with nutmeg. Roll up the dough as you would cinnamon rolls and cut it into 1½ to 2-inch slices.

Mix together the rest of the ingredients and boil the mixture for 3 minutes to make a sweet sauce. Place the dough slices in a pan and pour this sauce over and around them. Bake them at 350° until brown.

Variations: Diced apples may be used instead of rhubarb.

FRUIT TAPIOCA

1 small package gelatin powder
  (any flavor)
¼ cup minute tapioca
2½ cups water, fruit juice, or syrup
  from canned fruit

¼ teaspoon salt
½ to ¾ cup sugar

Mix together the ingredients and let the mixture stand for 5 minutes. Bring it to a boil over medium heat, stirring it often. Allow it to cool for 20 minutes, then add any fruit desired. This recipe makes 6 servings.

WEDDING TAPIOCA

9 cups water
½ teaspoon salt
1½ cups tapioca (baby pearl)
1 cup sugar

2 small packages pineapple gelatin
  powder
1 small package orange gelatin powder
1 small package lemon gelatin powder

Bring the water and salt to the boiling point. Add the tapioca and boil it until it is clear, stirring it constantly. Remove it from the heat and stir in the sugar and gelatin. Chill this mixture.

Variations: Whipped cream, nuts or fruit such as pineapple, bananas or orange slices may be added if desired.

VANILLA SOUFFLE

¼ cup butter, melted
¼ cup flour
1 cup milk, scalded

¼ cup sugar
3 eggs, separated
1 teaspoon vanilla

Make a white sauce of the butter, flour, milk and sugar. Add the beaten egg yolks and vanilla, and mix these ingredients thoroughly. Then fold in the stiffly beaten egg whites. Pour the mixture into a greased soufflé dish, set it in a pan of hot water and bake it in a moderate oven (350°) for 40 to 45 minutes or until the soufflé is firm to the touch.

SHORTCAKE

2 cups all-purpose flour
4 teaspoons baking powder
¾ teaspoon salt
1 tablespoon sugar

⅓ cup shortening
⅔ cup milk
1 egg, beaten

Make crumbs with the flour, baking powder, salt, sugar and shortening. Add the milk and egg to the crumbs, then spread the mixture into a small cake pan. Make the following topping and spread it on top of the batter before baking it at 350° until done. Serve this cake with fresh fruit and milk.

½ cup sugar
½ cup flour
3 tablespoons butter

Mix together these ingredients.

WHOLE WHEAT SHORTCAKE

1 pound granulated sugar
1 pound whole wheat flour
1 pound pastry flour
1 teaspoon salt

1 quart buttermilk or sour milk
1 tablespoon soda
1 teaspoon vanilla
2 tablespoons melted butter

Put the dry ingredients, except for the soda, into a bowl. Combine the buttermilk and soda, then add it to the dry ingredients. Add the vanilla and butter last. Mix it well to create a dough that is not too thick. Bake it at 350° until done, then serve it with milk.

SUDDEN COMPANY DESSERT

Pour 3 cups of canned, thickened cherries into a graham cracker crust. Top it with whipped dessert topping, or whipped cream mixed with white cream cheese. Sprinkle graham cracker crumbs on top.

CREAMY VANILLA SAUCE

¼ cup sugar
⅛ teaspoon salt
1 teaspoon flour

1 egg, beaten
1 cup light cream or top milk
1 teaspoon vanilla

Combine the sugar, salt and flour, then stir in the egg. Gradually stir in the cream or top milk. Cook this mixture over medium heat, stirring it constantly until it thickens and coats a spoon. Remove it from the heat and stir in the vanilla. This recipe makes 1⅓ cups.

VANILLA TOPPING

2 egg whites
1 teaspoon vanilla
¾ cup light corn syrup

Beat together the egg whites and vanilla, and gradually add the syrup while still beating. Continue to beat the mixture until it is stiff and holds peaks.

This topping may be used on pies and desserts as a substitute for whipped cream.

DANISH FRUIT DESSERT SAUCE

1½ cups juice or water
¼ cup gelatin powder (any flavor)
⅓ cup white sugar

¼ teaspoon salt
1½ tablespoons cornstarch

Heat to boiling 1 cup of the juice or water. Combine the gelatin, sugar, salt and cornstarch. Make a paste of it with the remaining ½ cup of liquid, then stir it into the boiling juice until it is thick and clear. Cook it for about 1 minute, then pour it over a mixture of drained, canned fruit. Chill it well.

ICE CREAM AND TOPPINGS

ICE CREAM

4 quarts rich milk
4 cups sugar (brown or white)
¾ teaspoon salt
2 tablespoons flour

2 tablespoons cornstarch
4 eggs, beaten
Cream or canned milk (optional)

Heat together the 4 quarts of milk, the sugar and salt. Mix the flour, cornstarch and eggs with enough cream or milk to make a smooth sauce, then stir it into the heated milk mixture and bring it to a boil. Add the vanilla and allow it to cool thoroughly before freezing. This recipe makes 6 quarts.

CHOCOLATE CHIP ICE CREAM

2 teaspoons melted butter
2 squares (2 ounces) sweet chocolate
2 teaspoons sugar

Mix the ingredients together in a saucepan. Put it on medium heat and stir it until the chocolate is melted. After the ice cream you have made is frozen (see Vanilla Ice Cream, page 211), open the freezer can, and with a long spoon make several holes on each side of the dasher as far down as you can. Dribble in the chocolate mixture and quickly close the freezer, giving it a few turns to turn the chocolate back into chips. This recipe makes enough chocolate for 1½ gallons of ice cream.

DAIRY QUEEN

2 envelopes unflavored gelatin
½ cup cold water
4 cups whole milk
2 cups sugar

2 teaspoons vanilla
1 teaspoon salt
3 cups cream

Soak the gelatin in the cold water. Heat the milk until it is hot but not boiling, then remove it from the heat. Add the gelatin, with the sugar, vanilla and salt. Let it cool before adding the cream. Chill it in the refrigerator for 5 or 6 hours before freezing.

This recipe makes 1 gallon. The ingredients may be varied to suit your taste.

Gelatin can be bought by the pound at some health food stores. It is much cheaper that way.

JUNKET ICE CREAM

1 quart cream, OR
1 pint cream plus 1 pint top milk
18 large marshmallows
5 eggs, well-beaten
2 cups sugar

2 tablespoons vanilla
½ gallon milk
½ teaspoon salt
6 junket tablets
¼ cup lukewarm water

Heat together but do not boil the cream and marshmallows until the marshmallows are melted. Add the combined eggs, sugar and vanilla, then the milk and salt. Pour this mixture into an ice cream freezer can. Add the junket tablets to the lukewarm water, then add this to the ice cream in the freezer can. Let it set for about 20 minutes before freezing it.

Variations: *Two boxes of junket mix or instant pudding may be used instead of the junket tablets.*

ORANGE PINEAPPLE ICE CREAM

9 eggs (or fewer), beaten
3¾ cups white sugar
½ package orange drink mix
14 ounces crushed pineapple or juice

1 quart rich milk
Cream or milk
3 junket tablets, dissolved

Beat together thoroughly the eggs and sugar, then add the drink mix and pineapple. Pour this mixture into an ice cream freezer can followed by the heated rich milk. Add cream or milk to fill the can to several inches from the top. Add the dissolved junket tablets and stir. Let it set for 15 minutes, then freeze it. This recipe makes 6 quarts.

Variations: *Omit the pineapple and orange drink mix and use vanilla or lemon flavoring.*

Try brown sugar instead of white.

GELATIN ICE CREAM

4 cups milk
5 eggs
2 tablespoons flour
2½ cups sugar
2 envelopes unflavored gelatin

1 cup cold water
2 cups whipping cream
2 tablespoons vanilla
Milk

Heat the 4 cups of milk to boiling. Beat the eggs together and add the flour and ½ cup of the sugar. Stir this into the boiling milk and cook it for 1 minute, stirring constantly. Pour it over the remaining sugar which has been measured into a large bowl. Dissolve the gelatin in the cold water, and pour it into the egg mixture. Add the cream and vanilla and enough milk to fill a 1 gallon ice cream freezer can to within 2 inches of the top. Freeze it. This makes 4 quarts.

Variations: The eggs may be omitted and 2 more cups of cream added. Or this can be made without any cream at all for a less rich ice cream.

Any flavor of gelatin may be used, using 1 box (3 ounces) of fruit gelatin powder for 1 envelope of unflavored gelatin.

VANILLA ICE CREAM

1 quart milk
2 cups sugar
½ cup cornstarch
¼ teaspoon salt
1 cup cold milk
4 egg yolks

2 tablespoons milk
1 package unflavored gelatin
3 teaspoons cold milk
1 quart thick cream
1 teaspoon vanilla
4 egg whites, well-beaten

Scald the 1 quart of milk, then add the sugar, cornstarch and salt which have been blended into the 1 cup of cold milk. Cook this mixture until it is thick. Add the egg yolks which have been mixed with the 2 tablespoons of milk, then cook it for 1 minute. Add the gelatin which has been soaked in the 3 teaspoons of cold milk. Remove the cooked custard from the stove and let it cool. Add the cream, vanilla and well-beaten egg whites, then freeze it. This recipe makes 1 gallon.

Variations: For CHOCOLATE ICE CREAM, mix ½ cup of cocoa with a little boiling water, and add it to the above recipe before freezing it.

Instead of cocoa, try adding crushed fruit.

FROZEN CUSTARD

1 quart milk
6 to 8 egg yolks, well-beaten
1 cup white sugar
1 cup brown sugar
½ teaspoon salt
1 pint milk

1 cup white sugar
1 package unflavored gelatin
½ cup cold water
1 large can evaporated milk
1 pint cream

Put the 1 quart of milk into a double boiler and add the egg yolks, 1 cup of white sugar, 1 cup of brown sugar and salt. Cook this mixture until it coats a spoon. In another pan heat the 1 pint of milk and add the 1 cup of white sugar, and the gelatin which has been soaked in the cold water. Combine the mixtures and add the milk and cream. Freeze it.

CHOCOLATE TOPPING

1 cup hot chocolate mix
⅓ cup milk

1 teaspoon vanilla
1 tablespoon butter

Mix the chocolate powder and milk. Cook it over medium heat until it boils, then boil it for 3 minutes, stirring it constantly. Remove it from the heat, add the vanilla and butter, and allow it to cool.

HOT CHOCOLATE SAUCE

1 cup white sugar
3 tablespoons cocoa
½ teaspoon salt

1 cup water
3 tablespoons flour
1 teaspoon vanilla

Combine the sugar, cocoa, salt, water and flour. Cook the mixture for 3 minutes before adding the vanilla.

BUTTERSCOTCH TOPPING

1 cup brown sugar
2 tablespoons corn syrup

¼ cup rich milk
3 tablespoons butter

Combine the ingredients and heat the mixture until it boils, stirring constantly. Then simmer it for 3 minutes.

HOT FUDGE SAUCE

1½ cups evaporated milk
2 cups sugar
4 squares (4 ounces) unsweetened
   chocolate or cocoa, or less

½ teaspoon salt
¼ cup butter
1 teaspoon vanilla

Heat the milk and sugar to a rolling boil, stirring constantly. Boil it for 1 minute. Add the chocolate and salt, stirring the mixture until the chocolate is melted. Then beat it with a rotary beater until it is smooth. Remove it from the heat and stir in the butter and vanilla. Serve this sauce hot on ice cream, or chill it if desired. This recipe makes about 3 cups.

STRAWBERRY TOPPING

1 quart mashed strawberries
1 quart sugar

1 package pectin crystals
1 cup boiling water

Stir together the strawberries and sugar until the sugar is melted. Dissolve the pectin crystals in the boiling water, bring it to a boil and immediately stir it into the berry mixture. Stir it for 5 minutes, then put it into jars and freeze it.

BREAKFAST TREATS

BUCKWHEAT CAKES

2 cups buckwheat flour
2 eggs, beaten
2 teaspoons sugar
2 teaspoons baking powder

⅛ teaspoon salt
1½ cups milk
½ cup water

Mix together the ingredients and bake the batter on a hot griddle.

YEAST BUCKWHEAT CAKES

1 cake yeast
1 quart lukewarm water (approximate)
2 tablespoons sugar or molasses
2 teaspoons salt
2 tablespoons melted shortening

1 pint sifted buckwheat flour
1 pint sifted whole wheat flour
½ teaspoon soda
2 tablespoons warm water

Dissolve the yeast in 1 cup of the lukewarm water, add 1 teaspoon of the sugar and let it set for about 5 minutes. Dissolve the salt and the rest of the sugar in the remaining water, then add the shortening, dry ingredients and yeast mixture. Beat it until it is smooth. Let it rise in a warm place until it is light and full of bubbles. This will take about 1 hour or more depending on the temperature. Then dissolve the soda in the warm water and stir it into the batter. Bake the cakes thoroughly on a heated griddle and serve them with butter and syrup.

If the cakes are wanted for breakfast, prepare the batter the evening before, using only ½ cake of yeast. Do not keep it too warm. Add the soda and 2 tablespoons of warm water in the morning before baking.

EASY PANCAKES

2 cups self-rising flour
½ cup buttermilk
2 eggs

2 tablespoons sugar
1 tablespoon melted shortening
Milk

Mix together the ingredients and add enough milk to make a batter of the right consistency. Fry the pancakes on a lightly greased griddle.

CORNMEAL PANCAKES

2 cups all-purpose flour
½ cup cornmeal
½ cup whole wheat flour
 1 teaspoon soda

½ teaspoon salt
2 eggs, beaten
Buttermilk or sour milk

Combine the ingredients and add buttermilk or sour milk for the desired batter consistency: use more milk for thinner cakes, less for thick cakes.

Syrup;

Bring to a boil 2 parts brown sugar to 1 part water. Add maple flavoring. Use the syrup while it is warm.

GRAHAM CAKES

1 cake yeast
2 cups warm milk
2 teaspoons brown sugar or molasses

3 eggs, separated
3 tablespoons shortening, melted
1¼ cups whole wheat flour

Dissolve the yeast in the warm milk with the brown sugar or molasses. Stir together the egg yolks, shortening and flour, then add the yeast mixture. Set it in a warm place to rise for 2 hours. Fold in the beaten egg whites just before frying.

GRIDDLE CAKES

1⅓ cups all-purpose flour
2 tablespoons sugar
3 teaspoons baking powder
3 tablespoons melted shortening or oil

1 egg
¾ teaspoon salt
1¼ cups milk

Combine all the ingredients and mix them well. Lightly grease a skillet for the first griddle cakes only. Fry them until they are puffy and bubbly, turning to brown the other side. Then serve them hot with butter and maple syrup. This recipe yields ten 6-inch griddle cakes.

PANCAKE SYRUP

1¼ cups brown sugar
¾ cup white sugar
⅓ cup molasses or corn syrup

1 cup water
1 teaspoon vanilla
Maple flavoring (optional)

Bring the sugars, molasses and water to a boil, stirring the mixture constantly. Simmer it on low heat for 5 minutes. Remove it from the heat and add the vanilla.

OATMEAL PANCAKES

2 cups all-purpose flour
2 cups whole wheat flour
2 cups quick oats
1 tablespoon each of baking powder,
   soda, salt

3 eggs, separated
½ cup cooking oil
1½ quarts sweet milk (approximate),
   warmed to lukewarm

Mix together thoroughly the dry ingredients. Add the egg yolks, oil and lukewarm milk, and mix. Fold in the beaten egg whites. Pour the batter onto a preheated, ungreased griddle, using about ¼ cup for each pancake. Turn the pancakes once.

WHOLE WHEAT PANCAKES

1½ cups whole wheat flour
½ tablespoon baking powder
¾ teaspoon salt
1 teaspoon soda

3 tablespoons brown sugar
2 eggs, beaten
1½ cups buttermilk
3 tablespoons melted shortening

Thoroughly mix together the dry ingredients. Combine the eggs, buttermilk and shortening, then add this mixture to the dry ingredients, and mix it until it is smooth. Fry the pancakes on a hot, lightly-greased griddle.

WAFFLES (CORNMEAL, RYE OR WHOLEWHEAT)

	Cornmeal	Rye	Whole Wheat
all-purpose flour	1½ cups	1 cup	
other flour	1½ cups cornmeal	2 cups rye	2 cups whole wheat
baking powder	1 tablespoon	1 tablespoon	2 teaspoons
salt	1½ teaspoons	1½ teaspoons	1 teaspoon
oil	⅓ cup	⅓ cup	¼ cup
milk	3 cups	3 cups	2 cups
eggs	5	5	4

Make a batter with the flours, baking powder, salt, oil and milk. Separate the eggs and add the yolks to the batter, then beat the whites until stiff and fold them. Bake the batter using a waffle iron. For pancakes, use a little less liquid.

GRANOLA

10 cups oatmeal
2 cups wheat germ
2 cups coconut
1 to 2 cups brown sugar
1 small package almonds

½ cup vegetable oil
½ cup honey
2 teaspoons vanilla
1 teaspoon salt

Mix together the ingredients and pour the mixture into shallow pans. Toast it at 275° for 30 to 40 minutes or until golden brown, stirring it occasionally.

Variations: There is no end of ideas on how the Granola recipe can be altered. Each person changes it according to his or her family's tastes. Following are a few suggestions.

—*For PEANUT BUTTER GRANOLA, heat the oil and honey until it is lukewarm, then stir in ⅓ to ½ cup of peanut butter.*

—*Add nuts (walnuts, pecans or whatever you prefer), wheat germ or coconut after the Granola has been toasted.*

—*Add about 1½ cups of water to the Granola and mix it, then toast.*

—*Omit the wet ingredients.*

—*Add any of the following: whole wheat flour, sesame seeds, sunflower seeds or 1 to 2 teaspoons of cinnamon.*

—*Coarse rolled oats can be used to make Granola more crunchy.*

—*Raisins and dates are also a delicious addition.*

COOKED GRAHAM CEREAL

1 cup cracked whole wheat kernels
4 cups boiling water
1 teaspoon salt

Into a pan measure the cracked whole wheat kernels, boiling water and salt. Boil this mixture for ¼ to ½ hour, stirring it occasionally. Remove it from the heat and cover it. Let it stand until it is ready to serve. Continue cooking it if the desired texture has not been reached. Serve this cereal hot with sugar and milk.

Variations: Graham Meal is also delicious. The flavor is greatly improved by using freshly ground whole wheat flour. Follow the above directions, but note that this need not be cooked so thoroughly.

Some people prefer Whole Kernel Wheat Cereal. It takes longer to cook but is an old-fashioned, chewy breakfast cereal.

Cooking the brown sugar with the cereal gives it a caramel flavor.

KALONA GRAPENUTS

5 cups flour
2 cups sugar
3 teaspoons salt
3 cups sour milk

6 cups graham flour
2½ cups cane molasses
3 teaspoons soda

Combine the ingredients to make a dough that is thick and hard to stir. Spread it in a shallow pan, and bake it at 250° for 1½ to 2 hours.

Put this into a plastic bag to avoid hard crusts. When needed, crumble it into grapenuts according to the Sieve directions (see page 219).

TOBE'S GRAPENUTS

5 pounds brown sugar
8 pounds whole wheat flour
1¼ tablespoons salt
2 tablespoons soda

2½ quarts buttermilk or sour milk
¾ pound margarine (melted)
1½ teaspoons maple flavoring
2 tablespoons vanilla

Put all the dry ingredients but the soda into a bowl, then add the milk in which the soda has been dissolved. Add the margarine and flavorings last. Mix this well. The thickness varies a little with your own whole wheat flour and store bought flour.

The dough should be fairly thick. If it is too thick, add a little more milk, and if it is not thick enough, add more whole wheat flour until it is of the right consistency.

Put the dough into pans and spread it evenly with a spoon or spatula. Bake it at 350° until done, then crumble it into grapenuts according to the Sieve instructions (see page 219). This recipe makes approximately 15 pounds.

SIEVE

This implement is required to crumble the grapenuts you have made. Make a strong rigid frame, approximately 14 x 14 inches. Over the top of this, stretch a ¼-inch wire mesh. Tack it in place, then put the frame over a large pan.

Cut the grapenuts into small pieces and rub them through the wire screen as soon as they have cooled. Spread the crumbs in pans and put them into a slow oven (250°) to toast to a golden brown. Stir them occasionally.

An inverted deep fat frying basket can also be used as a sieve.

Variations: A crumbling sieve is handy for cleaning shelled peas. Roll the peas over the screen and the dirt will fall through.

BREAKFAST CRUNCH

1 cup rolled oats	1 teaspoon soda
1 cup cornmeal	2 teaspoons salt
3 cups whole wheat flour	1½ cups milk
½ cup sugar	¾ cup molasses
2 teaspoons baking powder	

Mix together the dry ingredients. Heat the milk and add the molasses, then mix it with the dry ingredients. Bake this mixture in a shallow pan in a moderate oven (350°). Let it cool and slice it into strips, then when it is dry, grind it finely.

CREAMY OATMEAL

2 cups coarse oatmeal
½ teaspoon salt
1 quart cold milk

Heat water in the bottom of a double boiler to boiling. Into the top part put the oatmeal, salt and milk, then put it over the boiling water for 30 minutes. It may be stirred once or twice, if desired.

COFFEE CAKE

½ cup very warm (not hot) water	1 cup milk
1 teaspoon white sugar	1 cup lukewarm water
1 tablespoon yeast	¾ cup oil or other shortening
2 eggs	1 cup white sugar
1 teaspoon salt	3 cups all-purpose flour

Stir the teaspoon of white sugar into the very warm water, then add the yeast. Let it set in a warm place while beating the eggs. Add the salt, milk, lukewarm water, oil and 1 cup of white sugar. Stir in the yeast mixture, then add the egg mixture. Mix in the flour, slowly adding more until the dough is smooth and elastic. Let it rise until it is double in size, then punch it down. Let it rise again before cutting and putting it into 4 round pans. Bake it at 350° for 20 to 30 minutes. Sprinkle brown sugar, cinnamon or nutmeg on top if desired.

EGG ON TOAST

Spread 1 tablespoon of butter over the bottom of a small hot frying pan. Lay a piece of bread in the butter and break an egg on top of it. With a fork break the yolk and spread the egg over the bread. Sprinkle it with salt and pepper. When the bread is toasted, turn it over to fry the egg side for 1 or 2 minutes.

This is good served at lunch with mayonnaise and lettuce on top of the egg.

GOLDEN EGG

Make a Basic White Sauce (see page 49) while 4 pieces of bread are toasting. When the sauce is done, slice in 4 hardcooked eggs, reserving 1 yolk. Pour the sauce over the toast on individual plates. Press the remaining yolk through a strainer and sprinkle it over the sauce as a garnish.

Variations: Chipped beef or ham may be added to the sauce.

FRENCH TOAST

2 eggs
¾ cup milk
Bread slices

Butter
Salt

Beat the eggs before adding the milk, then dip pieces of bread into the mixture. Melt and lightly brown butter in a pan, and add the coated bread pieces, sprinkling them with salt. Fry them until brown on both sides. Serve French Toast with syrup or jam.

CANDIES

BUCKEYES

1 pound peanut butter
1½ pounds icing sugar
1 cup margarine

1 package (12 ounces) chocolate chips
½ stick paraffin

Mix the peanut butter and sugar like pie dough, then add the margarine. Roll the mixture into balls and chill them thoroughly. Then melt the chocolate chips and paraffin, and dip the balls into this mixture.

CANDY KISSES

3 cups brown sugar
½ cup water
Pinch of salt

1½ teaspoons rootbeer extract
1 egg white

Cook the sugar, water and salt until it spins a thread when dropped from a spoon. Add the extract and pour it over the stiffly beaten egg white, beating while pouring. Continue to beat it until the mixture is quite stiff, then drop it by teaspoonfuls onto waxed paper.

Variations: Instead of 3 cups of brown sugar, 2 cups of maple sugar and 1 cup of brown sugar may be used.

CARAMEL CORN

2 cups white sugar
¾ cup white corn syrup or sorghum
2 tablespoons vinegar
2 tablespoons water

¼ teaspoon salt
1 teaspoon soda
1 cup peanuts (whole or chopped)
5 quarts popped corn

Melt and lightly brown the sugar. Place it over low heat when it is almost finished to prevent scorching. Then add the syrup, vinegar, water and salt. Boil the mixture to a very hard ball when tested in cold water, so that it can be snapped into pieces. Remove it from the heat, add the soda and peanuts and stir it well. Pour it immediately over the warm popped corn. Stir it a few minutes until all the popcorn is coated, then stir it occasionally until it is cold.

CARAMELS

1 cup white sugar	½ cup cream
½ cup brown sugar (firmly packed)	1 cup milk
½ cup light corn syrup	¼ cup butter

Combine the ingredients and cook the mixture over low heat to 246°, stirring it constantly. Add 2 teaspoons of vanilla and pour it into an 8-inch square greased cake pan. Let it cool, then turn it out and cut it into squares. Wrap each piece in waxed paper.

GOLDEN POPCORN

1 cup sugar	1 teaspoon vinegar
½ cup baking molasses (dark)	¼ teaspoon soda
½ cup corn syrup	5 quarts popped corn
1 tablespoon butter	1 cup peanuts
2 tablespoons water	

Mix together the sugar, molasses, syrup, butter, water and vinegar. Cook the mixture until it forms a hard ball (265°) when dropped into cold water. Stir it frequently during the last part of cooking to prevent scorching. Remove it from the heat and add the soda, then stir it lightly. While it is still foaming, pour it over the popcorn and peanuts and mix them together. Pour the mixture into a buttered, flat pan, and when it has cooled, crumble it into small pieces.

POPCORN TREAT

1 quart corn syrup	½ pound butter
3 cups white sugar	1 teaspoon cream of tartar
2 cups brown sugar	Salt to taste

Boil the ingredients together to the hard crack stage (290°) on a candy thermometer. Into a large, buttered bowl pour the mixture over a lard can (4 gallons) of popped corn and stir it.

The popcorn may also be made into balls. Grease your hands well with butter or margarine and shape it into balls immediately, before the coated popcorn cools.

Use the following measurements with 2 gallons of popcorn.

2 cups corn syrup	¼ pound butter
1½ cups sugar	½ teaspoon cream of tartar
1 cup brown sugar	1 teaspoon salt

HOCOLATE-COVERED CHERRIES

p sifted all-purpose flour
up brown sugar
up butter or margarine
easpoon salt

18 maraschino cherries, well drained
and halved
6 squares (6 ounces) semi-sweet
chocolate, melted

nbine the flour and sugar. Cut the butter and salt into the flour mixture until it resembles a
dough. Press it into an 8 x 8 x 2-inch pan, and bake it at 350° for 20 minutes. While it is
m, cut it into 36 squares. Cool and place them in a pan lined with waxed paper. Place a
rry half on each square and cover each cherry with a spoonful of melted chocolate. Chill
m for a few minutes until the chocolate hardens.

UMMY CHOCOLATE SQUARES

package marshmallows
package (12 ounces) semi-sweet
chocolate bits
tablespoons butter

1 teaspoon vanilla
1 cup broken walnut meats
½ teaspoon salt
1 cup crisp rice cereal

elt the marshmallows, chocolate and butter over low heat, stirring the mixture constantly
til all is melted. Mix in the remaining ingredients and spread it in a well-buttered 8-inch pan.
ut it into squares after it sets.

FUDGE MELTAWAYS

½ cup butter
square (1 ounce) unsweetened
chocolate
¼ cup sugar
1 teaspoon vanilla

1 egg, beaten
2 cups graham cracker crumbs
1 cup shredded coconut
½ cup chopped nuts

Melt the butter and chocolate in a saucepan. Blend the sugar, vanilla, egg, graham cracker
crumbs, coconut and nuts into the butter/chocolate mixture. Mix it thoroughly and press it
into an 11½ x 7½ x 1½ baking dish or a 9 x 9-inch square pan. Refrigerate it while making the
filling as follows.

¼ cup butter
1 tablespoon milk or cream
2 cups sifted icing sugar

1 teaspoon vanilla
1½ squares (1½ ounces) unsweetened
chocolate, melted

Cream together the butter, milk, sugar and vanilla. Mix and spread it over the crumb mixture,
then chill it in the refrigerator. Pour the melted chocolate over the chilled mixture and spread it
evenly.

POPCORN BALLS

1 cup sugar
½ cup white or dark corn syrup
⅓ cup water
¼ cup butter

¾ teaspoon salt
¾ teaspoon vanilla
3 quarts popped co

Keep the popcorn hot in a slow oven. Stir and cook together the s
butter and salt until the sugar is dissolved. Continue cooking the m
until the syrup forms a soft ball (236°). Add the vanilla, then pour th
popped corn. Mix it well to coat every kernel. Grease your hands
shaping the mixture into balls. This recipe makes 12 medium-sized

CHEERIOS BARS

½ cup light corn syrup
1 package (6 ounces) semi-sweet
  chocolate pieces

1 teaspoon vanilla
4 cups Cheerios

Heat the syrup to boiling, then remove it from the heat. Stir in the chocol
until the chocolate is melted. Add the Cheerios and stir them until they ar
mixture into a 9 x 9 x 2-inch buttered pan. Let it cool for 1 hour before sli
recipe makes 3 dozen.

CHOCOLATE BALLS

1 square (1 ounce) unsweetened
  chocolate
1 can sweetened condensed milk

12 to 18 graham crackers
Coconut, shredded

In a double boiler, melt the chocolate, adding the milk. Remove it from the
crushed crackers. Form the mixture into balls and roll them in the cocon

CHOCOLATE CANDY

3 cups sugar
3 cups milk
5 tablespoons cocoa

1 tablespoon butter
1 teaspoon vanilla

Boil together the sugar, milk and cocoa, stirring it while it is on the stove. Boil the
soft ball stage. Remove it from the heat and add the butter and vanilla. Stir it un
then pour it onto a buttered plate and cut it into squares when it has cooled

CREAMY-SURE FUDGE

⅔ cup (1 small can) evaporated milk
16 marshmallows, OR
1 cup Marshmallow Creme
  (see page 228)
1⅓ cups sugar

¼ cup butter or margarine
¼ teaspoon salt
2 cups semi-sweet chocolate pieces
1 teaspoon vanilla
1 cup coarsely chopped walnuts

Mix the first 5 ingredients in a saucepan, stirring the mixture constantly. Heat it to boiling and boil it for 5 minutes only. Remove it from the heat, then add the chocolate, stirring until it is melted. Stir in the vanilla and walnuts. Spread the mixture in an 8-inch pan and cool it until firm. This recipe makes about 2 pounds of fudge.

SNOWY FUDGE

2 cups sugar
⅔ cup milk
1½ cups peanut butter

1 cup Marshmallow Creme
  (see page 228)
1 teaspoon vanilla

Cook the sugar and milk to 234° or until the syrup forms a soft ball which flattens when removed from water. Add the other ingredients and mix them well. Pour the mixture into a buttered 8 x 6 x 2-inch pan.

This candy can be stored for months and still be soft and edible.

STORE-AWAY FUDGE

4½ cups sugar
½ cup butter or margarine
1 can condensed milk
2 large chocolate bars
2 cups chocolate chips

1 pint marshmallows
1 teaspoon vanilla
½ teaspoon black walnut flavoring
  (optional)
½ cup chopped nuts (optional)

Bring the first 3 ingredients to a boil, then boil the mixture for 7 minutes or until the soft ball stage. Remove it from the heat and add the chocolate bars (cut into small pieces), chocolate chips, marshmallows (cut into pieces), vanilla, and flavoring and nuts if desired. Beat the mixture until it is smooth and pour it into a pan as you would regular fudge.

MARSHMALLOWS

2 cups sugar
¾ cup boiling water
2 envelopes unflavored gelatin
½ cup cold water
½ teaspoon salt

1 teaspoon vanilla
Icing sugar
Chopped nuts (optional)
Coconut (optional)

Boil together the sugar and water until a thread forms when the syrup is dropped from a spoon. Remove it from the heat. Soften the gelatin in the cold water, then add it to the hot syrup and stir it until the gelatin is dissolved. Let it stand until it is partly cool, then add the salt and flavoring. Beat it until the mixture becomes thick, fluffy and soft.

Pour it into an 8 x 4-inch pan thickly covered with icing sugar. Have the mixture 1 inch in depth. Let it stand in the refrigerator until it is thoroughly chilled. With a sharp, wet knife, loosen it around the edges of the pan. Turn it out onto a board lightly floured with icing sugar. Cut it into squares and roll them in icing sugar, chopped nuts or coconut.

MARSHMALLOW CREME

2 cups sugar
2½ cups corn syrup
1 cup water

½ cup warm corn syrup
3 or 4 egg whites
1 teaspoon vanilla

Cook the sugar, corn syrup and water to 242° (a medium-hard ball when tested in cold water). While this is cooking, place in a mixing bowl the warm syrup and the egg whites. Beat them slowly until they are mixed, then beat the mixture hard until it is light and fluffy. Pour the first mixture into this in a fine stream. When all is mixed, beat it hard for 3 minutes before adding the vanilla. Store it in cans or jars, but do not cover it until it is cold.

MINT CANDY

2 cups sugar
¼ cup butter
⅔ cup cold water

Mint flavoring
Food coloring

Boil the ingredients to 267 to 270°, then add flavoring and coloring. Pour the mixture onto a buttered marble slab or greased cookie sheet. Pull it like taffy, then roll it in icing sugar on brown paper. Cut the candy into squares and put it into jars. It will mellow in a day or two.

The candy can be made in different flavors—anise, wintergreen, peppermint and so on, and the coloring can be added according to the flavor.

HARD TACK CANDY

1¾ pounds white sugar
1 cup water
1 cup corn syrup

Cook the ingredients together to 280°, then add coloring. Leave the mixture on the heat until it reaches 290°, then remove it and add ⅛ ounce of the chosen flavoring (peppermint, spearmint, wintergreen, thyme, anise, cinnamon etc.—make each flavor a different color). Pour it at once onto a greased cookie sheet or marble slab. As soon as it is cool enough to work with (you can begin cutting at the edges almost immediately) cut it with scissors into strips and various-sized pieces.

IDA'S FONDANT CANDY

3 cups sugar
1 cup corn syrup
½ cup hot water

1 cup sugar
½ cup hot water
2 egg whites

Combine the first 3 ingredients in a saucepan and boil the mixture until it spins a thread. Do the same for the next 2 ingredients. Whip the egg whites until they are stiff, then slowly beat in the second mixture until it stiffens again. Add the first mixture to this, and beat it until it cools.

It may then be divided into parts so that different flavors can be added as desired. Then form the candy into shapes and dip it into melted chocolate.

MACAROONS

⅔ cup sweetened condensed milk
3 cups shredded coconut
1 teaspoon vanilla

Mix together the milk and coconut. Add the vanilla and drop the mixture by spoonfuls about 1 inch apart onto a greased baking sheet. Bake them in a moderate oven (350°) for 10 minutes or until delicately browned. Remove the macaroons from the pan at once. This recipe makes 30 macaroons.

OPERA CREAMS

1½ cups sugar
½ cup cream

2 tablespoons butter
1 square (1 ounce) chocolate

Boil the ingredients together to a soft ball (236°), testing it in cold water. Remove it from the heat and add 1 teaspoon of vanilla. Let it cool without stirring, then beat it until it becomes light in color. Drop it onto waxed paper.

PEANUT BRITTLE

1½ cups sugar
½ cup white corn syrup
⅔ cup water
1½ cups raw peanuts

½ teaspoon salt
2 tablespoons butter
1 teaspoon soda
1 teaspoon vanilla

In a 4-quart saucepan, combine the sugar, corn syrup and water. Cook this mixture to the soft ball stage (238°) on a candy thermometer, stirring it only until the sugar is dissolved. Add the peanuts and salt. Cook the mixture to the hard crack stage (290°), then remove it from the heat. Add the butter, soda and vanilla. Stir it thoroughly and pour it at once onto a well-buttered sheet or slab. Spread it thinly and let it cool before breaking the candy into pieces.

CHOCOLATE PEANUT CLUSTERS

½ pound sweet chocolate
⅔ cup sweetened condensed milk
1 cup peanuts

Melt the chocolate in the top of a double boiler over boiling water. Remove it from the heat, add the condensed milk and peanuts, and mix them well. Drop the mixture by teaspoons onto waxed paper, and allow it to cool.

NUTTY BARS

2 cups white sugar
1 cup corn syrup

1 cup water
¾ cup peanut butter

Cook the above ingredients until the mixture forms a hard ball when tested in cold water. Let it stand until cool, then add the peanut butter. Stir it until it is cold. Shape the mixture into rolls as thick as your thumb and 2 inches long.

1 cup corn syrup
½ cup brown sugar

2 pounds ground peanuts
Melted semi-sweet chocolate

Cook the syrup and sugar together until the mixture forms a hard ball when tested in cold water. Dip the previously prepared rolls into this mixture, then roll them in the ground peanuts while the coating is still hot. Coat them with melted semi-sweet chocolate.

SWEETENED CONDENSED MILK

Boil together 1 part sugar to 2 parts milk until the mixture thickens. This should occur at 225°, or 'jelly' on a candy thermometer.

ROCKY ROAD SQUARES

3 pounds milk chocolate
½ pound soft butter

10 ounces miniature marshmallows
3 pounds walnuts, broken

Melt the chocolate and stir it until it is smooth. Add the butter and mix it well (it will be thick but warm). Set the mixture in a cold place until it thickens around the edges, stirring it occasionally while it cools. Then put it in a warm place and stir it for 5 to 10 minutes until it becomes creamy and thinner. Add the marshmallows and walnuts. Pour the mixture onto a waxed paper-lined cookie sheet, and press it to a ¾-inch thickness. Let it cool to room temperature, then cut it into squares.

TAFFY

1 quart white sugar
1 pint cream
1 tablespoon gelatin dissolved in
¼ cup cold water

1 tablespoon paraffin
1 pint light corn syrup

Combine all the ingredients and boil the mixture until it forms a hard ball in cold water when dropped from a tablespoon (250° on a candy thermometer). Pour it onto a well-greased cookie sheet. When it is cool enough to handle, start pulling it. When an ivory color is obtained, pull the taffy into a long thin rope and cut it with kitchen scissors.

DRINKS

CANNING APPLE OR PEAR JUICE

Heat the juice, but do not boil it. Remove any scum with a spoon. Fill bottles or jars and seal them. Set them in hot water and bring them to the boiling point, then remove them from the water immediately.

By not boiling apple juice, it retains its fresh flavor.

CHOCOLATE SYRUP

4 cups brown sugar
2 cups cocoa
½ cup corn syrup
4 cups white sugar

2 cups water
2 cups water
4 tablespoons or ¼ cup vanilla

Mix the first 5 ingredients in a 6-quart kettle until all are blended. Add the remaining 2 cups of water and stir the mixture again. Bring it to a boil and boil it for 5 minutes. (Be careful as it is likely to boil over.) Add the vanilla. If you do not can the syrup, cover it until it is cool or a crust will form over the top. This makes approximately 3 quarts.

It will keep for 8 months (or through the school year) if it is put boiling hot into jars and sealed.

GRAPE JUICE

5 pounds grapes
1 pound sugar
1 quart water

Wash and stem the grapes, then add the water and boil them for 10 minutes. Strain, but do not press them. Add the sugar, stirring until it is dissolved, then bring the mixture to a boil. Bottle the juice. Add water before serving, about 50%.

Concord or Fredonia grapes are best for juice.

Variations: For GRAPE SAUCE, put the pulp through the sieve, add sugar to taste, and can the sauce.

233

CONCORD GRAPE JUICE

Wash fully ripened Concord grapes and spoon them into a quart jar until it is ⅓ full. Add 1 cup of sugar and water to fill the jar. Seal it and boil for 10 minutes.

FRUIT PUNCH

3 cups sugar
3 quarts water
4 large cans frozen orange juice

4 large cans frozen lemonade
1½ cups strong tea
4 quarts ginger ale

Boil together the sugar and water. Let it stand until it is cool, then add the frozen orange juice, frozen lemonade, tea and ginger ale. Add water to taste. This recipe makes enough for 75 people.

RHUBARB JUICE

Cut rhubarb coarsely. Cover it with water and boil it for 2 minutes. Drain off the juice. Cover the cooked rhubarb a second time with water, then bring it to a boil and drain it again. The rhubarb may be sweetened for canning.

Rhubarb juice may be added to other fruit juices, or with a little lemon juice to meadow tea for a deliciously refreshing cold drink.

QUICK ROOT BEER

2 cups white sugar
1 gallon lukewarm water

4 teaspoons root beer extract
1 teaspoon dry yeast

Dissolve the sugar in some hot water, then combine it with the rest of the ingredients. Put the mixture into jars, cover them and set them in the sun for 4 hours. The root beer will be ready to serve the next day. Chill it before serving. (There is no need to bottle it.)

ICED TEA SYRUP

4 cups boiling water
1 cup loose tea
2½ cups sugar

Let the tea steep in the boiling water for 15 minutes. Strain it, then add the sugar and boil it for about 10 minutes. This will make a quart of syrup, or 1 gallon of iced tea, depending on the strength desired.

To use it, put 1 tablespoon of the syrup in a glass, then fill it with water and ice.

GOLDEN PUNCH

7 packages orange drink mix
4 large cans frozen orange juice
5 large bottles (28 ounces each) lemon-
   lime soft drink

Mix the drink mix according to package instructions, then combine it with the rest of the ingredients. This makes 5 gallons.

GOOD LUCK PUNCH

1 quart rhubarb (2 dozen stalks)
Water to cover
3 cups sugar
2 cups water

Juice of 6 lemons
1 cup pineapple juice
Rhubarb juice
1 quart ginger ale

Cut the rhubarb into 1-inch pieces. Add enough water to cover it. Cook it until soft, for about 10 minutes, then drain it through a cheesecloth bag. This should produce approximately 3 quarts of juice. Dissolve the sugar in the 2 cups of water and cook it for 10 minutes to make a syrup. Add the lemon, pineapple and rhubarb juices. Pour this over a chunk of ice in a punch bowl, and just before serving, add the ginger ale. This recipe makes 1 gallon of punch.

SUMMER SPARKLE PUNCH

2 packages (3 ounces each) strawberry
   gelatin powder
2 cups boiling water

2 cans (12 ounces each) frozen
   lemonade, slightly thawed
3 bottles (28 ounces each) ginger ale

Dissolve the gelatin powder in the water, stir in the lemonade and add the ginger ale. This recipe makes 1 gallon.

PEPPERMINT WATER

Sweeten a pitcher of cold water. Dip a toothpick into a bottle of peppermint oil, then swish it off in the water. Do this a few times until the right strength is obtained. Stir the water before tasting it. (Synthetic peppermint oil is not recommended.)

This is a healthy drink and good on hot days for people working under the sun.

INSTANT SPICED TEA

2½ cups sugar
2 cups instant powdered orange drink
½ cup instant tea

2 teaspoons cinnamon
2 teaspoons cloves
2 large packages instant lemonade mix

Mix the ingredients together, and store the mixture in tightly sealed containers. To use it, place approximately 2 teaspoons of the mix into each cup of boiling water.

This is sometimes called Russian Tea. You may add to or reduce the amount of spices and lemonade mix according to family taste.

TOMATO COCKTAIL

1 peck tomatoes
2 bunches celery
2 green peppers
1 bunch parsley

6 small onions
1 cup sugar
¼ cup salt
½ teaspoon pepper (scant)

Cook the vegetables together until they are soft, then put them through a sieve. To the vegetable juice add the sugar, salt and pepper, then pour the liquid into sterilized jars. Cold pack them for a few minutes.

VEGETABLE DRINK

2 quarts celery
2 to 4 red beets
6 carrots
4 onions

Juice of 3 lemons, plus grated rind
2 gallons tomato juice
Salt to taste

Cook the celery, beets, carrots and onions separately until they are very soft. Mash them very finely, strain and add the lemon juice and rind and tomato juice. Add salt to taste, then cold pack the juice in jars for 10 minutes.

LEFTOVERS

LEFTOVER BREAD

Cut leftover bread into cubes and toast it in pans in the oven, stirring it a few times. When it is toasted and well dried out, store it in tightly sealed containers. It can be used in soups, dressings, tossed salads (adding them just before serving) and many other dishes.

Leftover bread can also be dried out completely over the stove, and stored in lard cans or jars. When you are ready to use it, place the bread slices in the steamer and steam them until they are heated through. Serve the bread warm. If you have no steamer, use a colander over a pan of hot water, and keep it covered.

You can pour bacon grease over pieces of leftover bread or toast, then let it harden. Put a string through the center of the bread and tie it to a tree branch for birds.

CHOCOLATE BREAD CUSTARD

2 squares (2 ounces) unsweetened
   chocolate
3 cups scalded milk
4 cups bread crumbs

¾ cup sugar
¼ teaspoon salt
3 eggs, well-beaten

Combine the chocolate and milk, then heat and stir the mixture until the chocolate melts. Add the bread, sugar and salt. Slowly stir this into the beaten eggs. Pour it into a greased 10 x 6 x 2-inch pan and set this pan in a pan of hot water. Bake it in a moderate oven (350°) for about 50 minutes or until a knife inserted comes out clean. Serve this custard warm with Creamy Vanilla Sauce (see page 208).

Old-Fashioned Bread Custard;

Omit the chocolate and add 1 teaspoon of nutmeg. Less sugar may be used if desired (⅓ cup).

LEFTOVER BUTTERMILK

Pour 1 cup of fresh water into your leftover buttermilk before storing it. Pour off the water which comes to the top when you are ready to use the buttermilk again.

LEFTOVER CAKE

Make large crumbs of leftover cake and put them into a serving dish. Cover them with the following sauce.

Nutmeg Sauce;

2 cups water
¼ cup sugar
3 tablespoons flour

2 tablespoons butter
⅛ teaspoon nutmeg

Mix the first 3 ingredients and bring them to a boil. Boil the mixture for a few minutes, stirring it constantly. Add the butter and nutmeg. Let it cool before pouring it over the cake crumbs. Sliced bananas or nuts may be added.

LEFTOVER HOMEMADE CANDY

Leftover candy and candy that did not turn out right can be used for cake frosting. Add water or milk to the candy and place it over low heat to melt it. Mix it to the right consistency.

LEFTOVER COOKED CEREAL

Stir milk into leftover cooked cereal before storing it. Serve it as a dessert by adding whipped cream, apples, raisins or other raw fruit. Leftover cake crumbs or apple roll may also be added.

LEFTOVER CREAM OF WHEAT OR ROLLED OATS

These may be added to hamburger or sausage. Mix it thoroughly and make it into patties or a loaf.

LEFTOVER CHEESE

Old cheese turns into a delicious spread when it is processed through a meat grinder with several chunks of onion.

LEFTOVER MACARONI

If there is not enough macaroni to go around, toast bread cubes in butter in a frying pan. Add the macaroni and enough milk to soak into the bread and to keep the macaroni from burning. Heat the mixture.

Leftover macaroni may also be added to vegetable soup, chili soup, potato salad or stews.

LEFTOVER COLESLAW

This is good when it is cooked before serving. Add a white sauce made with 1 tablespoon of flour and ½ cup of cream.

LEFTOVER FRUIT

FRUIT CAKE

1½ cups brown sugar
2 teaspoons soda
2 cups all-purpose flour
½ teaspoon salt

2 cups fruit (canned or fresh), mashed
2 eggs
½ cup salad oil

Sift together the brown sugar, soda, flour and salt. Make a well and add the fruit, eggs and oil. Mix these ingredients, then bake the batter at 350°. When it is done, top it with the following icing and return it to the oven for a few minutes.

¼ pound butter
¼ cup evaporated milk

¾ cup brown sugar
¾ cup chopped nuts

Combine the butter, milk and brown sugar, and cook the mixture for 1 minute before adding the nuts.

To use up leftover fruit syrup from canned fruit, add an equal amount of water to the syrup and thicken it with tapioca (3 tablespoons tapioca to 1 pint of liquid). A pinch of salt and a package of flavored gelatin powder adds to the taste. Whipped cream may also be blended into the cooled tapioca.

LEFTOVER PANCAKE BATTER

Do not throw out leftover batter. Add a little milk to make it thinner, then dip your hamburgers or other meat into the batter and fry them in hot oil.

LEFTOVER PICKLE JUICE

Save your leftover pickle juice for recanning. Use it for making relish, sandwich spread, or to can red beets (adding more vinegar, sugar, etc.) or make salad dressing. When you use the juice in salad dressing, omit the vinegar and sugar in the recipe.

LEFTOVER PICKLED BEET JUICE

Hardcooked eggs are good when left overnight in pickled beet juice.

LEFTOVER CHURCH CHEESE

Cut up the cheese and put it in the top of a double boiler. Add 2 tablespoons of margarine or butter and 1 tablespoon of water. Boil it until the cheese is melted. Pour it into wide-mouthed jars and seal them. Cold pack the jars for ½ hour, or until the cheese looks smooth. When you are ready to use it, put the jar into warm water until the cheese loosens from the sides of the jar—it will slide out easily. Slice and serve it.

LEFTOVER MACARONI AND CHEESE

Beat 2 eggs and add a little salt and 1½ cups of milk. Pour this over 4 to 5 cups of macaroni and bake it at 350° until brown. Extra cheese may be sprinkled on top if desired.

LEFTOVER NOODLES

Put about 1 or 2 tablespoons of grease into a frying pan. When it has melted, sprinkle in about 1 tablespoon of flour with a flour shaker. Cut the leftover noodles into slices and lay them in the floury grease. Fry them.

Leftover noodles are also good when added to vegetable soup.

LEFTOVER PIE DOUGH

HANS WASCHTLIN

Roll out the dough thinly. Spread it with apple butter and roll it up like a jelly roll. Cut it into ½-inch slices. Lay them on a pie pan with the cut side down, and bake them at 350° for 20 to 25 minutes.

These are a real treat for children.

SUGAR PIES

Roll out the dough thinly, then fit it into a small tin foil pan or any 4 to 6-inch pan. Onto the crust put 2 tablespoons of brown sugar, 1 tablespoon of flour, ½ cup of water and nutmeg to taste. A bit of cream may be added. Mix it with your finger or the back of a spoon, and bake it at 350° until the crust is done.

This makes a great treat for children.

BROKEN, BAKED PIE CRUSTS

These can be refreshed by putting them into the oven for a few minutes. Add them to applesauce just before serving. Then stir in cream (whipped or unwhipped) and blend. Cinnamon may also be added.

LEFTOVER POTATOES

To make Potato Filling with leftover mashed potatoes, cook the greenest part of 1 stalk of celery and 1 chopped onion. With juice and all, pour it over the mashed potatoes and mix. Add 2 eggs and milk according to the amount of potatoes used. Then add 4 or 5 slices of cubed bread which have been toasted in 2 tablespoons of butter. Pour the mixture into a buttered baking dish and bake it for about 1 hour at 350°. Leftover corn, peas, lima beans or diced meat may be added.

To approximately 2 cups of leftover mashed potatoes, add 3 eggs, ⅓ cup milk, 1 small chopped onion, 2 or 3 slices of bread made into crumbs and salt and pepper to taste. Mix everything together and put it into a hot, buttered skillet. Cover the mixture and heat it slowly.

Cold sweet potatoes are good when sliced very thinly, dipped into a beaten egg with a little salt added, then into flour. Quickly brown the slices in a skillet. Other potatoes may be treated in the same way.

Potato Salad may be made with leftover mashed potatoes, adding other ingredients the same as you do for salad made with diced potatoes.

FRIED POTATOES

Use fried, cooked or mashed potatoes. Put them into a hot greased frying pan and chop them. Beat an egg or two with a fork, pour it over the potatoes and fry them. (One tablespoon of flour blended with 1 beaten egg and ¾ cup of milk may be added instead of the 2 beaten eggs.) If there are not enough potatoes, toast bread cubes in the pan first, then add the potatoes. Add salt and pepper.

POTATO CAKES

2 cups medium grated, peeled, cooked
   potatoes, or mashed potatoes
2 eggs
½ teaspoon salt

1 medium onion, chopped
Dash of pepper
⅛ to ¼ cup chopped, leftover bologna
   or dried beef (optional)

Mix together the above ingredients, then fry the mixture as you would pancakes.

POTATO CHEESE PIE

Crust;

2 to 2½ cups leftover mashed potatoes
2 tablespoons flour
1 teaspoon baking powder

1 egg
2 tablespoons melted butter
Salt and pepper

Mix the ingredients thoroughly, then pat the mixture into a large, greased pie plate as you would dough.

Filling;

2 eggs
1 cup cream

Salt and pepper
¾ cup grated Velveeta cheese

Beat the eggs, then stir in the cream and seasonings. Pour this into the potato crust and sprinkle the top with the cheese. Bake it at 350° for 20 minutes or until a knife inserted in the center comes out clean.

POTATO PUFFS

1 cup leftover mashed potatoes
1 or 2 beaten eggs
¼ teaspoon salt

¼ to ½ cup flour
1 teaspoon baking powder

Mix the ingredients together well and drop the mixture by the ½ teaspoon into deep fat. Fry the puffs until brown on both sides.

POTATO SOUP

Cook a small chopped onion until it is soft. Add milk as desired. When it is hot, mix some in with leftover mashed potatoes until blended. Pour all back into the remainder of the milk, and heat it to the boiling point. Add a chunk of butter and a bit of chopped parsley, salt and pepper.

LEFTOVER SQUASH

Squash may be added to caramel pudding by mashing it and adding it to the milk.

It can also be used in pumpkin pie recipes, or made into custard by eliminating the crust. Just set the casserole into a pan of hot water to bake.

LEFTOVER RICE

This, like leftover cereal, can be prepared as a dessert. Prepare the Basic Custard Recipe (see page 189) then add leftover rice, and bake.

GLORIFIED RICE

2 cups boiled rice

1 cup pineapple, cubed or crushed

½ cup sugar

24 marshmallows

1 cup chopped apples

1 cup whipped cream

Cook the rice until it is soft, but not mushy. Let it cool. (Leftover rice can be used.) Mix together all the ingredients but the whipped cream and let it stand for 1 hour. Fold the whipped cream into the mixture just before serving. Garnish it with candied cherries.

LEFTOVER VEGETABLE AND MEAT DISHES

Use your leftover meat, potatoes, gravy and vegetables by placing them in layers in a pan or casserole. Add meat broth or tomato juice, herbs or spices. Make a plain biscuit dough and drop it by spoonfuls into the mixture and bake. Serve it with applesauce.

Mix together all your leftovers. Add beaten eggs, some milk and diced onions, and season the mixture well. Put it into a greased baking dish and bake it at 350° until bubbly.

Leftover meat, potatoes and vegetables can be made into dressing by adding diced toast, eggs, milk and seasoning.

Add canned hamburger to leftover meat gravy or tomato gravy. Add leftover string beans, put leftover potatoes on top and sprinkle paprika over the potatoes. Bake it at 350° until it is heated through.

Bits of leftover ham can be ground and mixed with bread crumbs which have been soaked in a milk and egg mixture. Shape the mixture into patties and fry them. This makes real hamburgers.

LEFTOVER CHICKEN

Cook macaroni until it is soft. Mix it with diced leftover chicken and gravy. Put the mixture into a baking dish and add milk to cover it. Season it with salt and pepper and top it with bread crumbs. Bake it at 350° for about 20 to 30 minutes.

LEFTOVER BEEF

Grind any leftover beef. Brown butter in a saucepan and add a little milk. To this, add the ground beef and enough milk to make the meat stick together. Stir in 1 tablespoon of flour and 1 egg. Drop the mixture by tablespoons into cracker or bread crumbs, coating it well. Then fry it in hot fat.

LEFTOVER ROAST BEEF

Prepare 1 package of onion soup mix according to the package directions, and add peeled chopped carrots. Cook it until the carrots are tender. Thicken it with a flour and water paste. Add sliced, cooked roast beef, then pour it into a greased casserole. Top it with mashed potatoes. Brush it with butter and brown it in the oven. Serve this with a crisp green salad and French bread.

SHEPHERD'S PIE

In a greased baking dish, spread out leftover meat. Top it with leftover vegetables and dot these with leftover mashed potatoes. Pour gravy over all. Bake this until it is heated through.

Tomato juice or ½ cup of milk blended with 1 beaten egg may be poured over the top before baking, instead of the gravy.

LEFTOVER WIENERS

Cook sliced potatoes in water, adding salt to taste. Add sliced wieners for the last 5 or 10 minutes of cooking. When they are about done, add a small amount of cream.

Instead of wieners, sliced smoked pork sausage is good. Cook the sausage with the potatoes.

CORNED BEEF PUDDING

3 eggs, slightly beaten
2 or 3 cups corn (fresh, frozen or canned)
4 tablespoons flour (scant)
¼ teaspoon pepper

1 teaspoon salt
2 cups rich milk
1 cup diced, cooked beef (or other meat)
2 tablespoons butter

Add the eggs to the corn. Stir in the flour and season it as desired. Add the milk and meat and pour it into a buttered baking dish, dotting the top with butter. Set the baking dish in a pan of warm water and bake it at 350° for about 35 minutes or until a knife inserted comes out clean.

TRAMP'S HASH

Cut up leftover sausage or beef. Cook 6 medium-sized potatoes (or according to family size) and 2 sliced onions with the meat and meat stock until they are soft. Before serving, add enough bread crumbs to soak up the meat stock.

OLD-FASHIONED POT PIE

Add 2 diced potatoes, 1 cup of finely cut celery and 2 tablespoons of minced onions (optional) to 1 quart of leftover meat broth (ham, beef or chicken). While this is boiling, make a dough of 2 beaten eggs, ¼ teaspoon of salt, ½ cup of milk, ¼ teaspoon of baking powder and enough flour to make a stiff biscuit-like dough. Roll it out thinly and cut it into squares. Drop it into the meat broth and cook it for 10 to 15 minutes. Add parsley before serving.

The dough may also be made as follows. Combine 2 beaten eggs, ¼ cup of water, 1 tablespoon of shortening and enough flour to make a thick dough. Roll it out, cut it into squares, then add it to the broth.

CORN FRITTERS

Separate 2 eggs for each cup of drained corn. Beat the egg whites until they are stiff, then add the corn and yolks. Form the mixture into patties and fry them in butter.

STRING BEAN CASSEROLE

Cook together until partly soft 1 quart of string beans cut into small pieces, 1 quart of diced potatoes and 1 or 2 diced carrots. Then mix in leftover beef and gravy, seasoned salt and salt to taste. Pour this into a casserole and bake it at 350° for 45 minutes. Serve this with a salad and dessert.

LEFTOVER GRAVY

Leftover tomato or meat gravy may be mixed with vegetable soup or stews.

TOMATO GRAVY

Chunk 1 quart of canned hamburger into a heavy skillet. Add leftover tomato gravy. If it is too thick, thin it with milk or tomato juice, or a little cream. This is good with corn bread or hot biscuits, or with cooked navy beans and applesauce. (If you have a small amount of fresh strawberries, mix them with the applesauce.)

LEFTOVER SOUP

Leftover soup which was made with hot milk and bread may be mixed with eggs and more bread crumbs if it is too thin, and fried in patties like pancakes.

SCHOOL LUNCHES

HINTS FOR SCHOOL LUNCHES

- *Do not cut lettuce wedges unless you want to use the remainder of the lettuce within a few hours. The edges of the cut lettuce will turn brown. With head lettuce, use it leaf by leaf and it will keep better*

- *Be sure that eggs are freshly cooked when you put them in a lunch bucket. When hardcooked eggs become too old, they may cause serious stomach disorders.*

SANDWICH OR SALAD SUGGESTIONS

Following are various ideas on the different combinations of foods that may be mixed with mayonnaise for a sandwich or salad.

—2 chopped, hardcooked eggs, 2 chopped pickles and a handful of peanuts, lightly crushed

—mashed cooked eggs (egg salad)

—flaked tuna and hardcooked eggs (tuna salad)

—ham, chicken, ground canned beef, liverwurst, or any meat which may be diced

—a variety of flavors may be added to ground meat: diced onions, dash of garlic, sprouts, pickles (with some pickle juice), grated carrots, finely diced celery, lettuce and chopped cabbage, as well as spices, seasonings or herbs, parsley, dill, chives, Worcestershire sauce and sage

—grind 1 tongue, chop 2 medium-sized sweet pickles and 1 large sweet apple, adding salt to taste (tongue salad)

—½ cup grated Cheddar cheese, 1 tablespoon of honey, ½ cup of pitted, chopped dates, mixed with milk, cream or mayonnaise

Spread peanut butter on bread. Top it with mayonnaise and lightly chopped or thinly sliced bananas.

Put salad dressing in the sandwich, and the lettuce in a plastic bag so that the child can add the lettuce at school. It will be crisper this way.

Try softening a package of cream cheese and adding some chopped nuts. Spread it on slices of Date and Nut Bread (see page 23).

For unusual flavor treats, try creaming one of your favorite seasonings into the butter. Mustard, horseradish, parsley, chives, curry powder, minced onion, celery salt and even a light hint of garlic will bring a welcome touch of flavor to the sandwiches.

247

ADDITIONAL SUGGESTIONS

—ice cream in a wide-mouthed thermos, served with a piece of pie

—freezer cabbage slaw

—cabbage wedges, with or without peanut butter

—carrot sticks

—grated carrots on buttered bread

—celery sticks filled with peanut butter or soft cheese

—apple halves filled with peanut butter

—prunes stuffed with cream cheese or nut paste

—dates, raisins, figs or dried apples

—sliced radishes on buttered bread

—popcorn

—hotdogs, sliced lengthwise, in a thermos, with ketchup or mustard on bread

—applesauce with strawberry gelatin

—cottage cheese, topped with applesauce

—cottage cheese with raisins and nuts

—soda crackers with peanut butter

—custard or pumpkin custard made in custard cups (set in hot water to bake)

—different kinds of bread for variety

—ground raisins, dates and nuts mixed with coconut

DESSERT SUGGESTIONS

DANISH DESSERT

Add 3 or 4 cups of water plus sugar to taste to 2 pints frozen or 1 quart canned strawberries. Let this come to the boiling point, then add enough cornstarch so that it is a little runny. Remove it from the heat and add 5 rounded tablespoons of fruit flavored gelatin. (This is cheaper when you buy it by the pound.)

Fill a week's supply of baby food jars with this dessert or with hot cooked caramel pudding. Keep it refrigerated. The jars often seal, which keeps the pudding from spoiling.

SCHOOL ICE CREAM

By the time winter rolls around, the young scholars are tired of the same things in their lunch buckets. A simple, yet delicious dessert can be made by cooking cornstarch (see Basic Vanilla Pudding, page 190). Cool it, then add whipped cream. Spoon it into a tumbler with a lid. When the children get to school, they set the tumbler outside and let it freeze (for those of you in northern climes!).

THERMOS POTATO SOUP

Dice and cook potatoes with parsley and onions. While they are cooking, melt a few tablespoons of margarine or butter in a pan. Add a heaping tablespoon of flour. Brown it slowly, then add milk, stirring it all the time. Let it boil then pour it over the soft potatoes. Grated hardcooked eggs may be added.

Variations: Fry bacon, then use the grease to make a pan sauce. Proceed as above, and add the bacon to the soup.

ADDITIONAL SUGGESTIONS

Crunchy or smooth peanut butter mixed in with leftover frosting, milk and icing sugar makes a very delicious snack. Put it between graham crackers.

Make a paste of icing sugar and milk. Add peanut butter to taste. Spread it between graham crackers.

Make Iced Tea Syrup (see page 234), then follow the simple directions for a quick tea to take to school in a thermos.

Homemade cereal is good to take to school. Send along a thermos with cold milk.

MIXES

BASIC CAKE MIX

10 cups all-purpose flour
5 tablespoons double-acting baking
   powder
5 teaspoons salt

7 cups sugar
1 cup dry milk
2½ cups shortening

Sift together the dry ingredients 3 times. Rub the shortening into this mixture until it takes on a cornmeal texture. Lift it lightly into containers and store it at room temperature. It may be kept for up to 3 months. (Dry milk may be omitted if whole milk is used instead of water for the batter.)

With this mixture you can make the following cakes.

Plain Cake;

4½ cups mix
2 teaspoons vanilla

1 cup milk or water
2 eggs

Bake the batter for 25 to 30 minutes at 375°.

White Cake;

Use the Plain Cake recipe, substituting 3 egg whites for the 2 whole eggs.

Buttermilk Cake;

In place of the milk in the Plain Cake recipe, use buttermilk, and add 1 teaspoon of soda.

Orange Cake;

Add to the Plain Cake recipe 1 tablespoon of orange rind, and omit the 1 cup of milk. Use ¾ cup of water and ¼ cup of orange juice.

Chocolate Cake;

Use the recipe for Plain Cake, and add ¼ cup of cocoa before any of the liquid.

Spice Cake;

Add to the Plain Cake recipe 2 teaspoons of cinnamon, ½ teaspoon of cloves and ½ teaspoon of allspice.

Applesauce Cake;

Omit the liquid from the Plain Cake recipe, and add the following.

¾ cup brown sugar
½ teaspoon cloves
½ teaspoon nutmeg
Raisins or nuts (optional)

1 teaspoon soda
2 teaspoons cinnamon
2 cups applesauce

Applesauce Raisin Bars;

Add to the Applesauce Cake ingredients ½ cup of margarine. After adding all the other ingredients, add 4 eggs, one at a time, and beat the mixture well. Add as many raisins as desired, cut up, whole or ground. Pour the batter into two 9 x 13-inch pans, and bake it at 400° for 30 minutes. Frost the bars with a powdered sugar icing.

Pineapple Upside-Down Cake;

Mix and pour the following ingredients into a greased 9 x 13-inch pan.

⅔ cup melted butter	1 cup brown sugar
¼ cup nuts	6 tablespoons pineapple juice
1 tablespoon flour	6 to 8 pineapple slices

Arrange pineapple slices in the bottom of the pan. Pour the Basic Cake Mix batter over the pineapple and bake it at 375° until done. Invert it on a large plate, then serve it with whipped cream or another topping.

Dessert;

Put fruit pie filling in the bottom of a cake pan. Top it with the Plain Cake batter and bake it at 375°. Use almond in the cake when cherry pie filling is used. Serve it with whipped cream, top milk or ice cream.

Chocolate Cinnamon Bars;

4½ cups Basic Cake Mix	3 teaspoons cinnamon
1 egg	1 egg yolk
½ cup margarine	

Mix together the above ingredients and press the dough into a greased 9 x 12 or 15 x 10-inch pan. Beat 1 egg white slightly and brush it over the dough, then sprinkle over it the following topping. Bake it at 350° for 25 minutes. Allow it to cool, then cut it into bars.

1 teaspoon cinnamon	1 cup chocolate chips
⅓ cup sugar	½ cup nuts

CHOCOLATE CHIP COOKIES

4½ cups Basic Cake Mix	2 eggs
2 tablespoons flour	1 small package chocolate chips
¾ cup brown sugar	Chopped nuts
⅓ cup cooking oil	

Mix together all the ingredients. Shape the dough into balls. Bake them at 375° for 10 to 12 minutes on an ungreased cookie sheet.

BASIC COOKIE MIX

10 cups all-purpose flour
7½ cups sugar
4 tablespoons baking powder

4½ teaspoons salt
3⅓ cups shortening

Measure the flour into a large bowl. Add the sugar, baking powder and salt. Blend these thoroughly, then add the shortening and work it into the mixture until it is uniformly blended. Put it into a tightly sealed container but do not pack it down. Store it at room temperature.

Mincemeat Bars;

3 cups Basic Cookie Mix
1 large egg
1 cup mincemeat

Mix together thoroughly all the ingredients. Spread the mixture in a greased 9 x 13 x 2-inch pan. Bake it at 400° for 30 minutes. If desired, sprinkle white sugar over the top while it is still hot. Let it cool in the pan, then slice it into bars. This recipe yields 36 (2-inch) bars.

Banana Coconut Bars;

3 cups Basic Cookie Mix
1 large egg
½ cup coconut
1 teaspoon vanilla

1 cup mashed bananas
¼ cup finely chopped candied cherries
⅔ cup chopped nuts

Follow the Mincemeat Bars recipe, but sprinkle part of the nuts on top.

Orange Date Nut Sticks;

3 cups Basic Cookie Mix
1 tablespoon grated orange rind
¼ cup orange juice

2 eggs
1 cup chopped dates
1 cup finely chopped nuts

Follow the same directions as for Mincemeat Bars, but cut the sticks about 1 x 2½ inches.

LYDIA'S PIE DOUGH MIX

9 pounds all-purpose flour
4 pounds lard
1 cup cornstarch

1 tablespoon baking powder
2 cups sugar, icing or brown, sifted
1 tablespoon salt

Use about 1½ cups of this mix for 1 pie crust. Wet it with water or milk.

BISCUIT MIX

8 cups all-purpose flour
8 teaspoons sugar
2 teaspoons salt
⅓ cup baking powder

2 teaspoons cream of tartar
1 cup powdered milk
1¾ cups shortening

Sift the dry ingredients together 3 times, then cut in the shortening. Pack the mixture loosely in an airtight container.

To make biscuits, add 1 cup of this mix to ⅓ cup of water. Bake the dough at 450° for 10 to 12 minutes.

You may omit powdered milk from the mix if using milk instead of water.

This biscuit mix may be used with the Cherry Pudding recipe (see page 194) and the Pizza Pie recipe (see page 78).

Custard Pie;

4 eggs, separated
½ cup Biscuit Mix
⅓ cup sugar
2 cups milk

3 tablespoons butter
1 teaspoon vanilla
½ cup coconut (optional)

Beat the egg whites until they are stiff, then add the remaining ingredients and beat the mixture well. Pour it into a buttered pie pan and bake it for 25 to 30 minutes at 400°, or until the pie is golden brown. The mix forms its own crust.

CRUNCH MIX

5 cups oatmeal
5 cups brown sugar
1½ teaspoons baking powder
5 cups flour

1½ teaspoons soda
½ teaspoon salt
2 teaspoons cinnamon.

Mix these ingredients together, and store the mixture in a tightly sealed container.

Method;

1 quart sweetened, slightly thickened
    fruit
3 cups Crunch Mix
⅔ cup butter

Place the fruit in the bottom of a buttered baking dish. Mix together the Crunch Mix and butter, then pour this mixture over the fruit, patting it down. Bake it at 350° for about 30 to 45 minutes. Serve it with milk or cream.

GINGERBREAD MIX

8 cups all-purpose flour
2¼ cups sugar
2½ teaspoons soda
2 tablespoons baking powder
3 tablespoons ginger

3 tablespoons cinnamon
1 teaspoon cloves
1 tablespoon salt
2¼ cups shortening

Sift together all the dry ingredients, then cut in the shortening. Store the mixture in a gallon jar, tightly covered, in a cold place. It will keep for about 3 months.

Method;

2 cups Gingerbread Mix
1 egg, beaten

½ cup molasses
½ cup boiling water

Put the mix into a bowl. Combine the rest of the ingredients and stir them into the mix. Blend this mixture until it is smooth, then pour it into a greased 8 x 8-inch pan. Bake it at 350° for 35 minutes. Serve it warm with whipped cream.

Maple Gingerbread;

⅔ cup maple syrup
⅓ cup sour cream

2 cups Gingerbread Mix
1 egg, well-beaten

Heat the maple syrup, then combine it with the sour cream, and stir it into the mix. Add the egg before pouring the mixture into a greased 8 x 8-inch pan and baking it at 350° for 40 minutes.

THREE-FLOUR MUFFIN MIX

12 cups fine whole wheat flour
6 cups sifted, all-purpose flour
6 cups oatmeal
3 tablespoons salt

8 tablespoons baking powder
3 cups sugar
3 cups lard

Mix together the dry ingredients, then cut in the lard to make a very fine, meal-like mixture. Store it in a cold place.

Method;

2¾ cups Three-Flour Muffin Mix
1 cup milk
1 egg, beaten

Mix the ingredients until moistened. Bake the batter at 425° for 20 to 25 minutes. This makes 12 medium-sized muffins.

Variations: Add raisins and carob flour, and bake the batter in an oblong pan like corn bread.

PANCAKE MIX

12 cups all-purpose flour   2 tablespoons salt
¾ cup sugar   ¾ cup baking powder
4 cups milk powder

Mix together well the above ingredients and store the mixture in a tightly sealed container.

To make pancakes, combine the following ingredients.

1½ cups of the above mix   1 cup water
1 egg, beaten   2 tablespoons salad oil

Variations: Buckwheat or whole wheat flour may be used as part of the flour.

Milk powder can be omitted if whole milk is used in place of the water.

PANCAKE AND WAFFLE MIX

4 cups all-purpose flour   2 cups buckwheat flour
2 cups cornmeal   1 cup raw wheat germ
3 teaspoons salt   4 teaspoons soda
4 teaspoons baking powder
⅔ cup liquid shortening (½ the amount
   for pancakes)

Mix together thoroughly the above ingredients. This mixture may be used immediately or stored in a cool place for future use. When using it, take equal amounts of the mix and milk (sour milk is best). For pancakes, use 1 egg to 1 or 2 cups of the mix. For waffles, use 1 egg to 1 cup of the mix.

FEATHER-LIGHT PANCAKES

8 cups all-purpose flour   2 tablespoons soda
1 cup sugar   2 teaspoons salt

Mix these ingredients, and store the mixture in a tightly sealed container.

2 eggs   2 cups milk
¼ cup vinegar   ¼ cup soft shortening

To make pancakes, beat the eggs well and add the vinegar, milk and shortening. Then add 2¼ cups of the prepared dry mix (making the ¼ cup quite full).

When dry milk is added to the mix, water instead of milk is required in preparing the pancakes.

WHOLE WHEAT MUFFIN MIX

24 cups finely ground whole wheat
   flour
3 tablespoons salt

3 cups sugar
8 tablespoons baking powder
3 cups lard

Mix together the dry ingredients, then cut in the lard to make a very fine, meal-like texture. Store it in a cold place.

Method;

2¾ cups Whole Wheat Muffin Mix
1 cup milk
1 egg, beaten

Mix the ingredients until moistened. Bake the batter at 425° for 20 to 25 minutes. This recipe makes 12 medium-sized muffins.

PUDDING MIX

½ cup cornstarch
1 cup flour

1½ cups sugar
1 teaspoon salt

Mix the ingredients together well and store the mixture in a tightly sealed container.

Vanilla Pudding;

3 cups milk
¾ cup Pudding Mix
2 eggs, beaten

2 tablespoons butter
2 teaspoons vanilla

Heat 2½ cups of the milk. While it is heating, make a paste of the Pudding Mix, ½ cup of the milk and the eggs. Add it to the hot milk with the butter and vanilla and cook it for 1 minute.

Chocolate Pudding;

3 cups milk
¾ cup Pudding Mix
5 tablespoons cocoa
¼ cup sugar

2 eggs
2 tablespoons butter
2 teaspoons vanilla

Cook these ingredients as directed in the Vanilla Pudding recipe, adding the cocoa and sugar to the Pudding Mix.

Butterscotch Pudding;

3 cups milk
¾ cup Pudding Mix
½ cup brown sugar

2 eggs
4 tablespoons butter
1 tablespoon vanilla

Cook these ingredients as directed in the Vanilla Pudding recipe, and top the pudding with nuts.

SHOO-FLY CRUMB MIX

4 pounds all-purpose flour
1 pound lard
2 pounds brown sugar

Mix these ingredients as you would for a pie crust, and store the mixture in a tightly sealed container.

Shoo-fly Cake;

2 cups Shoo-fly Crumb Mix
¾ cup hot water
¾ cup molasses
1 teaspoon soda (scant)

Mix together the above ingredients, then pour the mixture into a greased 9 x 9-inch cake pan. Top it with dry Shoo-fly Crumbs. Bake it at 450° for 10 minutes, then at 375° for about 40 minutes or until done.

Shoo-fly Pie;

For pie, pour the batter into an unbaked pie shell and bake it at 450° for 10 minutes, then at 375° for about 40 minutes or until done.

CANNING

HINTS FOR CANNING

- Boric acid is poisonous and should never be added to food.

- While peeling apples, pears or peaches, place the slices in slightly salted water. They will then retain their natural color. This also enriches the flavor.

- Do not peel pumpkins or squash. Wash them, take out the seeds, then put them into a pressure cooker with a very small amount of water (½ to 1 cup). Cook them for 10 minutes, timing after cooking starts. The shells then come off easily and the pumpkins or squash are ready to use.

- Use a melon ball tool or a measuring spoon to scoop out the centers of pears or apples.

- If you have a lot of peas to shell, place them in a bucket and pour boiling water over them. Cover, and let them stand for 10 to 15 minutes. They shell easier this way and will have a better flavor.

- Check cans to see if they are sealed while still warm. If any have not sealed, give them a few hard turns. This almost always eliminates the need to reheat the cans. Turning them upside down also helps.

- Boil used flats for 10 minutes in water with a little soda added to make them look like new. Be careful how cans are opened, then mark the lids. Use the ones you used for cold packing this time for pressure canning the next time.

MARASCHINO CHERRIES

4½ pounds pitted, white cherries
2 tablespoons salt

1 teaspoon alum
Water to cover

Soak the cherries overnight in a brine made from the 3 remaining ingredients.

3 cups water
Juice of 1 lemon
4½ pounds sugar

1 ounce red coloring
1 ounce almond extract

The next day, drain and rinse the cherries in water. Add the 3 cups of water, juice, sugar and coloring. Heat the mixture to the boiling point, then let it set for 24 hours. Bring it to a boil again the third day, and add the almond extract. Jar and seal the cherries.

COLD PACKING HUCKLEBERRIES

2 cups sugar
1 cup boiling water

Make a syrup of the sugar and water. Pack berries in a jar and add the syrup. Place the jars in water until the water starts to boil, then remove them from the heat and seal.

SPICED MELONS

2 cups sugar
½ cup vinegar
1 cup water

¾ teaspoon salt
1 tablespoon whole cloves

Boil the ingredients for 20 minutes to get the taste of the cloves. Put muskmelons in jars and pour the syrup over them. Cook them for 20 minutes. Do not can the cloves as they will color the melons.

CANNING PRUNES WITH SODA

Use 2 tablespoons of soda to 1 gallon of water. Bring the water to a boil, then drop in the prunes a handful at a time. When they rise to the top, ladle them out into a clean jar. When the jar is full of prunes, fill it with the hot syrup, then seal.

RHUBARB

There are many variations in canning rhubarb—some with pineapple and some without, and some with different flavors of gelatin powder. Use 2 small packages of gelatin powder to 6 quarts of cooked rhubarb. On each can write what flavor it contains so you can decide which flavor your family enjoys the most. While the rhubarb is boiling hot, pour it into jars and seal.

Rhubarb may also be canned for pies by putting the raw, diced fruit into jars and filling them with cold water. It need not be heated, as the acid in the fruit keeps it from spoiling.

CANNED STRAWBERRIES

3 quarts strawberries
2 cups sugar
½ cup water

The strawberries may be lightly mashed if desired. Boil the ingredients together for 8 minutes, then put the strawberries into sterilized jars while still hot, and seal them.

BAKED BEANS

8 pounds navy beans
4½ quarts tomato juice
1 pound brown sugar
½ teaspoon black pepper
1 tablespoon ground mustard

1½ pounds bacon or ham, finely cut
8 tablespoons salt
1 cup molasses
1 tablespoon cinnamon

Soak the beans overnight. Cook them until they are soft, then drain. Mix together the other ingredients, cook them a few minutes, then add them to the beans. Put the mixture into jars and cold pack them for 1½ to 2 hours. This makes 14 quarts.

Variations: Three pounds of wieners may be used instead of bacon. Slice and fry them before adding

The tomato juice may be doubled, or part of the juice from cooking may be added.

WATERLESS STRING BEANS

Wash the beans and pack them in jars. Drain off all the water and seal them, then cold pack them for 3 hours. There will be enough juice in the jars from the beans that no water need be added when preparing the beans for a meal.

To prepare the beans, melt a little butter in a saucepan. Then add the beans with some salt and sauté them.

CANNED CORN

Cut the corn off the ears, cover it with water and cook it for 5 minutes. Put the corn and liquid into pint jars. Add to each pint 1 teaspoon of salt, 1 teaspoon of sugar and 1 teaspoon of lemon juice. Boil the jars in a hot water bath for 3 hours.

CANNED PEPPERS

Clean peppers (cut them into strips if desired) and pack them in jars. Add 1 teaspoon of vegetable oil and 1 teaspoon of salt to each quart jar.

Syrup;

1 pint vinegar
3 cups water
3 cups sugar

Mix these ingredients then pour the syrup over the peppers while they are boiling hot. Seal the jars and cold pack them until the boiling point.

GREEN PEPPERS

Dice and fry green peppers in butter. Put them into small jelly jars and cold pack them until the boiling point, then remove them from the stove.

This is good for one-dish meals and casseroles.

Peppers for Casseroles;

These can also be diced and packed in small jars, adding about ¼ teaspoon of salt to 1 cup of peppers. Fill the jars with water and cold pack them. Bring them to the boiling point before removing them from the stove.

HOMINY

In a large kettle bring 1½ gallons of water and 3 tablespoons of lye to a boil. Then add 1 gallon of clean corn and simmer it for 10 minutes (no need to stir). Remove it from the heat and let it set for 25 minutes.

Drain off the lye water and add clean water. Wash the corn repeatedly until all the black ends are loose, changing the water often. Soak it overnight and follow the Hominy Canning recipe.

After the black ends are off, the corn can also be dried and kept in a cool place.

Hominy Canning;

Boil Hominy until it is almost tender. Fill jars ¾ full. Add 1 teaspoon of salt to each quart and fill the jars with boiling water. Process them for 3 hours in a boiler, or for 90 minutes in a pressure cooker.

Hominy with Soda;

Use 2 tablespoons of soda and 2 quarts of water for each quart of corn. Follow the same procedure as the Hominy recipe.

Household lime can also be used to remove hulls. Cook corn in lime water for 2 hours or until the hulls loosen.

Hominy Making Hints;

- *Always use stainless steel, iron or enamelware for making hominy.*
- *Stir it with a wooden spoon.*
- *The black ends may be removed by rubbing over a cloth on a washboard or by using a churn.*
- *Hominy is delicious even if the hulls and centers are not all removed.*
- *Hominy may be used in meat loaf.*
- *Do not inhale the steam from the lye water.*

STUFFED LITTLE PEPPERS

Make your favorite cole slaw and stuff it into small green, red and yellow peppers. Pack them into jars and cold pack them for 3 hours.

This makes a delightful and colorful addition to your salad plate.

CANNING POTATOES

Do not let newly-dug small potatoes go to waste. Scrape them, pack them into a jar, and add 1 teaspoon of salt. Cold pack them for 3 hours. To use, drain off the water and fry the potatoes in butter.

QUICK STEPS FOR CANNING PUMPKIN

Wash the pumpkins, remove the seeds and put the pumpkins into a pressure cooker with a very small amount of water. Cook them for 10 minutes, timing them after the cooking starts. The shell then comes off easily and the pumpkins are soft and ready to use. This eliminates peeling and cubing, and the pumpkins are nice in texture and not water soaked. If desired, the pumpkins may be put through a Foley food mill. Put them into jars and cold pack them for 1 hour.

CROCK KRAUT

Measure 3 tablespoons of pure granulated salt and sprinkle it over 5 pounds of shredded cabbage. Allow the salted cabbage to stand a few minutes to wilt slightly. Mix it well with clean hands or a spoon to distribute the salt uniformly. Pack the salted cabbage into a large crock. Press it down firmly with a potato masher until the juices drawn out will just cover the shredded cabbage. Place a water-filled plastic bag on top of the cabbage. This fits snugly against the cabbage and against the sides of the container and prevents exposure to air. Place the crock in a room with a temperature of 68 to 72°F.

Instead of covering the cabbage with a plastic bag you may cover it with a clean, thin, white cloth (such as muslin) and tuck the edges down against the inside of the container. Cover it with a plate or round paraffined board that just fits inside the container so that the cabbage is not exposed to air. Put a weight on top of the cover so the brine comes to the cover but not over it. A glass jar filled with water makes a good weight.

When fermentation is complete, remove the sauerkraut from the crock and heat it in a kettle to simmering. Pack the hot sauerkraut into clean, hot jars and cover it with the hot juice to ½ inch from the top of the jars. Adjust the lids. Place the jars in a boiling water bath and process them 15 minutes for pints and 20 minutes for quarts. Start to count the processing time as soon as the hot jars are placed into the actively boiling water.

Remove the jars from the canner and complete the seals if necessary. Set the jars upright, several inches apart on a wire rack to cool. An off odor indicates that the sauerkraut may be spoiled. It rots when it is not covered sufficiently to keep out the air.

EASY SAUERKRAUT

For this recipe it is best to use large bursted heads of cabbage. Shred and chop the cabbage, then pack it in jars. Add 1 teaspoon of salt to each jar, then fill them with boiling water. Do not seal them tightly. Let the cabbage stand about 10 days to ferment. Then turn the lids tightly and store the jars.

SIMPLE SAUERKRAUT

Shred cabbage and pack it loosely into a jar. Make a hole down through the middle with a wooden spoon or similar utensil and add 1 tablespoon of salt for each quart. Then fill it with boiling water and immediately seal the jar tightly. This will be ready to use in 4 to 6 weeks. More salt may be added if desired.

MARY'S TOMATO SOUP

1 peck ripe tomatoes	½ cup sugar
10 small onions	¼ cup salt
5 sprigs parsley	1 teaspoon pepper
3 bunches celery	½ cup flour
2 red peppers	½ cup butter

Cook the tomatoes and put them through a sieve. Boil down the pulp to nearly half. Grind the onions, parsley, celery and peppers through a food chopper and pour the mixture into the tomatoes. Add the sugar, salt and pepper. Make a thickening with the flour and enough water to make it smooth, then stir it into the pulp and tomato juice and boil it for ½ hour. Add the butter before removing it from the heat. Can the soup while it is hot. This makes 6 to 7 pints. To prepare it, add milk and heat.

PIZZA SAUCE

Cook ½ bushel of tomatoes and 3 pounds of onions for 2½ to 3 hours. Put them through a sieve, then add the following.

4 hot peppers, OR	1 tablespoon oregano
1½ teaspoons red pepper	1½ cups white sugar
2 cups vegetable oil	½ cup salt
1 tablespoon basil leaves	

Boil this mixture for 1 hour, then add 48 ounces (four 12-ounce cans) of tomato paste. Bring it to a boil, then pack it in hot jars and seal them. This makes 20 pints.

TOMATO SAUCE FOR PIZZA PIE

1 peck tomatoes
3 red peppers, seeded
3 onions

Cook the above ingredients together until they are soft. Drain them well then put them through a colander. Add the following ingredients.

2 tablespoons salt
½ teaspoon pepper
½ cup vinegar

2 teaspoons dried celery leaves
¼ teaspoon red pepper (optional)
2 teaspoons oregano (optional)

Put this into pint jars, seal and boil them for 30 minutes.

CHICKEN SOUP

4 chickens
Salt to taste
1 gallon noodles, cooked

Cook separately until nearly done ½ gallon of each of; celery, carrots and potatoes, all chopped. One cup of chopped onions may be added. Combine all the ingredients and cold pack the soup for 2 hours.

CHILI SOUP

1 pound hamburger
2 tablespoons butter
1 cup chopped onions
2 pints kidney beans
½ teaspoon chili powder

1 tablespoon salt
2 tablespoons prepared mustard
Pinch of black pepper
2 quarts tomato juice

Mix these ingredients as you would other Chili Soup (see page 000), then cold pack the soup for 3 hours. This makes 3 quarts.

BYLERS' CHILI SOUP

8 pounds hamburger
2 quarts red kidney beans
2 to 4 red peppers

6 quarts strained tomatoes
24 small onions
1½ teaspoons chili powder

Cook each ingredient except the spice separately, then mix all together. Put the soup into jars and seal them, then cold pack them for 2 hours.

MIXED VEGETABLES

Cook separately, carrots (diced small), lima beans, string beans, corn, soup beans, peas, potatoes (diced small) and green peppers (small amount). Salt each vegetable when cooking, then mix them together. (Be careful not to overcook them.) Cold pack the vegetables for 1 hour.

This recipe is good if you like variety in canning. The vegetables resemble frozen mixed vegetables available in stores. This is also delicious with meat broth for soup.

VALLEY TOMATO SOUP

1 peck tomatoes	4 cloves
8 onions fried in 2 tablespoons butter	1 stick cinnamon
6 sweet peppers, seeded	4 bay leaves
5 teaspoons salt	2 quarts water
5 tablespoons sugar	

Boil together all the ingredients before running them through a sieve. Put the mixture over heat again and bring it to a boil. Add 5 teaspoons of cornstarch mixed with ½ cup of cold water, and boil it for 15 minutes longer. Can the soup.

To serve, heat the soup and an equal amount of milk in separate pans, adding ¼ teaspoon of soda to 1 quart of soup. Mix the milk into the soup and let it come to a boil. Serve it with crackers.

VEGETABLE SOUP

10 carrots	½ bushel tomatoes, strained
2 heads cabbage	6 bunches celery
10 peppers	10 onions
½ gallon potatoes or macaroni	3 pounds hamburger or cut up chicken
½ gallon navy beans	1 pound butter

Cook each vegetable separately. Fry the onions and hamburger in the butter, then mix all together. Season it with salt, pepper and sugar to taste. Cold pack the soup for 1 hour. This makes 20 quarts.

PRESERVED BUTTER

Form butter into patties, then place them in a crock with salty brine strong enough to float an egg. Keep it in a cool place. In this way the butter can be kept for several months.

CANNED CREAM

When there is an overabundance of cream during the summer months, can it and keep it for the winter. First cook the cream, then seal it in pint or quart jars. Cold pack them for 1 hour. This cream can be whipped and used the same as fresh cream, and it has a good flavor.

CANNED NUTMEATS

Put nutmeats into cans with 2-piece lids. Heat them to 250° on a grate or rack in the oven for ¾ hour, then turn off the heat and let them cool on the grate.

INSTANT PUDDING

Thicken any kind of fruit or fruit combination such as pears and pineapple, sour cherries and raspberries or apples and raisins, using tapioca or cornstarch (tapioca should not be cooked until clear). As soon as the cooked fruit has reached the boiling point, fill the jars, seal them, and put them into the pressure cooker. Heat them to 5 pounds pressure. Let the steam out and the jars will seal. A hot water bath may also be used, or the jars may be placed in a hot oven for a few minutes.

This thickened fruit may be used for puddings or pie filling when unexpected company arrives.

CANNING SWEET CIDER

Never boil cider in a kettle to can it. Pour the fresh apple juice into bottles or cans, filling them to the top. Place them in a canner with cold water that reaches to the neck of the cans. Leave the cans uncovered. Bring the water to a boil. With a spoon or small ladle remove the scum that rises to the top. Continue to boil the cans until no scum appears. Then remove them from the water and seal.

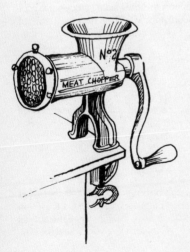

PICKLED FOODS, RELISHES, KETCHUP AND SPREADS

CHERRY PICKLES

1½ gallons cold water
1 cup salt
1 quart sweet cherry leaves

Place cucumbers in a mixture of the above ingredients and let them stand for 8 days. Remove, wash and cut them into desired pieces. Heat them in weak vinegar, then pack them in jars and drain. Cook together the following.

4 cups sugar
2 cups vinegar

2 cups water
1 tablespoon mixed spices

Pour this over the pickles and seal the jars.

CHUNK PICKLES

1 gallon cucumber chunks
½ cup salt
Boiling water to cover
3 cups sugar
3 cups vinegar
1 cup water

1 teaspoon allspice
1 teaspoon dry mustard
1 teaspoon mustard seed
1 teaspoon celery seed
½ teaspoon turmeric

Cut the medium-sized cucumbers into 1-inch chunks. Add the salt and cover them with the boiling water. Let them stand overnight then drain them. Combine the sugar, vinegar, 1 cup of water and spices, bring them to a boil and add the pickles. Green food coloring may be added if desired. Heat the pickles again to a boil, then can and seal.

CLARA'S PICKLES

Chunk 1 gallon of cucumbers. Add 1 cup of salt and enough boiling water to cover them. Let them stand overnight. The next morning drain them. Mix 3 cups of white sugar, 1 teaspoon turmeric, 1 teaspoon of mustard seed and 1 quart of vinegar, diluted. Pour this over the pickles and heat but do not boil them. Pack them in jars and cover them with the syrup. Seal the jars.

COLD PACKED PICKLES

Pack cucumbers in jars. To each quart add ⅓ cup of vinegar, 1 heaping tablespoon of salt and ½ teaspoon of sugar. Fill the jars with water, seal them and set them in cold water in a boiler. Heat the jars until the color of the pickles is completely changed or until the water boils.

CRISP PICKLES

1 gallon cucumbers, sliced ⅛-inch thick ⅓ cup salt
6 medium-sized onions, thinly sliced Cold water

Combine the above ingredients and let them stand for 3 hours before draining. Pack them in jars for cold packing.

1 cup water
⅔ cup strong vinegar
1¾ cups raw sugar (scant)

Make a syrup of the above ingredients.

½ teaspoon turmeric
½ teaspoon celery seeds
2 teaspoons mustard seeds

Tie the above seeds in a muslin bag and place it in the syrup. Cook the syrup a few minutes then lift out the seed bag. Add ½ cup of water extra and ⅛ cup more vinegar. When the syrup has cooled, pour it over the cucumbers and onions. Cold pack them 5 minutes, no longer. Use the leftover syrup for the next batch of cucumbers, but refrigerate it until then.

DOLLAR BREAD AND BUTTER PICKLES

4 quarts sliced cucumbers (40 to 50) 1 tablespoon turmeric (optional)
½ cup salt 1 quart vinegar
2 quarts sliced onions 1 tablespoon celery seed
4 cups sugar 1 tablespoon ginger
2 tablespoons mustard

Gently stir the salt into the thinly sliced cucumbers. Cover them with ice cubes and let them stand for 2 or 3 hours until the cucumbers are crisp and cold. Add more ice if it melts. Drain the cucumbers and add the onions. Combine the remaining ingredients and bring the mixture quickly to a boil, boiling it for 10 minutes. Add the cucumber and onion slices and bring them to the boiling point. Pack them at once in hot jars. Process them in a boiling water bath for 30 minutes. Remove the jars from the canner and complete sealing. This makes 8 pints.

EXCELLENT UNCOOKED PICKLES

Select good small cucumbers, and wash and dry them. Pack them into jars, then fill the jars with vinegar sweetened with saccharin to suit your taste. Do not make the vinegar too sweet or the pickles will wrinkle. Seal the jars as you would for cold packing. Put them into a boiler in cold water and bring the water to a boil. When it starts to boil, remove the jars and tighten the lids. This makes a very crisp pickle.

FROZEN CUCUMBERS

7 cups cucumbers, sliced thinly
1 cup peppers, diced
1 cup onions, diced

Mix these ingredients, then add the following vinegar solution.

1 tablespoon salt   2 cups sugar
1 teaspoon celery seeds   1 cup white vinegar

Let the cucumbers stand in the refrigerator for 4 or 5 days, stirring them every day. Then freeze them.

ICICLE PICKLES

2 gallons large cucumbers
1 pint salt
Water enough to cover

Mix the cucumbers, salt and water, and let them stand for 4 days. Drain and add boiling water to the cucumbers, then let them stand for 24 hours. Drain and cut them into strips. Pour water over them again, adding a lump of alum the size of an egg. Let them stand for 24 hours, then drain them again and pack them in jars.

Syrup;

2½ quarts vinegar   1 tablespoon salt
8 pints sugar (or less)   1 handful mixed whole spices (scant)

Boil these ingredients together to make a syrup. While it is hot, pour it over the pickles in jars before sealing them.

LIME PICKLES

7 pounds cucumbers, unpeeled, sliced
into 1-inch or thinner chunks
2 cups lime
2 gallons cold water
9 cups sugar (or less)

2 quarts vinegar
1 teaspoon mixed spices
1 tablespoon salt
1 tablespoon celery seeds
1 tablespoon whole cloves

Mix together the lime and water and pour the mixture over the cucumbers. Let them stand for 24 hours before thoroughly washing out the lime. Cover them with the sugar, vinegar and spice mixture. Do not heat the cucumbers at this time. The next morning simmer them for 40 minutes. Put them into hot jars and seal them. These pickles stay good and crisp.

MIXED PICKLES

8 cups sliced cucumbers
2 cups sliced onions
4 green peppers, sliced

1½ quarts cooked lima beans
¾ cup cooked carrots (or more)

Soak for 1 hour the cucumbers, onions and peppers separately in hot salted water, using 1 cup of salt for each gallon of hot water. Drain them, add the beans and carrots, then add a mixture of the following.

1 teaspoon turmeric
2 cups vinegar
2 to 3 cups sugar

1 teaspoon celery seed
1 stick cinnamon
Salt if needed

Boil the vegetables in this liquid for 20 minutes. Pack them in jars, fill with the liquid, and seal the jars while they are hot.

DELAWARE MIXED PICKLES

2 quarts carrots
2 quarts corn
2 quarts cabbage
2 quarts celery

2 quarts beans
2 quarts cucumbers
4 or 5 peppers
1 quart onions

Cook the above vegetables separately until they are tender, except for the cucumbers, peppers and onions. Mix the following ingredients and bring the mixture to a boil.

3 tablespoons mustard
3 pints sugar
1 cup flour
3 pints water

2 tablespoons turmeric
1 tablespoon salt
3 pints vinegar

Combine all the ingredients, then pack the vegetables in jars, filling them with the syrup. Cold pack them for 1 hour.

MUSTARD PICKLES

1 gallon vinegar
1 cup sugar (or use part saccharin)
1 cup dry mustard

1 cup salt
1 tablespoon mixed pickling spices

Boil together the above ingredients, then allow the mixture to cool. Put about 2 gallons of small cucumbers into a crock and cover them with the brine. (Make sure the cucumbers dry thoroughly after washing or they will become moldy.) Weight them down to keep them in the brine. Cover the crock with a cloth.

OVERNIGHT DILL PICKLES

Wash 20 to 25 dill-sized (4-inch) cucumbers. Put them into a pan of cold water and let them stand overnight. The next morning, pack them in hot sterile jars. Into each quart measure ⅛ teaspoon of powdered alum. Add 2 heads of dill (fresh with seed) and 1 small hot red pepper.

Combine 4 cups of vinegar, 1 cup of pure salt and 3 quarts of water. Heat the mixture to boiling, then fill the jars with this liquid. Seal them and allow them to stand for 6 weeks. A washed grape leaf or two can be put on the top for green coloring.

POLISH PICKLES

Cut 2 dozen cucumbers into quarters. Place them in salted water (1 tablespoon of salt to each quart of water) and let them stand overnight. Drain and pack them in jars. Fill the jars with the following syrup, which has been boiled for 3 minutes.

1½ pints vinegar
1½ pints sugar

¼ teaspoon red pepper
½ teaspoon turmeric

Put ¼ teaspoon of alum and a slice of onion on top of each jar before sealing.

REFRIGERATOR PICKLES

4 cups vinegar
1½ teaspoons celery seeds
1½ teaspoons turmeric

4 cups sugar
1½ teaspoons mustard seeds
¼ cup salt

This needs no boiling. Just pour a mixture of these ingredients over cucumbers and put them in the refrigerator. They will keep for months.

SEVEN DAY SWEET PICKLES

Day 1—Wash 7 pounds of medium-sized green cucumbers and cover them with boiling water.

Day 2—Drain them and cover them with fresh boiling water.

Day 3—Repeat procedure.

Day 4—Repeat procedure.

Day 5—Cut the pickles into ¼-inch rings.

Combine the following.

1 quart white vinegar	2 tablespoons salt
8 cups granulated sugar	2 tablespoons mixed pickle spices

Bring this mixture to a full boil and pour it over the sliced pickles.

Day 6—Drain the brine from the pickles, bring it to a full boil and pour it over the pickles again.

Day 7—Repeat Day 6 procedure, then jar and seal.

SOUR PICKLES

3 quarts water	3 tablespoons salt
1 quart white vinegar	7 tablespoons sugar

Soak cucumbers overnight in a mixture of the above ingredients. Then heat but do not boil them in this mixture. Pack the pickles in jars. Boil the liquid and pour it over the pickles before sealing the jars.

SWEET DILLS

Fill jars with sliced cucumbers, adding 2 bunches of dill and 3 or 4 garlic cloves to each quart. Pour the following liquid over the pickles.

1 quart weakened vinegar (may be ½ water)	¼ cup salt
1 pint water	4 cups sugar

Bring the mixture to a boil. Fill jars, then put on the lids. Set the jars in hot water and bring it to a boil, just long enough to seal.

CHOW CHOW

1 pint green beans
1 pint yellow beans
1 pint cucumbers
1 pint lima beans

1 pint carrots
1 head cauliflower
1 pint corn
3 or 4 stalks celery

Cook the above ingredients until they are just tender. Chop them to a uniform size, then salt and drain them. Chop and salt ½ dozen green tomatoes, and 3 red and 3 large yellow mangoes. Mix them well with the first ingredients and add the mixture to a boiling syrup made from the following.

3 quarts vinegar
5 cups sugar
1 tablespoon celery seed

1 tablespoon mustard seed
Other spices as desired
Onions (optional)

Heat, jar and seal.

PICKLED BEETS

3 quarts small beets
3 cups vinegar
2 tablespoons salt

4 cups sugar
1½ cups water
2 cinnamon sticks (optional)

Cook the beets. Combine the rest of the ingredients and boil them to a syrup. Pour the boiling syrup over the beets in hot jars, then seal them. Cold pack them for 10 to 15 minutes.

SPICED RED BEETS

2 cups sugar (raw if desired)
1 cup vinegar
½ teaspoon cinnamon
½ teaspoon cloves

3 cups water or beet juice
Juice of 1 lemon
½ teaspoon allspice
Salt to taste

Mix the above ingredients and pour the mixture over 1 gallon of cooked beets. Simmer them for 15 minutes. Then pack the beets in jars (without the syrup), and reheat the syrup to boiling. Pour it over the beets and seal the jars.

PICKLED PEPPERS

Into a clean cold jar, put pieces of green peppers (red peppers get mushy), or hot peppers. Add 1 tablespoon of pickling salt, and spices, garlic, pieces of celery or dried red peppers if desired. Fill the jar ⅔ full with cold water, then fill it to the top with cold white vinegar. Seal the jar with a screw cap and lid. These peppers will be ready to eat after 2 weeks, and they keep indefinitely.

CUCUMBER RELISH

4 quarts cucumbers, thinly sliced,
    unpeeled
6 large onions, sliced
½ cup salt

Mix these ingredients together and let them stand overnight. The next morning, wash them in clear water and drain. Make a syrup with the following ingredients.

4 cups sugar   1 quart vinegar (diluted if desired)
1 teaspoon turmeric   1 teaspoon celery seeds
1 teaspoon mustard seeds

When the syrup is hot, add the cucumbers and onions. Boil them together for about 15 minutes. Then make a paste with 3 tablespoons of flour and some vinegar, and add it to the pickles. Can the relish while it is hot.

RIPE TOMATO RELISH

18 firm, ripe tomatoes   2½ cups sugar (scant)
1 stalk celery   ½ teaspoon cloves
4 medium onions   2 tablespoons mustard seeds
2 green peppers   ½ teaspoon pepper
2 red peppers   2 teaspoons cinnamon
⅓ cup salt   1½ cups vinegar

Peel the tomatoes and chop them into small pieces. Chop the celery, onions and peppers in a food chopper with a coarse blade. Combine the celery, onions, peppers, tomatoes and salt. Let them stand in the refrigerator overnight, then drain them well the next morning. Mix together the sugar, spices and vinegar, then add this to the tomato mixture. Mix them well before putting the mixture into sterile jars. Cap the jars.

This will keep for up to 5 months in the refrigerator. It is very good on hamburgers, on different kinds of meat and on fried potatoes.

TOMATO CORN RELISH

12 ears corn   1 tablespoon salt
2 quarts ripe tomatoes   3 cups white sugar
2 bunches celery, finely cut   6 onions, finely cut
2 cups vinegar   ¼ teaspoon red pepper (or less)

Cut corn off the cobs. Peel the tomatoes and cut them into small pieces. Add the rest of the ingredients and boil them for 50 minutes. Put the relish into small jars and seal them.

TOMATO PEPPER RELISH

½ peck green tomatoes
8 red peppers
2 or more large onions

Put the above ingredients through a food chopper. Boil them for 15 minutes, then remove them from the heat and add salt. Boil them again for 15 minutes. Drain them through a colander, then add the following ingredients.

1 pint vinegar
1 pint sugar
2 sticks cinnamon

2 tablespoons allspice
2 tablespoons whole cloves

Boil the mixture rapidly, then add 1 tablespoon of celery seeds and 1 teaspoon of mustard seeds. Jar and seal.

SWEET PEPPER RELISH

2 ounces celery seeds
1 dozen sweet red peppers

1 dozen green peppers
1 dozen onions

Grind these ingredients in a food chopper, soak them for 10 minutes in boiling water, then drain them. Put the following into a kettle over heat.

1½ pints vinegar
2 pounds brown sugar (or less)
3 tablespoons salt

½ teaspoon pepper
1 teaspoon cinnamon
2 tablespoons mustard seeds

Add the chopped ingredients and boil them for about 10 to 15 minutes, then jar and seal.

CORN RELISH

12 ears corn
1 head cabbage
6 peppers
2 stalks celery
1 teaspoon celery seeds

1 teaspoon mustard seed
1 cup sugar
¼ cup salt
1 pint vinegar

Cut the corn from the cobs. Chop the cabbage, seeded peppers and celery in a food chopper using the coarse blade. Mix these with the rest of the ingredients and boil the mixture for 30 minutes. Jar and seal.

PICKLED GREEN TOMATOES

1 quart vinegar
2 tablespoons salt
2 tablespoons sugar

5 quarts green tomatoes (large if
   possible)

Mix together the vinegar, salt and sugar. Heat the mixture and add it to the green tomatoes
and garlic. Bring it to a boil, then put it into jars. Before sealing them add 2 dill sprigs or 2
teaspoons of dill to each quart.

Can the tomatoes whole, then slice them to use in sandwiches.

STORE-LIKE KETCHUP

½ bushel tomatoes
½ cup salt
4 cups sugar
2 cups vinegar

Dash of pepper
2 grated onions
1 ounce ketchup spices
Cornstarch (optional)

Mix the tomatoes and salt in a large crock. Weigh down the tomatoes and let them stand for 5
days. Each day dip off the water. On the fifth day, remove the white top and put the tomatoes
through a colander. Add the sugar, vinegar, small amount of pepper, onions and the ketchup
spices tied in a bag. Cook this for ¾ hour before removing the bag. The tomatoes may be
thickened with cornstarch if desired. Put the ketchup into bottles or jars and seal them.

WINTER KETCHUP

5 quarts tomato juice
1 pint applesauce
2 cups sugar
2 tablespoons pickling spices

6 onions
1 pint vinegar
Salt to taste

Cook the onions and put them through a sieve. Tie the pickling spices in a cloth and cook them
with all the ingredients for 1½ hours. Remove the pickling spices, then thicken the mixture with
1¼ cups of cornstarch. Cook it for 15 to 20 minutes. Put the ketchup into jars or bottles, and
dip the tops of them into melted paraffin to be sure they seal.

This ketchup can be made in the winter months.

PICKLE KETCHUP

1 pint onions, finely chopped
4 quarts peeled cucumbers, finely
  chopped
1 teaspoon pepper
½ teaspoon celery seeds
½ teaspoon turmeric
1 cup vinegar

1 small head cauliflower, finely
  chopped
1 bunch celery, finely chopped
2 cups white sugar
1 tablespoon salt
1 tablespoon dry mustard
1 tablespoon flour

Mix together all the ingredients and bring them to a boil. Put the ketchup into jars and seal them.

TOMATO KETCHUP

4 quarts tomatoes, finely cut
2 cups vinegar
2 tablespoons salt
1 tablespoon ketchup spices

3 cups sugar
½ teaspoon red pepper
1 teaspoon dry mustard
1 stick cinnamon

Boil the ingredients together for 2 hours. Put the mixture through a sieve and thicken it with approximately 3 tablespoons of cornstarch moistened with a little vinegar. Boil it for 10 minutes before sealing it in sterilized jars.

KETCHUP

1 peck tomatoes
1 tablespoon mixed pickling spices
4 onions
3 red peppers
6 peach leaves

1 cup vinegar
3 cups sugar
1 tablespoon salt
1 tablespoon turmeric
¼ teaspoon pepper

Peel the tomatoes and cook them until they are soft. Put them through a sieve. Tie the pickling spices in a bag, and add it with the remaining ingredients to the tomatoes, boiling the mixture until it is thick. Remove the bag. Put the hot ketchup into jars or bottles and seal them.

MUSTARD SANDWICH SPREAD

6 green peppers
6 red tomatoes
6 cucumbers

6 red peppers
6 onions

Grind together all the ingredients. Add 2 tablespoons of salt and let it stand for 2 hours. Drain it well, then mix the following and add it to the vegetables.

½ cup flour
4 cups sugar

2 tablespoons turmeric
2 cups vinegar

Cook everything together for 15 minutes, then add 1 quart of prepared mustard and cook it for 5 minutes more, stirring all the time to prevent burning. Put it into hot jars and seal.

SANDWICH SPREAD

3 to 4 quarts green tomatoes
1 quart onions

12 large peppers
2 large stalks celery

Grind the ingredients together and add 1 cup of salt. Drain the mixture overnight in a cloth bag, and press the remaining juice out in the morning. Add 1 quart of vinegar and 1½ quarts of sugar, then boil it for 25 to 30 minutes. When it has cooled, add 1 quart of mayonnaise (more if desired) and ½ small jar of mustard (optional).

PRESERVES

SIMPLE APPLE BUTTER

4 gallons apples, unpeeled, quartered
1 gallon corn syrup
6 pounds sugar

Put the apples into a heavy kettle or canner with a tight-fitting lid. Pour the syrup and sugar over the apples and let them set overnight to form juice. Bring the mixture to a slow boil and cook it, covered, for 3 hours. Do not open the lid or stir the mixture during the entire cooking period. Put it through a strainer.

Cider Apple Butter;

3 gallons snitz (dried apple pieces)   ½ gallon corn syrup
1 gallon sweet cider   4 pounds sugar

Follow the directions above.

STOCKMAN'S APPLE BUTTER

10 gallons fresh cider
8 gallons apples, peeled and cored
20 pounds sugar

Bring the cider to a boil in a copper kettle. Add the apples and bring it to a boil again. Add a lump of butter to keep it from boiling over. After the apples are well cooked, add the sugar and keep stirring it until it thickens. This makes 6 gallons of apple butter. When it is done, quickly remove it from the kettle.

GRAPE BUTTER

1 quart whole grapes
1 quart sugar
2 tablespoons water

Cook the ingredients for 20 minutes, then put them through a fruit press or colander. Pour this into jars and seal the tops with paraffin.

LEMON BUTTER

¼ cup lemon juice
Grated rind of 1 lemon
1 cup sugar

2 eggs, well-beaten
½ tablespoon butter

Cook the ingredients in a double boiler until the mixture thickens. Then pour it into jars and seal.

APRICOT JAM

2 pounds dried apricots
2 quarts water
8½ cups sugar

Wash the apricots and put them through the coarse blade of a food grinder. Then put the ground apricots with the water, into a large bowl. Let the mixture stand in a cool place for 48 hours, stirring it occasionally. Cook it for 15 minutes, then add the sugar and cook it slowly for 1 hour, stirring frequently until it thickens.

WILD GRAPE JELLY

Wash grape clusters and put them into a large kettle with enough water to cover them. Boil them for about 15 minutes. Pour the grapes into a cloth bag and squeeze out all the juice. Then add an equal amount of water to the juice. This is now ready for jelly making. Use 5 cups of juice, 7 cups of sugar and 1 package of pectin crystals.

Put the remaining juice into quart cans with ½ cup sugar per quart, and process it for 10 minutes at 10 pounds pressure, or for 30 minutes in a boiling water bath for later use.

PEACH AND PINEAPPLE PRESERVES

6 cups sliced peaches
2 cups crushed pineapple
6 cups sugar

2 small packages orange gelatin
  powder

Cook the first 3 ingredients together for 20 minutes, then add the gelatin powder. Pour the preserves into jars and seal.

In early spring, jams and jellies may be scarce. This recipe may be the answer to this problem.

PEACH PRESERVES

3 cups peaches, peeled and diced
3 oranges, diced or chopped
4½ cups sugar

Boil the ingredients until the mixture sheets from a spoon, about 20 to 30 minutes. Remove it from the heat and add a few chopped maraschino cherries. Pour it into jars and seal.

1-2-3-4 RASPBERRY SPREAD

1 cup water
2 cups red raspberries

3 cups chopped apples
4 cups white sugar

Cook the ingredients together for 10 minutes. Put the spread into jars and seal them with paraffin.

When choosing apples to use, Northern Spy work well with this recipe.

RHUBARB JAM

5 cups rhubarb, finely cut
4 cups sugar

Mix together the above ingredients and let them stand overnight. In the morning, boil the mixture for 5 minutes, then add 1 small package of strawberry gelatin powder. Boil it for 3 minutes, then pour it into jars and seal.

Variations: Try adding 1 small can of pineapple. Then only 4 cups of rhubarb are required instead of 5.

PEACH MARMALADE

5 cups sliced peaches
1 small can crushed pineapple
7 cups sugar

Cook the ingredients together for 15 minutes. Add 1 large or 2 small packages of orange or strawberry gelatin powder, and cook this mixture until the gelatin is dissolved. Pour it into jars and seal them. Use paraffin if desired.

PEAR BUTTER

Boil ½ gallon of pears. Then mash them as you would apples for apple sauce. Add 1 quart of white sugar and 1 quart of light corn syrup. Nutmeg or cinnamon may be added at this time. Bake the mixture in a moderate oven (350°) or simmer it on top of the stove until it is of the right consistency.

When cooking it on the stove, extreme care must be taken to avoid scorching.

FRESH STRAWBERRY JAM

3 cups strawberries, well crushed
6 cups sugar

1 package Certo crystals
1 cup water

Mix the strawberries and sugar together and let the mixture stand for 20 minutes. Stir it several times. Combine the Certo crystals and water. Boil this for 1 minute, stirring constantly. Mix it with the berries and stir it for 2 minutes. Put it into jars and cold pack them a few minutes to seal them. Store them in the freezer.

Variations: Other fruit may be used instead of strawberries.

STRAWBERRY JAM

1 cup strawberries, crushed or whole
2 cups sugar

Boil the ingredients for 3 minutes. Remove the mixture from the heat and stir in 1 teaspoon of Epsom salts. Pour it into jars and seal them.

STRAWBERRY PRESERVES

1 quart strawberries
2 cups sugar

Boil the ingredients for 5 minutes, then add 2 more cups of sugar and 2 teaspoons of lemon juice. Boil the mixture for 10 minutes more. Let it stand for 24 hours, then put it into glasses and seal them while cold with paraffin, or cover them with lids.

CARAMEL SPREAD

2 cups brown sugar
2 cups granulated sugar

1 cup corn syrup
1 cup water

Cook the ingredients together, bringing the mixture to a full boil. Then let it cool. Add 2 egg whites beaten stiff. Stir them together well and add maple flavoring.

PINEAPPLE HONEY

6 pounds sugar
5 pounds corn syrup
2 (19-ounce) cans (1 quart) crushed
   pineapple

Mix the ingredients well and bring the mixture to a boil. There is no need to boil it longer. Pour it into jars and seal. This recipe makes 1 gallon.

QUINCE HONEY

¼ cup corn syrup
1 cup water
3 cups sugar

2 cups quince, ground, OR
1 cup quince plus 1 cup apples, ground

Cook the ingredients together for approximately 5 minutes. Pour the mixture into jars and seal.

MAPLE SYRUP

4 cups brown sugar
2 cups boiling water

¼ cup corn syrup
2 teaspoons maple flavoring

Mix together the first 3 ingredients and bring the mixture to a good boil. Remove it from the heat and add the maple flavoring

Variations: Double this recipe plus ½, and mix it with 5 or 6 pounds of peanut butter. If it becomes too stringy at this point, add a bit of cold water. Then add 2 quarts of Marshmallow Creme (see page 228) to almost fill an 8-quart bowl.

GRAPE MOLASSES

1 pint corn syrup
1 pint grape juice
3 pounds granulated sugar

Boil the ingredients for a few minutes until the mixture is of the right consistency. Pour it into jars and seal them.

Variations: Raspberries, blackberries or elderberries may be used instead of grapes.

CHEESE

HINTS FOR CHEESE

- *One gallon of curds produces approximately 1 pound of cheese.*

- *To make hard, dry cheese, press it with 25 to 30 pound weights.*

- *If mold forms on cheese that is being used, just trim it off.*

- *Cheese may be kept longer while it is being used if it is kept in a large container with a cup of vinegar beside it. Cover the container tightly and set it in a cool place. Do not set vinegar with cheese while the cheese is aging.*

- *Rennet tablets and coloring may be purchased at drug or grocery stores. If they are not available in your area, they may be ordered from—*

  Hansen's Laboratory, Inc., 9015 West Maple Street, Milwaukee, Wisconsin, U.S.A. 53200

  OR

  Horan Lilly Company Limited, 26 Kelfield Street, Rexdale, Ontario, Canada.

- *Try scalding your milk for cottage cheese in a waterless cooker. The cooker has an insulated base. The milk will then require less watching and with a low fire is not apt to be overheated.*

EQUIPMENT NEEDED TO MAKE SOLID CHEESE

rennet tablet
yellow food coloring (for yellow cheese)
wooden spoon

sharp knife with long blade
thermometer (a clean weather thermometer is sufficient)

To press the cheese, use an old lard press, or 2 canners which fit together like a double boiler (put water into the upper one for weight), or a lard or jam bucket which can be obtained from restaurants. Holes (about 18) should then be punched from the inside out into the one side of the bucket bottom to drain off whey. Set it on the table with the holes extending over the edge. Place a bucket beneath to catch the whey. Put a lid over the cheese with bricks on top.

GENERAL DIRECTIONS FOR CHEESE MAKING

1. Let milk set in a cool place overnight to ripen. A commercial starter may be added to hasten ripening, using 1 cup per gallon of milk.

2. The next morning warm the milk slowly to 86°.

3. Dissolve the cheese color tablet in ¼ cup of water and add it to the milk. Use ¾ tablet for 10 gallons of milk. Never mix the cheese coloring with the rennet tablet solution.

4. Dissolve the cheese rennet tablet in ¼ cup of cold water. Mix it with the milk at 86°. Ice cream junket tablets may be used instead of the rennet.

5. Remove the milk from the stove. Stir it gently but thoroughly with a wooden spoon for 2 minutes.

6. Cover the container and let it stand by a warm stove for 1 hour or until it is thick enough. To test it, put your finger into the milk and bring it up like a hook. If the curd breaks clean across your finger like jelly, it is thick enough.

7. Cut the curds into cubes using a long-bladed knife that extends to the bottom of the kettle. Cut ½-inch squares, then cut them diagonally. A wire bent in a U-shape may be used to cut the curds horizontally, using the 2 ends as handles. Cutting should give a clear whey.

8. Let the curds stand for 5 minutes. Return them to the stove, then stir them slowly and gently to keep the pieces from sticking together while the temperature is slowly raised to 100 to 102°, and kept there. Then stir them only occasionally so the pieces will not stick together.

   Instead of returning the curds to the stove, some of the whey may be taken from the top, strained into a dipper, then brought to a boil. Slowly pour the hot whey back into the curds, stirring the curds all the time. Continue this process until the temperature has risen to 100 to 102°. The curds are ready when a handful, squeezed firmly, does not squirt out between your fingers, but almost falls apart when your hand is opened. This takes about 1 hour.

9. Pour the heated curds into a colander which has been lined with cheese cloth, organdy or gauze diaper cloth. Catch the whey; it is a healthy drink, it may be used in recipes calling for water, and it is also a good tonic for flowers.

10. Gently work salt into the curds, about 1 tablespoon to 2 gallons of milk, or according to taste.

11. Leave the curds in the cloth, with only 1 thickness over the top, and place them in the prepared press—a lard press, bucket or cans. Do not use an aluminum container. Place the lid on top of the cheese. Weigh it down with 2 bricks, or the equivalent in weight. In the evening turn the cheese and double the weight. The next morning, remove the cheese from the press. Keep it in a warm room for 36 to 48 hours. Laying it in the sun by a window for ½ day will hasten the aging process.

12. Seal the cheese by brushing it with smoking hot paraffin, but be careful, for hot paraffin catches fire like oil. If the cheese is not solid, do not seal it. Instead of paraffin, vegetable or mineral oil may be rubbed into the cheese to keep it from becoming moldy. Another method to prevent mold is to mix only ½ of the salt into the cheese, then rub salt over it every few days. If mold appears, wash the cheese in warm salt water and salt it again. Turn it every few days.

13. Place the cheese in a room (cellar) with a temperature of about 60° and turn it every other day for 3 to 6 weeks. If it is kept longer, turn it twice a week. Cheese may be kept for several months. The longer it is cured, the sharper it becomes.

BUTTERMILK CHEESE

Let a quart of buttermilk set until it is thick. Pour 1 quart of boiling water over it, stirring it at the same time. Let it set for a few minutes. The cheese will go to the bottom. Pour off the water. Put the cheese into a cloth to drain for ½ day. Add salt according to taste.

CREAM CHEESE

1 quart light cream of good flavor
¼ cup fresh sour milk

Mix the ingredients well in the top of a double boiler or stainless steel bowl. Cover the mixture and let it stand at room temperature until it is thick. Skim the thin layer off the top if necessary. Cut it into squares and heat it over warm water to 110°. Make a few strokes across the bottom while warming. Handle it carefully so the cream does not get thin and drain off with the whey. Pour it into a cloth bag. After 15 minutes place the bag on a rack in the refrigerator with a bowl underneath to catch the whey. Drain it for 10 hours or so. Press the curds with a weight on top of the bag, until the curds are pasty. Turn them into a bowl, and with a fork or mixer, work in salt to taste (about ¾ teaspoon). Mix it thoroughly.

This cheese is good with crushed pineapple, or served on drained pear chunks.

MARVEL CREAM CHEESE

Make yogurt (see page 293). One quart makes about 6 to 8 ounces of Marvel Cream Cheese. Instead of refrigerating the yogurt once it has formed, pour it into a colander lined with a triple thickness of cheese cloth, or an old clean gauze diaper. Catch the whey by placing a bowl under the colander. Allow the whey to drip for 1 minute, then lift up the 4 corners of the cheese cloth and tie them together. Hang the bag at the sink faucet or elsewhere and let the whey drip for 6 to 8 hours. It is then ready to be removed from the bag and stored in the refrigerator. This cheese is almost identical to commercial brands of cream cheese.

CROCK CHEESE

Place a gallon of thickened sour milk on the stove. Stir it constantly and heat it to about 102° until you can press curds of milk together with your hand. Pour the curds into cheese cloth and thoroughly press out the whey. Melt 2 tablespoons of butter in a hot skillet, then add the curds, 1 teaspoon of soda and salt (approximately 1 teaspoon or according to taste). Stir it with a potato masher. Cook it until it is smooth, then add cream or milk to the thickness desired. Pour it into a bowl and it is ready to serve.

MUENSTER CHEESE

Let 2½ gallons of sour milk set until it is thick like junket. Scald it until it is too hot to hold your hand in, then pour it into cheese cloth. Let it hang until the curds are dry, overnight or for about 12 hours. Crumble the curds and mix 2 heaping teaspoons of soda and ½ cup of butter into them. Let them set for 2 hours then put them into a double boiler. Add 1 cup of sour cream and melt the cheese. When melted, add another cup of sour cream and 1 tablespoon of salt. Mix it well. Pour it into a buttered mold and let it set until it is completely cold before slicing it.

PROCESSED CHEESE

Let 5 gallons of skimmed milk sour until it is thick. Then scald it on top of the stove until it is hot enough to be uncomfortable for your hand, or until you can squeeze the whey out of the cheese with your hand. Then strain it through a cloth and squeeze it until it is very dry.

Grind the cheese finely in a food grinder. Then cook 5 cups of this dry cheese with the following in a double boiler until it is smooth (for approximately 1 hour or a little more.)

1 teaspoon soda	½ cup butter
2 teaspoons salt	1 to 1½ cups cream or milk

Stir it occasionally while it is cooling. To make a softer cheese add more milk. This recipe makes approximately 3 quarts.

SMEAR KASE

Take drained dry cheese and add salt, pepper and milk or cream. Mix it until it is smooth, then spread it on bread. It may be topped with molasses or apple butter.

STINK KASE

Put about 5 cups of dry curds into a dish. Mix in 1 teaspoon of soda and let it stand in a warm room until mold has begun to form over the top. The older it is, the stronger the flavor. Add 1 teaspoon of salt and then proceed with the same directions as for Crock Cheese (see page 289), by heating and adding milk or cream.

SOFT CHEESE

Select a quantity of very rich milk. Mix with this 3 to 5% of its bulk in clean well-soured skim milk or this amount of a commercial starter. Add dissolved rennet (2 ounces for each 10 pounds of milk) and set the mixture at 80°. When it is well thickened, cool it down to 60° by placing it in the refrigerator or by letting cold water run around the container. Care should be taken not to break the curd. After it has cooled for 24 hours, turn it into a cheese cloth sack and allow it to drain for another 24 hours. Add salt to taste. (The presence of fat makes a smooth, soft cheese.) This cheese can be molded into balls or printed in a butter printer and wrapped in oil paper or aluminum foil.

SPREADING CHEESE

Let 2½ gallons of skimmed milk sour until it is very thick, then heat it until it is too hot to hold your hand in, but not boiling. Drain it through a coarse cloth bag, putting only ½ of the milk through at a time, so as to be able to squeeze out as much water as possible. (If it is too hot, hold the bag under running water a minute to cool it.) Put it into a bowl and crumble it. This makes 4 cups or a little more of crumbs. Let it set at room temperature for 2 to 3 days, or longer if a stronger taste is desired.

To 4 cups of the crumbs add 2 teaspoons of soda, and mix. Let it stand for about 30 minutes, then stir in 1½ cups of warm water (scant). Set the bowl in a dishpan of boiling water or use a double boiler. Heat the mixture to the boiling point, then stir it vigorously. Add ⅓ cup of butter and 2 level teaspoons of salt. Add 1 cup of hot water, a little at a time, stirring after each addition. Cook it for 10 to 12 minutes longer or until the crumbs are mostly dissolved. If necessary, put it through a strainer. Stir it occasionally until it is cold. This makes approximately 1½ quarts of cheese.

Variations: Use milk instead of water with only 1 teaspoon of soda. One cup of hot cream may also be added.

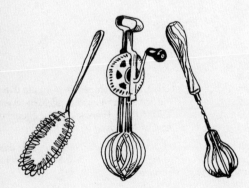

MISCELLANEOUS

MAKING YOGURT

Add 3 tablespoons of yogurt culture to 1 quart of warm milk. Set it in a warm place (about 100°) until it thickens. Do not serve all of the yogurt but let at least 3 tablespoons remain. To this add 1 pint of milk. Set it in a warm place until it thickens, then it is ready to serve. Repeat this process to make more yogurt from yogurt. Eventually it is necessary to buy fresh yogurt again as a starter.

YOGURT

To make yogurt, simply buy a small quantity of plain yogurt and stir 3 tablespoons into 1 quart of milk that has been slowly warmed to 98°. Keep the milk in a warm room for 5 to 6 hours. When it has thickened, the yogurt is ready to use. Keep it refrigerated.

More yogurt can be made from this yogurt by following the simple directions above.

JAR YEAST (SOURDOUGH)

4 medium-sized potatoes
3 pints boiling water
½ cup bread flour
½ cup sugar

2 teaspoons salt
1 cake yeast, dissolved in
¼ cup water

Pare the potatoes and boil them in the boiling water until they are soft. Mash them, or put them through a strainer, then return them to the water. Use the hot water mixture to scald the flour, sugar and salt. Let it cool, then add the yeast and set it aside to rise. There should be 1 quart of this mixture. (Use 1 cup of sourdough (jar yeast) instead of 1 cake of yeast.)

Always save 2 cups of starter from each baking. To this, add the same amount of water that was used from the jar and store it in a cool place for the next baking. This may be done for a long time, but occasionally a fresh starter needs to be made.

JAR YEAST (YOGURT CULTURE)

Heat 1 cup of milk to lukewarm, then add ⅛ cake of yeast. Cover it and set it in a warm place until the next day (24 hours). Take ½ the liquid and pour in 1 cup of warm milk. For 7 days add ½ cup of warm milk to ½ the liquid. Always keep the yeast milk in a warm place. On the 7th day use all the yeast milk and add 2 cups of warm milk. Let it set for another 24 hours. This makes 3 cups of yogurt starter.

HOW TO FREEZE EGGS

Stir up 2 or 3 eggs at a time as for scrambled eggs, and freeze them in small containers. They can be used later for baking, but not for any other purpose.

PRESERVING ELDERBERRIES

2 gallons elderberries
1 pint vinegar
4 pounds sugar

Boil the ingredients until thick. This can be used for pie. Store it in crocks.

Plums can also be cooked this way but they need no vinegar as they are sour. Water should be added before putting plums into a pie crust.

BATTER FOR DEEP FRYING

1 cup flour
¼ teaspoon salt
2 teaspoons baking powder

2 eggs, separated
⅔ cup sweet milk
1 tablespoon melted butter

Sift and measure the flour. Add the salt and baking powder and sift it again. Add the beaten egg yolks and milk, then the beaten egg whites and melted butter. This is good for fish or cooked chicken. Two batches make enough for 3 fryers.

TEETHING COOKIES

Break 2 eggs into a bowl. Stir them in one direction until they are creamy. Add 1 cup of sugar. Continue stirring in the same direction. Gradually stir 2 to 2½ cups of sifted flour into the mixture and continue stirring it until the mixture is stiff. Roll out the dough with a rolling pin, between 2 lightly floured sheets of waxed paper, to a thickness of ¾ inch. Use a drinking glass and a salt shaker to cut out doughnut shaped cookies. Place the cookies on a lightly buttered cookie sheet. Let the formed cookies stand overnight (10 to 12 hours). Bake them in a preheated oven at 325° until they are lightly browned and hard. This recipe makes approximately 12 durable and relatively crumb-proof teething biscuits.

GRAHAM CRACKERS

2 cups sugar
4 cups graham flour
1 teaspoon soda
1 teaspoon salt
1 teaspoon vanilla

2 cups all-purpose flour
1 cup shortening
1 teaspoon baking powder
1 cup milk

Make a dough with the ingredients, then roll it out thinly. Cut it and prick it with a fork. Bake it at 350° until nice and brown.

SOFT PRETZELS

1 envelope yeast
1¼ cups warm water
1 teaspoon sugar
2 teaspoons salt

4 to 5 cups all-purpose flour
Butter as needed
4 teaspoons soda
Coarse salt for sprinkling

Dissolve the yeast in ¼ cup of the water. Then stir in an additional cup of warm water, and the sugar. Pour the yeast mixture into a bowl and add the salt. Beat in the flour to make a stiff dough. Knead it for 10 minutes or until the dough is elastic. Place it in a bowl and spread it with butter. Cover it and let it rise for 45 minutes or until double in size. Shape the dough into sticks or twists. Make it ½ the thickness of the desired finished pretzel.

Bring 4 cups of water to boiling with the soda. Drop in 3 pretzels at a time. Boil them for 1 minute or until they float. Remove and drain them, and place them on buttered cookie sheets. Sprinkle them with coarse salt. Bake the pretzels at 475° for 12 minutes or until golden brown. To make them crisp, lay them on a cookie sheet and place them in a warm oven (200°) for 2 hours.

NOODLES

6 egg yolks
6 tablespoons water

3 cups all-purpose flour (approximate)
1 teaspoon salt

Beat the egg yolks and water for a few minutes. Add the flour to make a dough as stiff as possible but still workable. Divide it into 4 balls, then roll them very thinly. Lay them separately on a cloth to dry. They are ready to cut when they are almost dry and do not stick together.

How to Quick Cut Noodles;

Put as many as 12 sheets of noodles on top of each other when they are dry enough to cut. Roll them tightly and cut them with a sharp butcher knife. After they are cut, lay them out on a table in a warm place, cover them with a cloth and let them dry thoroughly. Store them in a tightly closed container.

HOW TO DRY CORN

Cook corn for 10 minutes as for roasting ears. Cut it from the cob. To each gallon of cut corn add ¾ cup of sweet cream (optional), ½ cup of white sugar (optional) and salt to taste. Pour it into flat pans and place them in the oven at 200° to dry. Stir the corn often so it will dry more evenly.

When using the oven for drying, do not forget to leave the oven door open.

CORNMEAL

Dry selected ears of field corn or sweet corn in a slow (275°) open-door oven for several days, or until the corn shells easily by hand. The cornmeal is tasty when the corn has been slightly browned. Shell the corn, then take it to a mill to have it ground. Put it into an oblong pan and bake it in a slow oven for a more toasted flavor. Stir it occasionally. Place the cornmeal in a tightly covered container when it is cool.

CORN MUSH

Bring 3 cups of water to a boil. Make a thickening with 1 cup of cornmeal, 1 teaspoon of salt and 1 cup of milk. Add it to the boiling water. Stir it until it has reached the boiling point, then stir it occasionally. Cook it for 15 to 20 minutes then pour it into a deep baking dish. Let it cool, then slice and fry it.

To clean the mush kettle after the mush has been poured out, put 1 or 2 cups of water into the kettle. Add 1 teaspoon of soda. Cover it, then bring it to the boiling point. Set the kettle aside, but keep it covered until dishwashing time.

DRIED FRUIT

These are lunch box treats for children as they are naturally sweet.

Pears—Take firm pears, peel them, then make small snitz (dried pieces). Dry them as you would other fruit.

Peaches—Cut them into quarters, unpeeled, then dry them. They can also be mashed, spread in a thin layer on pie plates and dried in the oven. This is called PEACH LEATHER and is a great snack.

Prune plums—Cut them in half. Remove the pits. Place them in a dryer.

Apricots—Cut them in half, remove the pits and dry them.

Plums—These can be dried but if they get too hot, they become mushy.

Apples—Quarter peeled slices, then lay them on a dryer. When put through a food cutter and dried they make a delicious snack or addition to breakfast cereals.

Elderberries—They can be dried in the sun on a warm, sunny day. Spread them thinly on a sugar bag or a brown paper bag in a warm, dry, sunny place.

DRIED TOMATOES

Pour boiling water over ripe tomatoes. Let them stand for a few minutes. Slip the skins off then cut them into pieces. Put them through a Foley food mill. Fill greased pie pans with them about ½ full, then put them into a slow oven (275°). After they are dried only a thin layer is left. Fold them and put them into a dry container. When ready to use, add water and cook them up again.

DRIED GREEN BEANS

Cook beans for 15 to 30 minutes or until the green color disappears. Spread the beans in thin layers on pans. Dry them in a slow oven at 250° until dry. Store them in a tightly sealed container for winter use.

How to Use Dried Beans;

Fry ¼ pound of bacon. Pour off the grease then add 3 cups of dried beans, 1 teaspoon of salt and water to cover them. Cook them until the beans are soft and most of the water is absorbed; OR

Pour boiling water over 2 or 3 cups of dried beans. Let them set for several hours, then drain them. Add water to cover them and cook for 1 to 1½ hours. The cooked beans may be added to meat and gravy and vegetables as a one dish meal.

HOW TO ROAST SOYBEANS

People have different methods of roasting soybeans. Even if they do not quite agree on method, they all agree that roasted soybeans are delicious as well as nutritious. Here the different ways of preparing them are all merged into one recipe. The reader can decide his or her own method of roasting them.

Wash the beans in cold water and remove the debris. Some soak the beans overnight, some 6 hours, others 3 hours and some only 10 minutes in warm water. Drain them well by placing them on a towel. (Some prefer to cover the soybeans with water and freeze them, thawing them before roasting.) Place the soybeans in oil that has been preheated to 375 to 400°. (They may be put into a colander to set in the oil.) Cook them until they begin to crack in ½ and float to the top and the oil stops bubbling—some keep them in for 3 minutes, others for 10 minutes, and still others for 20 minutes. Watch closely, for soybeans burn easily. Drain them and add salt. (Add more oil if the beans cook dry.)

Oven-Roasted Soybeans;

Soak washed soybeans overnight. Boil them for 1 hour in salted water. Spread them in a shallow pan and roast them at 350° until brown. Sprinkle them with salt while warm.

GREEN TOMATOES FOR PIE

Wash and trim out the stalks from 1 gallon of green tomatoes. Slice them quite thinly. Add ½ crock of white sugar and boil this mixture until it is thick. Add 2 lemons, thinly sliced, about 15 minutes before removing it from the stove. This can be kept in crocks and used as needed.

Before putting the tomato mixture into a pie shell, add water to make them thinner. Place a crust on top.

CORN COB SYRUP

Boil 6 red corn cobs, washed, for 1 hour in 3 quarts of water. Strain them, then add 3 pounds of brown sugar and water enough to make 3 quarts. Boil this mixture until it is the consistency of maple syrup.

Be sure to select clean corn cobs, free from mold. Light colored cobs will make a lighter syrup and give a better flavor.

BURNT SUGAR SYRUP

Into a heavy skillet that heats uniformly, pour 2 cups of granulated sugar. Melt the sugar over low heat, stirring it constantly with a wooden spoon to prevent scorching. When the sugar becomes a clear brown syrup, remove it from the heat. Slowly stir in 1 cup of boiling water and return it to a low heat, stirring the syrup until it is smooth again. Let it cool, then pour it into a clean pint jar. Cover it tightly and store it at room temperature. It keeps for 6 to 8 weeks. This recipe makes 1⅓ cups of syrup.

INDEX